The life and times of
Cat Stevens

The Boy Who Looked at the Moon

by David Evans

The life and times of
Cat Stevens

*Friends and colleagues look back on what led
this charismatic poet-singer to turn his back
on superstardom and convert to Islam.*

BRITANNIA PRESS PUBLISHING

First published in Great Britain by Britannia Press Publishing, 1995.
This edition published in 1995 by Britannia Press Publishing.

British Library Cataloguing in Publication Data. A catalogue record for this book
is available from the British Library.
    Evans
    The Boy Who Looked at the Moon,
    The Life and Times of Cat Stevens

    ISBN 0-9519937-7-1

Printed and bound in Great Britain by WBC, Bridgend
Cover photograph: Rex Features

Britannia Press Publishing, 72 Chalk Farm Road, London NW1 8AN

IF FOR SEX AND SLEAZE YOU LOOK
YOU'LL FIND NEITHER IN THIS BOOK.
THAT WHICH DAYLIGHT CAN CONCEAL
MAY BY MOONLIGHT BE REVEALED.
TO BE IMPERFECT IS THE FATE
OF ALL WHO QUEUE AT HEAVEN'S GATE.
TO SIT IN JUDGEMENT'S NOT FOR ME
FOR THOSE I JUDGE MIGHT WELL JUDGE ME.

This book is dedicated to the memory of TONY BECKLEY. He was a good friend to Cat Stevens and to me.

Walter shrugged: *"Trouble is,"* he said, *"my songs don't change one single thing"*...
She said to her new friends: *"I think, as one gets older, it's perfectly all right to turn one's back on certain things."*

Rose Tremain, *"Sacred Country"*. Sinclair Stevenson Ltd.

My gratitude is the only reward I can give for the help I have received. This assistance has been invaluable and, other than the individual contributors to whom I am most immediately indebted, I would like to thank... Nigel Quiney, as always and above all; Robert and Caroline Lee; Roger and Val Woodburn; Charles Negus-Fancey; Harry Payton Evans; James Newton; Matilda Quiney; Sarah Standing; Mike Ashwell; Rae Coates; Brian Harding; Sarah Harrison; Peter Burton; Linda Cairns - Hugh Middleton School; Annie Woolston; Vicky Bruce and finally, André Delanchy.

CONTENTS

INTRODUCTION

David Evans worked for Barry Krost, Cat Stevens' second manager as Personal Assistant between 1970 and 1976 and was privy to the inner workings of the staff and strategies which facilitated the career of one of the least understood and most secretive and mysterious talents which emerged on the music scene. After setting the social milieu for the first Cat Stevens hit in 1966, David Evans uses his unique memories, together with the recollections of many other friends, colleagues and contemporaries of Cat Stevens, to chart some of the events and explore some of the possible reasons why this enigmatic and charismatic poet-singer withdrew from superstardom and embraced that faith which ensured he would never again play and sing in public.

David Evans is the author of three novels *SUMMER SET* , *A CAT IN THE TULIPS* and *A HOLLYWOOD CONSCIENCE,* as well as a book of tributes to his friend the late Freddie Mercury, *THIS IS THE REAL LIFE...* and a collage biography of Dusty Springfield, *SCISSORS AND PASTE*

CHAPTER ONE

CHANGES A-COMIN'

A lot has happened since the end of World War Two. For starters, the world has changed. Completely changed. The second World War finished off what the first had started and, in the Western World, laid forever those ghosts which were the hangovers of an inflexible, authoritarian and un-democratic world.

The phenomenon that was the career of Cat Stevens was only possible because of this changed world. The life of Steven Giorgiou, upon whose back the Cat Stevens edifice was built, in some way denies this new world of widened horizons. Born into freedom and tolerance and broadcasting these qualities for personal as well as pecuniary profit, his latter life suggests that he was un-comfortable in the reality of such freedom as he opted to live under the established and well-worn parameters of, possibly, the world's strictest religion.

However, when he was growing up, he and his life were very different. Cat Stevens cannot be properly understood without knowing something of the context of his young life.

By the 1950's it seemed that people were free to think what they wanted and do what they pleased. The new generation, dubbed teenagers, felt that this new world was indeed their oyster and that their power was limitless. It was the first time in the history of the world that the young had the opportunity to express themselves with impunity without first being granted the rubber-stamp approval of their elders. No longer were their elders auto-matically their betters. Free thinking individualism began to re-place mass conformism and relentlessly started to wreak havoc in classrooms, Sunday schools and, above all, the workplace where merit, ability and opportunity replaced seniority, age and length of service as qualifications for the higher salaries which quick-buck prosperity and inflation bred.

In the arena of the arts, boundaries were tumbling too. In the theatre, the Me, Myself, I trend begun by people like John Osborne in the 1950's and re-inforced by the chaotic individualism of Joe Orton in the 60's did not in general make theatre-going particularly more accessible but it allowed dramatists to lay new ground rules upon which the television playwrights were able to build for the truly wider audience. In the film world, a grittier, more realistic genre was developing with continental roots led by people like Lindsay Anderson and John Schlesinger. In the bookshelves, writers such as Gillian Freeman with her *LEATHER BOYS*, John Braine with his *ROOM AT THE TOP* and the Irish sagas of Edna O'Brien sliced through the blubber of strictly aristocratic and middle-class creativity and product and paved the way for less euphemistic glimpses of the human condition. All these and many, many more unsung works were echoed as the 50's aged and turned into the 60's and nowhere were the echoes more resounding than in the tin-pan alleyways of popular music.

In the streets in and around Charing Cross Road and Denmark Street in London's West End, publishers and producers of popular music began to listen to the work of young men and women writing and singing about intensely personal, apparently anarchic and certainly rebellious feelings resulting from their own quests for hearts and minds of their own. What existed of a British youth culture before the war was already deeply influenced by the music and songs promulgated by the Hollywood movies. The arrival of real life flesh and blood Americans during the war with their affluent ways symbolised the new world for which many Britons were fighting and sacrificing. This secular occupation cemented the fabled 'special relationship' between the two cultures. More significantly, as well as their tanks and guns and Liberty ships, the Americans brought consumer hardware. The gramophones, the record players and the records. After the war, both British and Continental electrical goods manufacturers turned swords into ploughshares and suddenly there was the Dansette! And it was affordable! Now everyone could play records. Not only was dreaming and self-expression no longer the exclusive preserve of the elitist artistic groups of society, when Elvis Presley first swivelled his hips in the mid-fifties and when Bill Haley sweated his way around that rock and roll clock, it was a signal to everyone that dreaming and wish-fulfilment and sex were okay and here to stay.

By the mid-sixties, it seemed that all social and economic barriers had been scaled. Life in the second half of the twentieth century had been tossed in the air. However, for both the older generations as well as the young, life on it's way back to earth became vastly complicated and confusing. As they were struck off, the old balls and chains clanked and rattled distractingly against an enormous amount of newly-generated, widely available disposable income. This money wasn't only for well-disposed parents to distribute. It was there for the young to earn themselves and once earned, it was there not to be always and unquestioningly saved but to be spent. No longer were parents in sole charge. Hundreds and thousands of households had to cope with the agonies of pride and place as fledging young were seen coming home with more in their pockets on payday than their parents.

A floodgate had been opened and the marketplace found itself brimful of new opportunities for coaxing this new money out of the punters' pockets and into the coffers of overnight fortunes. The western world's cash registers were ringing simultaneously in the ears of both the greedy and the gullible.

In the business of popular music, it seemed to the watching vultures as much to their unwary prey that all one had to do was to write that one song, to sing in that special way in order to have that hit to reap the incommensurate benefits. And incommensurate was certainly how the rewards were seen. Young men and women earning, for those days, fabulous amounts of money was banner-headline news in the new lowest common denominator yellow press and this news was both fuel to the fire of years of suppressed ambition for the working classes and yet also fuel for the damning reaction which the fearful middle classes saw as the visible cause of the erosion of the fundamental precepts of their world.

Throughout British society, a lot had indeed been lost. Life would truly never be the same again. Sufficient troops, seamen and airmen had certainly been rounded up for the second world war in 1939 but there was a big difference in their attitudes from the initial gung-ho bash-the-Bosch perspectives of the Derby conscripts of 1915. The 1939-ers did not want to go. They had been born and raised in a world already well-served by the media of communication. These young men and women knew the horrors of the first great war and the majority of the class of 1939 sure as hell didn't want the same to happen to them.

But the same did happen. The carnage was, if anything, worse. Not only were lives lost in muddy, bloody trenches but they were lost beneath falling carpets of bombs and through the phenomenon of a mass cruelty and inhumanity, the horror of which gradually emerged in the guise of The Holocaust and the awful suffering of millions of the civilian population across Europe and the Far East.

However valid the cause may have been, the actual cost of the struggle against the Axis Powers was always in question. And so were the methods. For all the well-worn stories of heroism and triumph and victory there are equally, if not more, stories of ineptitude, lack of command, indecision and waste of both time and life. My own father, after five years of prison camp incarceration in Poland and Germany refused the medals offered to him upon his demobilisation with as much bitterness as my grandfather at the end of the first world war had accepted his with pride. There were many thousands like my father who felt the same. A national cynicism had been bred and by the cessation of hostilities it had escaped between the stiff upper lips and was soon abroad in the land. Side-by-side by cynicism, idealism pales. The British people had had enough. They had been led not to mistily-eyed trust but instead to doubt their leaders who were certainly no longer their traditional masters.

The people wanted their own voice, not necessarily spoken in the cut crystal tones of the Bee Bee Ceee. The people wanted their own culture to be recognised, transplanted from the Music Halls and Variety circuits and nurtured by the national air waves. They were, of course, to get what they wanted as we all, in our fashion, got what we deserved. But what inexplicably was to survive virtually intact was the British class system, the very structure which had perpetrated the shibboleths of wealth, privilege, nepotist influence and dynastic power which the new world decried. The British class system merely adapted its methods of manipulating power. Their first exercise was to ensure that power was to be seen by the people to be flowing upwards from the base of the pyramid rather than from the top down. However, beneath the cosmetic facade, the supposed revolution was nothing more than a badly struck bargain between the new and the old which was ultimately to empower very few.

Happily, it was at least recognised that jingoism and appeals to better natures were no longer available as tools of control and government. Though the British people's individual homes would remain inviolate and sacrosanct, it was reluctantly understood by those who still retained control that it would have needed a doorstep invasion of Kent by demons and Visigoths to mobilise the British en masse again to defend their realm. In 1945, the British embraced the promise of socialism with as much relief as the prodigal son was welcomed when he stumbled out of the wilderness back into the bosom of his family.

Traditional values had been overthrown. The communities which had harboured them were too being eroded as extended families were broken up by post-war relocation. New industries were introduced and old ones crumbled. Whole areas found themselves faced with a Damoclean future. The emerging individuals, no longer able to rely on the support of stable families living in permanence, raced to create alternative security. The rush to succeed in the new materialistic world became a stampede. Many found that being an individual was neither as easy nor as cheap as had been advertised. There were no easy terms.

Before the war, individual failure had been relatively unknown. Conformity under God's umbrella had been both a comfort and a haven from adversity. Industries had failed, sure. Governments and Prime Ministers had failed, certainly. Harvests had failed many times but individual failure was hardly known in the tight-knit, traditional communities of the mining villages, in the cotton towns and also on the land for the idyll of the English village too had become tarnished. No longer the domain of millions of Mrs. Minivers, the countryside and its farmers were facing up to an expensive industrialisation and rationalisation process; the old, land-rich families, the backbone of country life both socially, politically and economically were feeling the pinch. Paternalism and fore-lock tugging were fast becoming politically incorrect. The ground rules were being set for the sixties liberal backlash against two centuries of deprivation and poverty. Indeed, without the welfare state and its agencies which urged on the reaction, the old world could not have been made to disappear for the new world's individuals were fast to become completely dependent on the welfare state, in some respects more enslaved to forces beyond their control than they had ever been before.

Unlike America, Britain never properly learned the lesson of individualism with any philosophy or perspective. Learning that in order to succeed someone else had to fail was essential in participating in the new competitive spirit abroad in the post-war world. Competition is all very well whilst dressed in sacks or playing in a brass band or on the village cricket team but when given a price tag, goaded by greed, lured onwards into debt and fuelled by untrammelled avarice, many competitors found that they were prepared to do anything if not to win then at least to finish amongst the leaders.

Between the wars there had been a census taken in churches of all Christian denominations throughout the land one Sunday morning. It was found that less than forty percent of the population attended church. The second world war came and went and still less was found to be the hold of the Churches of England over their flock. The people sought other gods, listened to different prophets for the people still wanted to believe in something.

As its established religion waned, the very nature and fabric of the country was changing, helped in no small part by greatly increased immigration from the former British colonies and imperial possessions. Blacks from Africa and the Caribbean, Hindus and Muslim from the Indian sub-continent, Buddhists from the Far East, Russian and Greek orthodox from the Middle east, the Levant and the Mediterranean Protectorates. Once again, the British melting pot was being stirred and once again, Britain found itself noticeably becoming a multi-cultural society. Each influx of new population either by invasion, immigration or asylum has brought fresh impetus to the enrichment of the fabric of British culture. By the late 1950's was it any surprise that the artistic and creative life of the old country bloomed in a torrent of fresh ideas like a desert after a hundred year drought?

Nowhere was the transfusion of blood-stock and the flowering of life, leisure and culture more noticeable that in the West End of London; the West End had traditionally been a true melting pot of a neighbourhood drawing from and bolstered by the hungry intellectual enclaves of Chelsea, Notting Hill, Hampstead and Bloomsbury whose very proximity to the West End and the new, exploding youth culture lent both authority and legitimacy to emerging artistic developments. Inherent in all new art is the very thing which its patrons and husbandmen - the intellectuals, lawyers, accountants and business people - need to survive and thrive. Money.

And such was the tie that bound. The newly financed young and working class wanted to spend it; the business world wanted to earn it. Well ... earn, for how much - how much indeed, as the old music hall one liner proclaimed - does a Grecian Urn? Out of the clay pots and into a magnificent golden chalice. Whatever the analogy, whatever the allusions, the 'You've-never-had-it-so-good' world proclaimed so unforgettably by Harold Macmillan was a union between the wannabees and the wannabee-makers, a union truly made on earth with no regard to heaven whatsoever, a loveless arranged marriage between the givers and the takers on the entertainment exchange.

For the talent spotters, it mattered not from where the new talent came ... from never-mind what, provincial backwater, suburb or walk of life. Whatever the accent, the money talked louder. Whether a book publisher in Bloomsbury, whether a theatrical impresario in Regent Street, a film producer in Soho or Mayfair, a writers' agent in Covent Garden, all it seemed necessary to do each morning was merely to wake up and go to work. Between the street and the office door there was a side-walk arguably paved with gold. Bright, fresh, newly-minted talents were queuing up. New 'discoveries' were announced daily and frogmarched into the service of Mammon. Talent was turned into product and the product was put on the shelf for us, the new teenagers, to buy. The talent itself was dressed up and burnished bright and lo and behold, the people also had something to believe in. And idols was how the new stars were dubbed. Pop Idols.

The creation of the new product was a necessary symbiosis between the young and the not-so-young. To succeed, the young talent had to be enabled. To be used, one must first meet a user. The users were usually older and presumed wiser. Whatever. They wrote cheques and for both sides at the outset of such a process, the goal was mutual success. Nothing else mattered. Young innocents were not going to be permitted to obstruct the onward momentum of the show business juggernaut and neither were they going to allow the colossus to roll by without attempting to jump on. No sacrifices were made and no prisoners taken.

Many of the new young recruits were ignorant of just how talented they were. Some, either with success under their belts or with the talent way past the sell-by date, still don't know to this day. At the time, many became casualties of their ignorance; some even died. Very few, once aboard the gravy train ever had the strength of mind to get off when they realised just how much of their integrity, principles and values they had had to sell.

Most only got off when they fell or if they were pushed and ninety five percent either fell or were pushed for reasons no more graceful than those of expediency. The minders of these talents, that incipient breed of manager/agents were subtle but sturdy pushers because they needed the room. When the travel cards of the older passengers began to expire, the overcrowded train had to be weeded out in order to make room for the replacements. You only have to read one of the umpteen available histories of rock 'n' roll to realise that most of pop's heroes and heroines no longer strut the weary stage. For those who have not made new lives for themselves, these fret in total obscurity ... Not even the requisite Sunday paper exposé or a cursory mention in another's biography. Oblivion.

The survivors in the main are those whose staying power was tremendous or who never had to sell themselves short, never becoming so entirely dependent on the fickle organisations which they believed supported them. So many artists, believing that they had successful careers in limitless perspectives, forgot that it was their minders and mentors and managers whose careers took precedence. The survivors are always the ones who stayed in control.

There is only one person in my certain knowledge who has ever voluntarily turned away from the enormous success which those times generated. In those heady sixties, he too was a young hopeful looking for his facilitator. Perhaps the greatest advantage that this young man had was that he both lived and wrote his songs in the centre of the bubbling cauldron which was London's West End, a source which attracted hundreds of thousands of people like me as powerfully as a magnet.

Unlike those of us who were still scheming and dreaming of one day making it to London, this particular young man didn't have far to go to try and climb aboard the gravy train. The Charing Cross Road wasn't even a bus ride away. He could walk it in two minutes.

London has a great deal to do with this story. Had the young man in question been born in another town, his rise to fame and fortune might never have happened. Taken separately, his attributes, qualities and talents might have been considered too disparate, even contradictory. His family background might have conspired to clip his wings. His provincial horizons might have been wide enough only to hem him in. His musical style could well have found celebrity on the regional folk club circuit. His dark looks could well have been considered too Levantine to be properly aesthetic, his songs too precious to survive against an industrial background of silent chimneys and sooty streets. There were others who would emerge from those backgrounds with different songs and from a different family and ethnic background.

Our young Londoner presented a package of potential assets which, when having been discovered and assessed all together, found a ready niche in the hungry maw of the music machine mashing its way through new material not a few yards from our young man's front door.

His name was Stephen Dimetre Giorgiou although you will know him lately as Yusuf Islam. He is now in his later forties. For a time, however, for some fifteen years, he was best known by the world as Cat Stevens. By me and those of his friends and colleagues who have contributed to this book, his name was Steve.

Very little has been written about Stephen Giorgiou alias Cat Stevens. A great deal has been said about Yusuf Islam, mainly by Yusuf himself. However, it is the paucity of appreciation of the work which Steve produced whilst in his Cat Stevens period which I am attempting to augment and elucidate. It is not that I have no interest in Yusuf Islam but I have to define the parameters of this book and these I have set merely to ringfence some of the elements of a life which ultimately conspired to convince Steve that Cat Stevens should be escaped from or killed off. Many people are still confused as to his reasons why. Why? Why indeed ...

I don't know if Steve thought that, having abandoned it, the body of Cat Stevens would be easier to bury than it has proved or that it would decompose less conspicuously but Steve had too much effect on too many people's lives both in his own life and also, mainly, via his work to be allowed to merely slough one skin and inhabit another adopted skin un-noticed.

CHAPTER TWO

PLAYGROUNDS
AND PLAYMATES

The postal address of Steve's childhood home was actually Shaftesbury Avenue although the building, co-incidentally, presented and still presents two faces to the world, one to New Oxford Street to the north and one to Shaftesbury Avenue to the south. Looking north, Steve would have gazed out of windows which gave onto an area of London celebrated for the edifice of the British Museum, for several colleges and the Senate House of London University, respected medical and hospital centres as well as the locations of illustrious publishers' offices and homes of a reasonable residue of the writers and thinkers who were known en bloc as 'The Bloomsbury Group'. Bloomsbury was and is a very learned and esoteric neighbourhood, perhaps somewhat daunting to the child of a Greek Cypriot father who earned his family's living by cooking and a Swedish mother who was mutely loyal and supportive to her patently chauvinistic husband. From the other side of his home, Steve would have looked out on a small triangle of ground, mostly paved but from where grew tall plane trees populated by large numbers of pigeons whose droppings spattered the pavements beneath. Across this barren ground stood the red-pink edifice of the Shaftesbury Theatre whose neon marquees clicked into life after dark, advertising the theatre's current production. The Shaftesbury marks the northernmost outpost of London Theatre land. I remind people that the London production of Rado and Ragni's *HAIR!* opened and ran for several years at the Shaftesbury only to give perspective to a project which in some ways gave, if not birth then at least, huge impetus to Steve's renaissance in 1969-70. Over his growing years Steve must have looked out at many famous stars' names in lights.

The Giorgiou family home is still there, still a restaurant. There is no blue plaque although it would seem important that there should be as the family who lived there brought up one of the finest and least celebrated talents that British popular music has produced. This was Steve's house and the streets were his garden.

There are many testaments in this book about Steve's mother, Ingrid who sadly died in 1990 and also about Steve's sister Anita, the eldest of the three Giorgiou children. I can personally attest to the fact that both these women were exceedingly kind, very proud of Steve, the 'baby' of the family and also extremely indulgent to the whims of both baby, boy and man. Ingrid had a wonderful serenity and patience and she appeared to be a very uncomplicated woman. She spoke very gently, in a distinct but soft Swedish lilt. Almost musically. I'm reminded of her each time I see Liv Ullman or, even, Ingrid Bergman. Perhaps it's the Swedishness but rather, I think, because of a certain stoic, resigned quality which lends dignity to that particular embattled reality of life displayed by people who haven't been blessed from the outset with silver spoons and safety nets. I suppose the quality is of perseverance, of quiet determination. Anita, though physiognomically very different from Ingrid shared these qualities. I only knew her as a 'grown-up', married as she was and still is to Alex Zolas to whom she is devoted. I never distinguished temper or spirit in either woman although there was oodles of sensitivity. Emotions were, plainly, deeply felt. I felt instinctively that both women had the ability to observe and absorb in plenty.

Steve's father, Stavros Giorgiou, I knew hardly at all. He was a direct immigrant, from Cyprus and in his youth was obviously a very handsome man. He was as dark and Mediterranean as Ingrid was fair and Nordic. Their union could not have failed to produce striking children. But Stavros was in middle age when I knew him; he had thickened, coarsened and still spoke with a heavy accent. I hazard that Stavros was not greatly educated. I further hazard that neither Stavros nor Ingrid appreciated that in wanting their sons and daughter to do well at school and to better themselves as first generation British-born subjects that those children would inevitably drift first apart and then, away.

I don't know if others called him Stavros but I always addressed Steve's father as 'Mister Giorgiou' and his mother as 'Mrs. Giorgiou'. There was never any indication that that formality should be broken. Further or deeper conversation I never had with Stavros other than a polite 'Good Morning' when I called for Steve at the restaurant. I always thought it strange the place was called The Moulin Rouge. It must have been so-called by previous owners although when Steve arranged to have the place 'done over' in the mid-seventies, the restaurant was re-christened 'Stavros' and the menu widened from the chips-with-most-things offerings it had advertised for so long.

I am left now with the impression that Stavros Giorgiou looked at London and at Great Britain with the same eyes which had become used to Cyprus. Carl Miller, Steve's tour manager and confidante for many years, tells a story wherein he, Carl, is eating his meal at the Moulin Rouge one day whilst waiting for Steve to come downstairs. Carl always had to pay for his meals and had duly paid for the one he was eating that day, served to him by a waitress who was new at the job. One of the constituents of the platter was peas. Halfway through eating, a forkful poised at his mouth, Carl was aware of Stavros at his side with the new waitress in tow and half the portion of peas being swept from his plate and onto a spare. *"Izza too many peas!"* Stavros exclaimed crossly to the new waitress. *"Izza too many peas!"* Carl was ignored completely. Presumably Stavros saw him as merely an employee of Steve's or even just part of the cafe's furniture. Carl was certainly not someone considered worthy of his apology.

Immigration had not made Stavros British in anything else but name. He remained indubitably Mediterranean and exuded that characteristic machismo. That Stavros was intensely proud of Steve was obvious. That he didn't understand his son is equally plain. Maybe the whole family were slightly in awe, not necessarily of Steve but certainly of Cat Stevens. The lyrics Steve wrote for *FATHER AND SON* say more than perhaps even Steve intended. The strains and stresses felt by a son struggling with the guilty knowledge that he will never be and doesn't want to be like his father are undisguisable. And yet still the son wanted the father's love. Very difficult. To have been brought up in such a Mediterranean culture of fathers and sons only to realise that life has cast you as an extreme individual unable to slot naturally into the place that family and destiny has allotted you must have placed the young Steve beyond the pale of his own comprehension. To want to be part of something and yet know you are inexplicably not a part produces confusing and conflicting reactions in a growing male perspective. And so he grew, the son, becoming the pacifist poet prince striving to make the warrior king, the father, proud. It's the stuff of legends.

Stavros was a man who I always felt would act before he thought, a man possessed of volatility, impulsiveness and passion. I fancy he wore beneath his chef's apron all the colours of blood and wine and sunsets and centuries of loves and hates and memories of battle glories. Stavros' maleness was distinct at a hundred yards.

All this leads me to David, Steve's elder brother. Not only was David elder but he was bigger. David was beefier than Steve. Not quite as swarthy as Steve. There was a deceptive softness in David's features, almost a feminine roundness. He was earth to Steve's air and fire. Try as he could, David never managed to fly like his brother. I knew him as David Gordon though I cannot tell where Gordon came from. In their choice of adult names, it is interesting that both brothers chose spectacularly British handles, a million miles away from Giorgiou.

In the culture of fathers and sons, the eldest son always occupies a special place as the next head of the family, God willing. The eldest naturally deserved, willy nilly, the respect of all younger and certainly all female siblings. David, I'm sure, saw himself in this role. Though they'd been blessed with the same parents, David was not blessed with Steve's conflicting, contradictory nature which embraced both yin and yang. David Gordon was all yin.

I also think David was something of a bully. The violent streak which Steve at times displayed was just as resident in David. David was not a man I would ever have sought cause to cross. I'd known boys like David at school. One either avoided them, passed them by at a wise distance or, at worst, toadied and fagged for them to keep in their good books, as far away as possible from the inevitable stinging slap or other tenderly devised torture.

All the time I knew Steve and David, David's endeavours always appeared to have something to do with Steve's and Steve's career. Whether Steve found this irksome, I don't know for Steve never displayed any emotion regarding his elder brother other than the slightly second-place, deferential vibes I would have expected from an entirely un-famous and otherwise insignificant younger sibling. David by this time was also married, to a Swedish girl and had fathered a couple of children. Very important, children in that Mediterranean culture of fathers and sons and man-hood and virility and continuity and fierce pride.

I never saw Steve and David clash and I never heard and never was told that Steve ever said publicly anything whatsoever about his feelings or thoughts about his elder brother.

Conversely, what effect Steve's greater material and public success and achievement had on the elder brother again can only be guessed but I feel it right, for the sake of comprehension, to raise the question. David too was brought up streetwise in the Soho of the 1950's and early 1960's. David also liked to be noticed, to be thought of as 'someone'. To have nothing specific to do as an alternative when suddenly confronted by your younger brother's huge success presented an opportunity for David which he didn't miss as the initial Cat Stevens career gathered momentum in 1966 and 1967. Steve, thankfully for family peace, was notoriously generous and indeed even profligate with money as far as his family was concerned and, after all, specifically needed someone at his side on a day-to-day basis other than Mike Hurst, his initial manager and producer, and his staff. David Gordon filled that every-day management position then and played the 'minder' role.

In the second career, although David Gordon was always around, he was never involved with Steve's professional affairs as far as we who worked in the management company were con-cerned. David, however, was always popping into the office, always had ideas and projects, was always seeing Barry Krost, Steve's second manager, for meetings, introducing this new part-ner or that with a view to this new venture or that. But closer than this or that he never got to Steve's career. I can only surmise that it must have been more than irritating to David that he wasn't more closely involved at the helm.

I've been told that it was David who bought Steve a copy of the Qur'an for his birthday in 1974. It was the year when Steve and Barry Krost were beginning to drift apart. At such times of trouble, families tend to close ranks against those perceived as the enemy. It had happened before. But as well as protecting, such family unity can also tend to stifle and to trap. Those family members more at home adventuring outside and alone often find that they have to discover ways of avoiding the tentacles of the dear octopus. 1974 for Steve turned out to be a year of that classic trap: "*... nowhere to run to, nowhere to hide ...*".

Sadly the family that once lived all together at the Moulin Rouge proved to be an insufficient refuge for Steve as did many of the other relationships which had underpinned his daily life. Steve needed more than family and David always knew it. Steve's final split with the music industry after his ultimate conversion to Islam at least meant for David Gordon that he had been released from ever again being perceived merely as Cat Stevens' brother although by being so released, the continuity of the Giorgiou family as it had come down through Stavros' line would be irrevocably threatened.

But before such unfathomable complications began to mar the life of the young singer, there were Steve's own golden years. Going to school, he attended Hugh Middleton's school in Sans Walk, London EC1. The school has now moved to new premises in Middleton Street in the same district and is about to celebrate its centenary. The teacher I spoke to, Linda Cairns was unaware of the illustrious alumnus when I telephoned. It seems that Steve also attended Hugh Middleton Secondary School at least until the age when his parents decided he would benefit for some reason more from a private secondary education.

Growing up in London's West End, however extraordinary and enviable it might seem to me, must have been, inevitably, pretty much everyday stuff for the young Steven Giorgiou.

Anita Bovingdon remembers this everyday stuff very clearly. She was born one of ten children, five boys and five girls and her family lived in a house in Museum Street, just north, across New Oxford Street, of the Giorgiou family home. Now a researcher working in film and television, Anita's memories provide a rich background and some interesting insights.

ANITA BOVINGDON: "Steven I remember very, very well and for one simple reason. He was my elder brother Eddie's best friend. They were the same age and they went everywhere together. It's all the more poignant for me to remember because Eddie sadly died in 1981 and he's still talked about. Ten of us there were, and now there's nine. Eddie was unforgettable. Larger than life, full of hope and energy. It's more for him that I'm talking as he's not here to help you. However, I've spoken to Alex, my eldest brother and also to Mickey who was next youngest to Eddie and they've both jogged my own memory and contributed some memories of their own.

Our part of the West End was very mixed. You got some very wealthy people and there was a lot of poverty. We lived in Museum Street, in the top three floors above a shop. Our entrance was in Gilbert Place and the back of our house overlooked Helen Graham House, part of the YWCA. I rather fancy that a lot of the local boys would hang around at the back of Helen Graham just to see what they could see!

Although there wasn't much Afro-Caribbean presence then, there was starting to be an Indian one. I remember Merou, an Indian boy whose family lived off Drury Lane. Merou was very much a part of Steve and Eddie's group of friends and later went on to become a wrestler. I believe his professional name was The Black Panther of Pakistan!

I remember Steve because he always used to be at our house. Ours was that kind of house. Open all hours it seemed. Everyone loved coming there. My parents weren't the sort that frightened kids off. They were never judgemental although that didn't stop other parents being judgemental about us! My mum was always cooking and there was an atmosphere where everyone was welcomed. She always had enough love to go round not only for her own children but for all their friends as well. I hear horror stories of kids and their growing up and they sound alien to me because all we ever knew was love and security and a strong sense of being protected. I remember one day Steve got bitten quite nastily by a dog while he and Eddie were playing in a car park. They were playing with a Manchester United Football and kicked it accidentally into the car park which was being guarded by a big German Shepherd. Steve went in after the ball but instead of retrieving only his own ball also picked up the dog's! For some reason, he wouldn't go back to his own house but insisted that my mum see to his wound. Like my brother, people still talk about us as a family and, obviously, always about my mum who was the powerhouse behind it.

I didn't know David, Steve's elder brother but then being kids, even being a year younger is like a huge gap. My elder brothers, Alex and Mickey never knew David Gordon although for some reason we all remember Anita, Steve's sister, perhaps because she used to work in the hairdresser's opposite but I can never remember going to The Moulin Rouge, Steve's parents' cafe although I knew who they were well enough. The boys would go there, though and always get some chips from Stavros or, if he was feeling generous, some chicken.

You have to understand that because we had no gardens, we all went outdoors from what I suppose would now be considered a very early age. Just outside Steve's house there was a drinking fountain. In those days, we used to call the fountain and the island it stood on 'Lousy Island' for some reason but it was nevertheless a favourite gathering place for the young kids. There was a shop on the opposite corner of Shaftesbury Avenue which sold every kind of cheap item that we kids would spend what little pocket money we had on.

I also have to explain that our freedom was never random. It had boundaries just as children born then in the country had limits to what they could and couldn't do. We were just as strictly brought up and although it would seem a busy bustling place, the West End had eyes and ears for its own if you happened to be a resident. Being a girl too, your brothers wouldn't let you get away with anything.

Having said that I have to enlarge upon saying that freedom for boys and freedom for girls were very different animals. Boys definitely got the better deal in that department although there were times, football matches for example, when our parents considered that there would be likely to be too great a risk of loutish behaviour in the West End for any of us under teenage to be safely allowed out. There was certainly a world for boys and a world for girls. As girls, we not only had limits to our world and our lives, there were frontiers. Although I went up and down Charing Cross Road as much as I liked and was allowed to ride my bicycle down Oxford Street on Saturday afternoons when all the shops shut after lunch and it was deserted, I never went into Soho proper. If I had, the jungle drums would have sounded for sure. I remember once being told by my brothers that I'd strayed too far over the line when I passed a friend of theirs standing in a doorway. I later learned that the place was a Strip Club. Irish Micky, as he was called, from Victoria had apparently been heard calling out something like "'*Ello, darlin'*," as I had walked by. And I was censured. NOT a proper situation for a girl to be in!

Steve'd come up to our house either on his own with Eddie or with Andrew, who I always remember as being a cousin of his. Andrew was a very important part of Steve's growing up too, I'd imagine because I always remember him being around. Even at the age of sixteen or seventeen, Steve was pretty frail. He didn't look too strong. One day, he was up in our house and my mum thought he looked very poorly. She told him to go straight back home and see his own mum. She told us all that she thought he had jaundice, his skin was all yellowed.

Anyway, having Eddie and Andy around him can't have harmed Steve's welfare as he was finding his feet in the West End. I remember Andy and Steve would always get the white hankies out when they came to our house and show off their Greek dancing. Steve was very much one of the lads, often getting into spots of bother at school or elsewhere when his 'gang' would rush off to provide either moral or physical support.

One of the things I remember most about Steve and Eddie's friendship was that they were forever making up songs. They'd go off round the streets or into the parks and gardens and make up lyrics. Their 'gang' was very much a part of this process. The Indian boy Merou and Steve's Greek friend Andy were always around and the 'gang' turned into something of a band. It was the days when bands were springing up all over the place. It was big news that the Beatles wrote their own words and music and Steve and Eddie's band were heading in the same direction.

Eddie always used to joke when Steve became famous that HIS songs were MUCH better than Cat Stevens'. I do fancy Steve had a guitar in those days but I'm afraid I can't be sure. Both Alex and Mickey assure me, though, that the band were pretty far advanced. Mickey especially remembers going up with the other four to Steve's room above the cafe and singing. He remembers clearly that the band had learned that Tommy Roe song SHEILA and that Stavros had bought Steve a tape recorder. The band recorded SHEILA as well as a lot of the other songs that Steve and Eddie made up themselves. They even went one day to a proper recording studio off Monmouth Street somewhere and did some tapes.

My brothers certainly remember where a lot of those early lyrics or at least the inspiration for them came from. We had a lovely dog when we were little called Prince which sadly died. Then Eddie got another one called Rex. He really loved those dogs. Alex remembers there being a wholesaler too called Matthew and Son somewhere around Gilbert Place and it was well-known in our family that Steve was very much captivated by the story of a robbery at a gunshop in Poland Street. All these of course were just little snippets of neighbourhood West End life which Steve saw fit to treat in his own way. Mickey remembers another song they all wrote together called DARLING NO although as far as they know, it never surfaced in a Cat Stevens context.

Of course, you lose touch with so much as time passes. The worst is when you lose people all together. I haven't seen Steve in years and years but one of my brothers bumped into him not so long ago. Steve was by this time only using his Islamic name, Yusuf and he was with his wife. My brother told him that Eddie had died and my parents too. Steve was very polite, acknowledging this sadness and asking to be remembered to the rest of the family but my brother said he felt odd, felt he wanted to hug Steve or something but couldn't, felt that the intimacy would not have been welcomed, that they really did now live in different worlds. Sad, really. Sort of makes the memories of the old times even more poignant ..."

More than a hint of the fuller flavour of Steve's school-days is provided by Ian Warner. Ian's history emerges in the text although to add to his testament, since 1974 when he left Carlin Music to look after publishing at Tony Stratton-Smith's Charisma group and B and C records, Ian has worked at Screen Gems but left when EMI acquired the Columbia Pictures interest in 1976. That same year, he moved to Vancouver to work for Mushroom records where his main responsibility was the band HEART. Ian returned to work in this country in 1991. I met him whilst he was working with my colleague David Minns. David Minns happened to mention I was writing this book and Ian casually said: *"Oh, really. I went to school with Steve."*

IAN WARNER: "Well ... It's a very long story so I'd better get on with it. My father was in the rag trade. His company, whose factory was located in Rathbone Place just off Tottenham Court Road, made ladies' skirts and slacks. My parents lived in St John's Wood and I was the youngest of two children, my sister being a few years older than me. I was a London boy but a nice London boy.

In their wisdom and with obviously high hopes, my parents had sent me as far away from London as they could between the ages of eight and thirteen to the Queen Mother's School in Stagenhoe Park at St Paul's Walden near Hitchin, Hertfordshire. It was one of those schools where great ladies in even greater hats descended periodically through the year. Sports Days and beginnings and ends of term we could cope with but the Queen Mother always seemed to light upon my bath night as an appropriate moment to check the welfare of the charges of a school that stood on Bowes-Lyon family land. Even at that tender age, no dispensation was granted to remain decently covered by two inches of murky grey bath water. Upstanding we had to be for Her Majesty. Ugh! The embarassment!

Because they wanted me to cram for the common entrance exam which might possibly get me into a public school, at the end of prep school days at Stagenhoe Park, my parents decided to send me to a crammer in London. The crammer they selected - though how and why is still a mystery - was Hyde Park College. This small, fee-paying, private day school was located in a building on the corner of Leinster Gardens in Bayswater, a building which is now a Toy Museum. The school was run by Donald Evans and his Russian wife Ilona. I suppose in the terms of the time, it was no different to many private schools established and run by ex-colonial service or ex-army people. Most didn't last long and few developed into anything more than one generation affairs affording meagre incomes for the families who operated them.

Hyde Park College to the world outside its gates can't have been considered that different in its mould although it must have been perceived as in some way 'better' than the state schools. I fancy that the education meted out by state primary or private prep was pretty equal but that the latter was thought somehow more socially respectable and more likely to advantage pupils in future life.

Well, as far as I was concerned, I'd landed in clover. For starters, there were girls! Hyde Park College was co-educational and coming from a single sex school in the country with puberty rattling my hormones alarmingly, I found the presence of the opposite sex, at first, just unbelievable. I also had money in my pocket. Tiny amounts compared to today, maybe but five shillings to be spent as I wanted on fares, chocolate bars for break-time ... It was amazing!

And I got to sit next to Steven Giorgiou.

As you can imagine, being in that area of London at that time, Hyde Park College sported a very cosmopolitan spectrum of pupils. There were Jewish, like me, Greeks, Italians, Levantines as well as English and, even in those days when there'd been very little Afro-Caribbean immigration, a couple of black kids. The Paliaci family who ran the delicatessen in Shaftesbury Avenue, lots of people in catering and many of the families who had settled in London's Soho district sent their children to Mr. and Mrs. Evans to be bettered.

We sat in double desks in classes of between fifteen and twenty and I can't even start to talk about being at school with Steve without mentioning his relative Paul. Whilst Steve was small and thin and tough, Paul at age fifteen was huge, strong and tougher. He was the Goliath. To see Steve and Paul swaggering away from school in that green uniform with the gold braid, caps perched jauntily on the backs of their heads, pinned on to very well-combed thick hair in the highest of current style, the one so tall and big, the other so small by comparison is a sight I will remember for ever.

To be brutally frank, Steve and Paul were the terrors of the school - to staff and pupils equally. Of all the West End and Soho people, Steve and Paul were the street-wisest and they were tough. They meant business and you did NOT mess with them. With his 'minder' Paul behind him, Steve wasn't at all the shy, retiring type. Quite the reverse. He was perfectly prepared to resort to violence to get what he wanted, get his own way. He'd think nothing of bullying when he thought he could get away with it, treading on your shoes and grinding his foot over yours. Not mine I hasten to add because for whatever reason, maybe because I'd ended up sitting next to him, he and Paul took me under their collective wing and proceeded to show me their ropes.

Apart from Paul, Steve had a lot of ammunition in his armoury at school. He was the lippiest kid. He seemed to be able to talk his way out of anything. His smile was wonderful. Teachers, grown-ups would melt and he'd turn on that smile like a switch. In class, when the teacher's back was turned, Steve and Paul would get up to terrible things. Far worse than just talking out loud. They'd fool around, misbehave and even, as we got older, try making out with some of the girls in the class. I remember two girls especially who often found their blouse buttons being tampered with; they were sisters, one slightly older and they were frequently, and never unwillingly, the objects of these adolescent fumbles. But when whichever teacher it was turned round, there would be Steve looking like a saint, a beatific smile radiating innocence and charm.

Of course, he didn't always get away with cheek. He'd occasionally get a clip round the ear from one of them - Mr. M who taught English and French and whom we all thought was gay; and there was the classic Jimmy Edwards type too, handlebar moustache bristling ... More likely there'd just be a telling off. *"Giorgiou, shut up!"* When Steve was chastised, either physically or verbally, he would be overcome with embarassment at being brought down and embarrassed in public and would blush noticeably even with his Mediterranean colouring.

One teacher who must have fetched up in this country as a refugee from one of the Eastern European states when the Iron Curtain came down taught us maths. Poor guy. When his back was turned as he wrote on the blackboard, Steve would say in an obvious stage whisper: *'Bloody communist!'* The teacher would get so mad. He'd turn round and almost scream at us in his heavy middle-European accent: *'Communist! Vot you mean, communist? I've been through bloody hell escaping from the communists! Why do you say zis to me?'*

Despite his bad behaviour, Steve was a good student. He was very bright indeed although it must have seemed to the teachers that he was forever fighting against being educated. I think his native intelligence was bridling against the imposition of learning that the school was trying to achieve. Steve bridled against so much control, almost struggled to stay outside the pale of that educative process.

Schoolboys. I don't know. They really were the days of the old school yard and, as Steve himself wrote, we certainly used to laugh a lot. Steve was as good as he was bad. Yes, they smoked in the playground; yes he was always the guy with the pack of cards with the naked girls on the back, yes he'd either bully, cajole or bribe people to do his and Paul's homework but he was fun. He created a lot of fun and laughter and he was never downright malicious. He was operating. He was a strong character and he found it only logical to express this strength, this confidence in being a cool, smooth, natural operator and as you'll see, he was only doing what came naturally.

The impression of the Steve of those days which has remained with me most is that he really didn't care whether he won or lost. He knew he could mostly win and so I suppose that helped. He really didn't give a shit one way or the other. His intelligence came very much to bear because I know he had weighed up the consequences of either eventuality and ten to one knew how he would try and wriggle out if the worst happened. To me he was a free spirit, almost untied by discipline, right, wrong, good, bad ... he was a complete pragmatist.

Games we hated. Once a week, on Mondays, we'd schlep out to a playing ground on Warwick Avenue where there were pink concrete football pitches. Ugh! We hated it and just stood on the sidelines or bunked off for a smoke and if challenged would come out with the standard and un-workably lame excuse: *'Forgot my kit, sir!'* It worked because it worked. No boots. No footie.

I thought Steve was magical and I followed the sound of his drum willingly, gladly. He was the best and I suppose the worst possible friend an impressionable adolescent could have made at school. Every parent's nightmare.

Most of my strong memories of Steve however concern those times when we were off school premises. He and Paul were forever trying to bunk off and inescapably I was drawn into this truancy too. We'd often spend most of a whole day in Selfridges ... Can you imagine that? A whole day in Selfridges? Or we'd go into Wimpy Bars, the big new thing then, and wile away the hours. At lunch-time, faced with the school's offerings which numbered amongst other unappetising, puke-making items as mashed potato with no salt and custard made with no sugar, Steve and Paul would take me with them to buy one-and-eight penny bags of chips from the fish shop around the corner from Leinster Gardens or at the cafe in Whiteleys. You see, Steve always had money in his pocket. It must have come basically from his parents who, after all, were running a cash business with their cafe. Lots of the kids from the catering backgrounds were the same. Always had money, unlike poor little me with the rationed-out five bob. Also, being brought up in catering, you ate when it was convenient to eat. The family, I imagine, rarely ate together. Meal-times weren't sacred institu-tions and food was always around ... It was nothing special unlike in homes like mine where a mother's status depended on her providing meals at set times from her specific efforts. Life with Steve and Paul was like going on the dodgems with the people who owned not only the ride but the whole bloody fair.

After-school hours and out-of-school hours were more than magic. They were enchanted, probably because to me they were forbidden. I always felt guilty when I was with Steve at, say, his parents' cafe. I always felt that I shouldn't be there, that I was being very daring. It was probably because Steve's parents were so unlike mine. Though he was doted on, he lived completely outside their control. It was Steve who had the control, control over his own life. It seemed that he could and did do exactly what he wanted. In fact, I can't honestly remember much about his parents. Now you mention whether I was aware that Mrs. Giorgiou was Swedish, I have to say that it's news to me.

I, on the other hand, was always under control or at least felt the invisible parental hand on my collar most of the time I was away from home. It was only on a very few occasions that Steve came back and stayed, pre-arranged with his folks, at my house. I much preferred being in the West End.

The temptation to be as bad as I thought Steve and Paul were was too much. Come four o'clock we'd be off. I had to be home by 6.30 for dinner in St John's Wood and I'd either spend the intervening time with Steve and Paul and take the bus home or I'd race to catch my dad who'd leave his factory around six to drive home for dinner. That all important dinner time.

Had we remained in school the whole day, at four o'clock Steve, Paul and I would walk from the school up to Paddington tube station. Outside the station there was a shop which sold everything - electrical things, cameras. There were always naughty items like nudie pin-up postcards. If I saw one I liked and said so, chances are that Steve would turn up the following day with the same card or one very like it for me. When I tell you he certainly didn't steal, how, you might ask would a fourteen year old schoolboy come by such things so easily?

The explanation is simply that Paul's father's business was strip clubs. I was given to believe that he owned, organised and ran clubs in Soho and it was to Soho that we would take the underground everyday after school. Thank God my father worked in Tottenham Court Road and not Tottenham High Road.

The rather raw truth of what was a paradoxical situation was that Paul was expected to attend school each day like a perfectly normal, ordinary boy only to be equally expected to start work in the box office of the strip club as soon as he got home. I must confess that while I initially found the whole thing crazily exciting, after a while I kind of backed off. Big and hefty as Paul was he was still only a fifteen year old and when I saw him getting grief if he was a few minutes late for work from some man I remember as always being in a white shirt, I felt for him and felt embarrassed and didn't want to be around. I hated seeing one of my heroes being cut down to size by a grown-up.

I also vividly remember the abusive way the strippers were treated by the people who ran the club. I hate to admit it but these women were treated less kindly and with even less respect than one would have shown to a horse in harness. Of course I used to show off to my other friends and when we'd scrape into the West End on Saturday nights, I'd always tip up to the strip clubs just to prove that I DID know the people on the door. Privately, I was always rather frightened of the enormity and also confused, disillusioned that something which ought by rights to have caused a healthy fourteen year old an almost continuous orgasm was treated by Paul and Steve like just another piece of chewing gum, as nothing special. It was as though my friends were anaesthetised to something that excited me to my very guts. What being around such places for so long must have done to their characters, I can only conjecture.

But at least they remembered to send me postcards.

Presumably Steve and Paul stayed at Hyde Park College until they were sixteen but I don't know because I was sent at almost fifteen to Harrow High. Presumably they had some sort of a stab at GCE 'O' levels although again I don't know, I was surprised afterwards to hear that Steve had gone to Art School. I can't remember him displaying any talent for the graphic arts at school and there was certainly no hint of a musical future. I can't remember him having learned or learning either the guitar or the piano and we didn't even talk about music or bands particularly. I remember we used to like THE OUTLAWS and THE FLEEREKKERS but we never went to record stores or anything like that or collected or swapped records. As he never even hinted at it, I can be fairly sure that Steve wasn't anywhere near writing songs then and it now seems almost an impossibility that he grew up to be Cat Stevens.

After I left Hyde Park College there was a temporary lapse in my friendship with Steve. And, after I left Harrow High, I too went into show business. As my mother has famously remarked about the cost of my education: *'All that money and you end up a bloody beat drummer!'* Whilst Steve was learning instruments and writing songs and preparing for his debut with Decca, I was 'doing a Beatles'... Strange how from the same class in the same tiny school, two such different people with no connection to music should wind up in the music business which is really very small.

In the sixties, you didn't run away to join the circus, if you wanted to run away you headed for a rock 'n' roll band. I went to Germany and joined David Bridger's group which went under the name of DAVEY SANDS AND THE ESSEX. It was, for non-cognoscenti and anyone under forty, a piece of wordplay on DAVID ESSEX AND THE SANDS.

As well as presenting our own identity, we were also contracted by bookers like Roy Tempest, John Salter, Don Arden and Alan Eisenberg to appear on American bases and other German venues backing American artists like Tommy Roe when they toured Europe. The Germans hated the American occupying forces. There were endless fights, constant vicious attacks and more often than not we were caught in the middle, as much of the violence occurred in the dance halls and the clubs where we'd be playing. If I mentioned bodies in the boots of cars being driven away at top speed under the cloak of night, of course I wouldn't be talking about anything real ... Life on the German road was certainly a baptism by fire into the business.

Brian Somerville was David Bridger's manager and after our ultimate and, I suppose, inevitable deportation, although Brian drove us back into Germany once more, life there was never the same and we found ourselves once more back in England.

Though we hadn't seen each other much, Steve and I had kept in touch and he came to see me. Typically generous, he had a song for me. He must have met up with Mike Hurst and Chris Brough by this time although my memory for the exact times and dates is a bit wobbly. I was far more concerned with my own precarious career at the time. I'm sure Mike Hurst needs no amplification but it should be remembered that Chris, son of Peter Brough of ARCHIE ANDREWS fame, supplied equal input into their production concern. Whether I LOVE MY DOG had already been done by the time Steve brought us THAT song, I'm not sure but one thing is for sure and that is he turned up at my place one day with a tape of HERE COMES MY BABY.

I jumped on it. I played it to the guys in the band and Steve gave us the go-ahead to record it. The way Steve had originally composed HERE COMES MY BABY displayed all his trademarks - the fractured rhythms and sudden staccato tempos. We recorded it and then my cousin and I went away for two weeks holiday in the

South of France. I can't say I was thrilled with our version but I went off fondly thinking HERE COMES MY BABY was our song.

It's said that a week's a long time in politics. To that you have to add ... 'But it's short compared to a week in rock and roll.' By the time I came back from holiday, Len 'Chip' Hawkes, Chesney's dad, had been poached by the TREMELOES and had left the band. HERE COMES MY BABY had been recorded by the Brian Poole-less TREMELOES and of course it became a massive hit and restored the TREMELOES' fortunes not to mention what it did for Steve Giorgiou's coffers.

Meantime, we put on a brave face and hired another bass player as we had a gig to do at Major David Watts' venue at Oakham on the Rutland Estate - the same Major Watts featured in the KINKS' song title I WISH I COULD BE MORE LIKE DAVID WATTS. Co-oincidentally, we were to appear on the same bill as the TREMELOES who, like ourselves, were sponsored by Ruddles Ales to the tune of equipment as well as engagements. The TREMELOES were on the same bill. I saw no reason to perpetuating grudges especially as the TREMELOES' Alan Blakeley was our producer as well. I went up and congratulated Len Hawkes who was flying high on having been given a £100 a week retainer and a new Fender guitar and amplifier by his new band. I was sincerely pleased for him.

Thereafter, I wasn't long for the DAVEY SANDS band and left to play for a while with a group called THE PLAYGROUND which mutated, without me, into HARMONY GRASS. Tony Rivers from the CASTAWAYS did all the vocal arrangements for THE PLAYGROUND. MOVE IN A LITTLE CLOSER, BABY sung by Tony Rivers as HARMONY GRASS became one of the first hits for the publisher Cyril Shane. It then happened that Cyril who was looking for a promotions man asked the TREMELOES if they knew of anyone and they kindly suggested me. Just the chap, they said and that's how I started on the other side of the microphone. I promoted the recorded product around the media whilst Cyril stayed in the office trying to place the original material with his contacts in the business. Cyril was a great importer of foreign songs which Jack Fishman would translate. We placed songs with loads of people - HERMAN'S HERMITS, Malcolm Roberts, AMEN CORNER whose IF PARADISE WAS HALF AS NICE was originally an Italian song.

I used to see Steve on and off at places like THE CROMWELLIAN and THE SPEAKEASY. The Speakeasy played a huge role in our lives. You could go in there at one or two in the morning and still get your steak sandwich and load up on the fashionable scotch and coke or Bacardi rum and coke. Where else could you do that, pick up a road crew if you needed one and watch people like HENDRIX getting up on stage to jam with YES, then the club's house band?

I have to say that when I saw Steve as Cat Stevens, the act that Mike Hurst and Chris Brough had moulded, I sensed he wasn't too happy. Mike Hurst was a very powerful man. He was really dominant and had huge self-belief. He saw himself as a sort of British Phil Spector. I know Steve was the successful one of the pair of us at the time and I wasn't but I don't think it's jealousy talking here. He was uncomfortable. I know it. Steve was never one to stand for any bullshit but he was obviously willing to sacrifice for I felt that Hurst and Brough and done a music biz number on someone who was patently a fresh and original talent. Perhaps that's a little unfair in that the business was not structured in those days to allow the talent to present itself. However, it was obvious to me that Steve was being packaged in those Deram days, branded with a gimmick, landed with an image and sent out there to live up to both. I actually felt embarrassed for him sitting up there in the cowboy hat and the whip thing or whatever it was in I'M GONNA GET ME A GUN.

They were the days of the '45', days which engendered and bred a '45' mentality throughout the music business whose legacy to some extent persists today in broadcasting and television media circles. I was away in Vancouver and LA for fifteen years and when I came back, although things had changed, some of the fundamentals were still in place. Like the people - same brains and same attitudes. The only thing that had changed was the number of wrinkles and the colour of their hair.

The '45' mentality affected recording and publishing alike. I'm sure that Steve's publishing wasn't considered by his early mentors as much as it later proved it should have been. People really did think in terms of three singles contracts, six sides - Try 'em, fly 'em and see if they buy 'em. Careers weren't countenanced. The unsuccessful were merely discarded and ignored with little hope of any renaissance. Singers weren't considered artists and as such, even if, like Steve, they did write, they weren't contracted on blanket publishing arrangements. It was still song by song by song. Thank heavens for people like Steve who helped change all that old fashioned, rather exploitative view of short-term gains from the sweat of creative brows. Okay, it's not perfect now but it's better for a lot than it was when the industry was run basically by cowboys bred on the wide open spaces of agency and booking work, sitting fatly in West End offices all hungry for their ten percents, banking most of their commissions from ill-conceived and hurriedly-begotten touring road-shows which only served to further impress the '45' mentality into the perceptions and expectations of the great British public. Gigging and touring was, even in the early seventies, the only way of promoting recorded product in Great Britain. In the United States the proliferation of radio stations had to an extent pre-empted touring. Sure, you could tour and really establish your credibility but radio could do it just as well. If you were like Steve and came over brilliantly on vinyl, radio would make you a star. It's why so many American acts never came to England. The venues were too small and the grosses not tempting enough and where was the ultimate exposure to sell the product and earn on the publishing?

People drift apart and certainly Steve and I did. The last time I saw him to speak to was on a beach on the Greek island of Mykonos in the summer of 1972 where I was on holiday with my wife. Steve was with Alun and Val Davies, his accompanist and great friend whom I'd also met on some project or other we had going at Carlin Music. I couldn't believe the smallness of the world and, again, the now inevitable co-incidence.

Of course we talked and went and had dinner and a couple of bottles of retsina together but Steve wasn't overtly friendly. I knew he had become a serious artist but you can be serious and still be fun. Steve'd definitely changed. The wild spark had certainly gone out entirely somewhere along the line and the Steve I spent that evening with was a very distant relation to the one I'd known. Perhaps I was drinking retsina with Cat Stevens and not Steve Giorgiou?

I know there are periods in all our lives during which we lose our innocence. I have a feeling that Steve lost his very quickly. Almost overnight. Was it his illness which deprived him of the sense of fun and mischief and devil-may-care which had so inspired me as a 'nice London boy' to join him in so many wicked escapades? Serious illness can and does have that effect. I was thirty five when I had a major heart attack. I was in the shower. Things do change when you're faced with mortal possibilities. You realise just what is important. For me it was my relationships, my friends. Suddenly, what other people thought about me was insignificant. Money definitely took a back seat. We may, after all, not be here on the day we intended to spend it.

I actually think there's something else. I suppose I shouldn't be but I never cease to be amazed by how many people who, after working so hard and achieving their precious success, discover that the success they wanted isn't what it was cracked up to be ... Doesn't necessarily solely apply to people in show business. Suddenly you wake up and realise that in order to carry on, to continue just to exist you have to re-take control ..."

It's difficult to imagine that the adolescent youngster sketched by Ian Warner could possibly have developed with any shred of sensitivity for it seems certain that at fourteen and fifteen, he displayed little. Certainly all the traits of character which were the least appealing of the adult Steve's characteristics were all in place. And the contradictions. He had obviously learned at an early stage whom he could pick on and still retain the upper hand of control and yet he could be both generous and protective to those he liked. It would seem the duration of his loyalty was always questionable but on the other hand he was always buoyed up by the presence of both immediate and extended family members. He didn't particularly NEED friends. Outwardly, he seemed to have cause to be more than secure enough in his childhood. He certainly had confidence enough for several children.

His being aware so brashly and matter-of-factly and at such a relatively early age of sex would seem to suggest that he missed out on something of the build-up, something of the mystery. I can't help feeling instinctively that something of the emotional connotation of sex had been lost on Steve by the time he was able to profit from emotional rewards of his sexual relationships.

But something finer must have rubbed off from somewhere or have been inculcated by someone. Steve left school at the earliest opportunity and for a while attended Hammersmith College of Art. He must have been doing a lot more than toying with the idea of developing his graphic talents for at some time between fifteen and seventeen, Steve learned to play the guitar. Did he also go through a stage of going to see other performers or buying records and playing them alone in his room or, as most of us did, practise the peacock struttings of our favourite singing stars in front of our bedroom mirrors?

CHAPTER THREE

A LONG WAY
FROM NOWHERE

There were few places in the centre of London where the new talent could be assessed directly and 'discovered'. The relentless touting of songs by writers to publishers was a tried and tested tradition in music publishers offices in the West End but rarely was it heard of for the writers to also want to be the entertainers. Playing their song on the piano in the publisher's office was not entertainment; it was merely to ratify that the song was fit to be passed to another to sing properly. The Noel Cowards of pre-war London had been few and far between. In the 50's and 60's young performers joined the queuing ranks of song writers touting themselves for discovery. The legion of actors and singers who legendarily paid their dues whilst working as entertainers in British Summer and Holiday Camps or schlepping endlessly up and down the country from one Variety theatre venue to another is well-known but gradually, talent agents and managers and A and R (Artists and Repertoire) staff at the record companies were beginning to seek out talent at its grass roots.

The prime venue where new work in the even newer vein of rock music could be seen was London's MARQUEE CLUB. I was lucky enough to be able to talk at length to John Gee who has good reason to remember the teenage Steven Giorgiou.

JOHN GEE: "In 1965, I was in overall charge of THE MARQUEE CLUB. The Marquee had started off in Oxford Street, beneath the Academy cinema which, like many phenomena from that period, no longer exists. THE MARQUEE had been spawned in the world of jazz. I myself was initially employed by the National Jazz Federation under whose aegis many renowned musicians and their bands had prospered. Through working for some of the earlier big bands like Ted Heath's, I had graduated both in my musical tastes and my working arena into Jazz which in the late fifties and early sixties was incredibly popular. The Reading Festival, administered by THE MARQUEE organisation, was hugely attended and the BBC's TRAD TAVERN television show was a hit programme. The MARQUEE CLUB was a natural and permanent extension of the tours and gigs and appearances made by Chris Barber who, with Harold Pendleton, founded the club which soon became a national institution, one of the internationally celebrated London homes for jazz.

As well as Chris Barber's, Johnny Dankworth's and Humphrey Lyttleton's bands, the raunchier Alexis Korner had discovered rhythm and blues whilst on tours in America and had fallen under its spell. Chris Barber too fell under the influence and Korner and Barber and their bands would get together more and more regularly to play rhythm and blues at the Marquee. The purity of THE MARQUEE's original brew was being diluted and by 1965, it was well on the way to becoming the British equivalent of Doug Weston's Troubadour in Los Angeles, a venue that was to be as significant as THE MARQUEE to the older Cat Stevens in 1971.

In 1964, THE MARQUEE club moved its premises to Wardour Street.

I'm giving you this background because it's important to know both where the sixties music came from and why I was so particularly engaged when the young Steven Giorgiou, as he was then, appeared at The Marquee. As far as I was concerned, being at The Marquee for me was just a job of work. We'd moved from Oxford Street to where the Club ended up in Wardour Street. Of course we were never a dancing sort of club, never a disco. People would crowd round the stage and it was to hear the music. Very much so. By the time we're talking about, the jazz was taking very much a back seat. I remember we'd already had Manfred Mann on Mondays, THE WHO on Tuesdays and THE STONES on Thursdays and THE STONES were a support act in those days, 1962 to 1963, to Alexis Korner, Cyril Davies and BLUES INCORPORATED. (Club members paid four shillings to get in, non-members paid five. Twenty pence or twenty five! THE STONES then or now, take your pick!)

I have to say that I found this sort of music very loud. Over-loud and rather vulgar, I thought. It had nothing to do with the sort of music that I was into and which I'd been brought up with. You couldn't even distinguish the actual music half the time let alone the lyrics. Lyrics. Ha! Words didn't end in anything ... They just trailed away to nothing. You see, I met Steve in about 1965. No. Probably 1966.

American music had of course always been popular although it was to England, after the huge success of THE BEATLES and the other bands from Liverpool, that the American music business began to turn and it brought with it a corporate identity previously unknown in the relatively hit and miss atmosphere of the British music scene where hits had always just happened. As business men saw what huge sums of money could be made from relatively small investments, hits were being made. Success was being bought and sold. Managers, agents, publicists ... the biz had become an industry.

I encountered many people in those days at the Marquee. The need to find new talent, to discover the next BEATLES or whoever, was very strong and so we were all on the 'qui vive', as it were. On Wednesday nights, the Marquee presented Folk acts and music that wasn't quite so rock oriented. I can't for the life of me think how it came about or who booked him because it certainly wasn't me, but I distinctly remember the first time I heard Steve playing. It was as though someone had rolled back the cloud of noise and a shaft of real music had pierced through the gloom of that smoky club. As the set went on, I was quite amazed. There was this stunningly good-looking young chap of about seventeen or eight-een with what I considered a splendid voice. When he sang, you could hear the lyrics clearly. His diction was impeccable, delivered in a beautiful, resonant voice and of course he was playing all his own material. His whole presentation was so refreshing. He had that charisma, that overwhelming quality which distinguishes a star from the dross.

I introduced myself after he'd finished his set and we went out and had a coffee. He was very well-dressed and seemed incredibly together. He was very clear in his head about what he wanted and he wanted, basically, to get on and become a success. He very much wanted to be successful. I explained to him about the Marquee set-up, that we had management and agency facilities and I told him about all our other interests such as the Reading Festival and the other 'ins' we had with platforms to promote new young talent and I really did sense that the young Cat Stevens was very talented. There was this special spark, a creativity so distinctive that it immediately set him apart in my mind from all the others around at the time. We arranged to meet again. I remember meeting him in his room above the cafe his father had on Shaftesbury Avenue, a room filled, as I recall, with guitars. We went out for drinks somewhere and I told him that depending on what my superiors at the Marquee felt, I would like to make a deal with him. As I had a reasonably established track record in finding new artists - for example THE MOODY BLUES - I was reasonably certain that something could be worked out for Steve.

It was then that Steve explained, in all fairness, that mine wasn't the only interest floating around in his nascent career. Mike Hurst, he revealed, was more than interested. As you'll remember, Mike was one third of THE SPRINGFIELDS although by that time he was a record producer working mainly at Decca. Mike had already offered Steve a deal but Steve assured me that he would hold off signing until I'd been able to discuss a deal with the Marquee management and get back to him.

Sadly, the Marquee management were hesitant. They were interested but they weren't sure. Perhaps Steve's material was just too different even for those days but, whatever the reason, I couldn't finalise their agreement to back my hunch. The Decca offer to Steve involved money. Those were the days when 'the advance' had reared it's head and, of course, when it was a question of the career of a solo artist, money was of vital necessity as backing musicians had to be bought and paid for and touring expenses were, relatively, as expensive then as they were soon to become. However, the Marquee management perhaps were still of the mind that any advances from record companies were paid for bands, groups of three or four people who didn't require back-up. They could also have been of the old-school thinking that advances were paid to managers who then doled out money to the guitarists, the optional keyboard players and the drummers like pocket money until the big bucks rolled in from chart hits.

So, I couldn't be definite with Steve and Steve wanted things definite. His Decca arrangement also meant recording immediately. I told him I didn't want to hold him back and so off he went.

He became huge. When he'd had his two or three hits as he did in succession the following year of 1967, I booked him to come back to the Marquee. It was a disaster. You see, the punters at the Marquee were seriously into music and what Steve had become wasn't what they thought of as music. Steve had become a "pop star" and the audience that turned up were screaming girls who ahd bought he records and followed the hysterical publicity which ensued.

I'd booked him because he was a friend but I soon realised that Cat Stevens wasn't the same person as Steven Giorgiou whom I'd met a year earlier. There was a host of people fussing around him, there was a backing band. He did an hour spot and he told me he was very happy with the way things were going. At least, that's what he said ...

Why didn't I believe him? Something wasn't ringing right. That special essence in his work which had so impressed me had been somehow shaped into something else, something that fitted more conveniently into the slot that the industry knew could be profitably filled."

Something definitely wasn't ringing right but however much John Gee felt Steve's work to be threatened, it wasn't a patch on what was happening to Steve's health. In 1969, Steve was admitted to hospital just outside London suffering from tuberculosis.

JOHN GEE: "Of course, I read about it and I read about it with perhaps more knowledge than most for I too had contracted and recovered from TB some seven years before and had been in Harefield, then celebrated as a sanatorium for the treatment of this disease. I went in during the summer of 1962. It was a momentous period both in world history and in the revolution taking place in popular music. It almost seemed a natural co-incidence that Kennedy and Kruschev faced up to each other over the Cuban missile crisis as THE BEATLES were emerging from THE CAVERN in Liverpool onto the world's stage.

Being at Harefield was a time for much reflection. Most of the six months I spent there was spent in bed, complete rest and relaxation being basic prescription. Putting it bluntly, it was a time to live or, if the worst should happen, to die. Fortunately, by the time I, and Steve, contracted the disease, drugs were available to effect a 99.9% total recovery rate. But it was, in historical terms, a recovery snatched by the skin of our teeth. In my case, the doctors told me that fifteen years earlier I would have died.

Most of my time was spent reading and then reading some more as well as playing chess and what time remained was spent in contemplation. I guess Steve must have done very much of the same. Perhaps it was here that he first felt the need to explore further than the immediate boundaries of life and the religious aspect of his later character began to form. Certainly, from what I can observe, his material changed dramatically when he returned to his career.

I wrote an article for JAZZ NEWS in August 1962 which I called simply, 'Reflections in the Ward'. One section I think deserves reiteration as I believe it might have reflected Steve's feelings too as a musician communicating with his audience ...

'I've been thinking. In fact, I've been thinking long and hard which is one of the few consolations of being in hospital for any great length of time as I am at the present. I've been thinking for example of how lucky I am to play even a small part in this business of jazz music. Often one gets to thinking it's one big rat race and begins to despair. And then the unexpected happens! Look at me. Since I arrived in hospital, I've been receiving many letters, cards and gifts, not only from musicians and friends in the business but from complete strangers too ... They fill me with a great sense of humility and a realisation (forgotten so many times) of the responsibility that rests on the shoulders of all writers endeavouring to communicate to their readers ...'

Quite by chance in the summer of 1970, I ran into Steve again in Oxford Street or Wardour Street, I can't be precise. Anyway, I was amazed that he was with Paul Samwell-Smith. I'd known Paul when he was in THE YARDBIRDS, a band which had often played at The Marquee. We went off and had a drink somewhere. Steve had always been articulate, again so different from many of the mono-syllabic yobs I often had to deal with. Of course we discussed TB which I obviously sympathised but I also sympathised with him when he confessed how much thinking he'd been doing, thinking which had perforce to encompass the real issues of life and death. He told me he had completely rethought his career. Cat Stevens the pop star had obviously not been happy and what I had sensed had been correct. He told me about the new deal he had signed with Island Records, a new and lively company, itself so different again from Dick Rowe's Decca. I felt as happy for Steve as he obviously felt for himself. I knew both Chris Blackwell and Muff Winwood from Island who had signed two or three acts they had heard on their talent-scouting expeditions to the Marquee.

The rest is history, as we're well aware. Steve was a musical pioneer, I don't think that's too strong. I'm glad I was right when I thought he was something special. Of course, we said we'd keep in touch but, of course, we never did. I've met so many people in my life and many of them via the Marquee who've gone on to be incredibly rich and famous. Like John Baldry said about all those rich and famous people when I last saw him in Canada where he now lives quite quietly and happily: *'Good luck to them.'*

I cannot stress too heavily how lucky the young Steve was to have met up with and been accepted by the music business professionals he happened across. There are others he could have teamed up with and whom he more than likely met who were indeed as monstrous as their reputations. Men - and some women - of completely vulgar taste, some with no taste whatsoever and upon whom Steve's sensitive work would have been lost. Perhaps he did meet such people and wisely avoided them. His fertile teenage mind was throwing up so many urgent images as evidenced by the lyrics of his contemporary material. Such work would have been truly lost on many a philistine ear.

I've tried so hard to get inside the head of the young man I imagine Steve to have been. Thirty years later, standing outside Stavros' house in the daytime throng of current West Enders, the hustle and bustle breeds no tangible atmosphere in which I can sense Cat Stevens' presence. Or Steven Giorgiou's for that matter.

But what would standing in this same spot engender in my imagination late at night, way past the time the theatre disgorges and the trippers go home, way after the electric marquee's neon is shut down and lights are turned off in all the offices and buildings around? In the middle of the night, that time for dreams, well before dawn, what would it have been like to be a handsome, well-made, talented, beloved, ambitious, sensitive, thoughtful, shy, reserved, teenaged young man returning from a night out in the

West End? What would Steve have felt as he stood, fumbling for his key, outside that sleeping restaurant in the almost silence and looked up, through the waving branches of the plane trees overhead and looked full at the face of the moon?

Even in my imagination, I know there must have been such moments for the young Steve Giorgiou. There are times for all of us when our smallness is proclaimed by something else's hugeness and what is there bigger than the tantalising proximity of the moon, set like a diamond in the endless blackness of infinite space? Though he may have not recognised their disruptive nature or even cast them onto the back burner of his mind, I instinctively feel that Steve experienced some such thoughts, strange and original feelings provoked by looking at the moon in all it's shapes and phases. Lunar thoughts which pull us, water that we are, first this way and then that, sometimes making us feel that we are all but mad for lunatics are what mad people were once called. Now, of course, now we are civilised, there are no longer mad people. Madness is the name of both a pop group and a television series, not necessarily a human condition.

However civilised, people still seem to spend a great deal of their valuable reality looking at the moon, even as a metaphor. There must be madness in us all. Those disturbing yet exciting thoughts are still engendered and in turn stir our souls to make those incommunicable, painfully private feelings well up.

Thankfully there always have been a very few people who can express those thoughts and feelings for without those people, the rest of us, the majority, would go under, suffocated by the weight of what we cannot express. Ask most of us to write down those strange, deep, apparently unique human feelings and out would come some lyric lines that by themselves would spell only gibberish, an un-crackable code to the hidden emotional turmoil.

So let us consider seriously those whose gibberish can be understood for these people are called poets. Some of these poets are the luckiest of all for this tiny residue can actually set their words to music, creating songs which as if by magic somehow strike the same chords in the hearts and minds of millions, enabling whole generations of people to realise that they are not alone, that they are part of something comfortingly bigger which can be explained and which does not threaten them and which can be embraced.

As you will have guessed, the earth moves for me when I try

and describe the creative process. Obviously I can't say what it was like for Steve because these are my words and my thoughts and I'm not him. But in a way, that doesn't matter. For a creative artist, the end is often the means, for new means soon come to displace the old ends. A song, like a poem or a novel or a painting, once created becomes achieved and itself turns into a stepping stone on which the artist treads to develop further. For the listener, it is the ends which are all important and as a listener to Steve's songs, I am only me. But as me, I am one, one of the millions who heard the songs and felt the same thing and who used his ends to come away with a little of the magic for themselves, having shared those few moments of their lives with Steve in his role of troubadour, a neo-Blondel come to cheer and revivify us languishing Lion-hearts; the Cat Stevens whom I knew emerged as that minstrel, the traditionally rootless, wandering broadcaster of hopes, dreams and fancies, whimsical fantasies so powerful that once heard, his music bred memories of sound and cadence which could soothe whomsoever heard them. His words and music seemed to vindicate us and we felt ourselves somehow richer for the hearing of them, for the experience of listening. Popular music may be cheap but many a dark night of the soul has passed to the sound of it.

CHAPTER FOUR

PRAISE FOR THE SINGING...

On October 20th 1966, the Decca Record Company released a single entitled I LOVE MY DOG on its brand new DERAM label. The single was by a hitherto unknown singer called Cat Stevens and, upon examining the label, those interested would have seen that the young man had written the song himself. I LOVE MY DOG climbed to the twenty eight position in the charts before it began to fall away. It spent eight weeks falling away.

This statistic is as bald as it could also have been un-memorable for it was only the beginning and so many other young talents had stood poised at the number twenty eight position before and many have stood there since. Most are now safely filed away in the obscurity of the pop pundits' glossaries. It seems safe to assume that none returned to obscurity through choice. There are few publicised mortals who have actively turned their backs on success, wealth and celebrity of any sort. At this point it also seems safe to assume that turning his back on success was a course of action that didn't even figure as a possibility on the young Steve Giorgiou's horizon. It must have been hard enough to get to that initial twenty eight position.

John Gee has already indicated Steve's involvement with Mike Hurst and, from what John has said, it is interesting that Steve was still casting around or at least allowing people to think he was still available whilst technically committed to Mike and the Decca deal.

Mike Hurst is a man of high energy and, therefore, great enthusiasm. His dynamism is still, plainly, infectious. He is the sort of man whom you meet and then feel you really have to get up and

DO something. He is not only a wonderful raconteur and a fund of stories and anecdotes but he is also a great listener. His memory is so sharp and crystal-clear that he remembers songs he heard and recorded over twenty years ago with ease, even down to who played what and where and how long the session lasted. He is a caring man who, by instinct, understands the creative spirit as much in others as he does in himself.

In those early glory days of the mid-60's, the fledgeling music business ran on favours. It was fuelled and lubricated by friends doing favours for friends. Perhaps it was small enough to run like that because today, huge and might and imposing and remote as the industry has become, it sure don't run on the same gas! In the days when fuel itself came in bigger cans, good honest gallons and not nit-pickety litres, favours were never measured or counted although they were always, always returned. Talent too seemed bigger, more complete, less reliant on gizmos and gadgetry. Or am I just another old man with a rose-tinted memory?

Mike Hurst's whole life seems to have been concerned with talent and, the way I see it, it was a good job that he and Steve met up because if Mike hadn't cared enough to put his own reputation on the line, Steve might easily not have had those early hits and without those hits it is inconceivable somehow that he would have even been considered for a second go around the track.

MIKE HURST: "I was born into this business, bred in a Variety background. It was when Variety was coming to an end, admittedly, but I was glad of the experience because the Variety tradition carried on in the entertainment business way after the halls and theatres themselves closed down. The agents, the bookers, the musicians, the dancers as well as the artists themselves had to carry on working and so they moved one step sideways into the new music, radio and television businesses which expanded as music hall and variety died. Well ... Not died as in 'dead and gone'. You think something's died but it never has, really. There's always that regeneration, that transubstantiation and things reappear in a different guise.

My mother, Flavia Pickworth, (Pickworth being my real name), ran a troupe called FLAVIA'S STARLETS. My earliest memory of performing was with the STARLETS on the same bill as MAX MILLER at the Met in the Edgware Road.

Jumping on a good many years, I'd taught myself to play the

guitar by the late fifties and found myself in the early sixties as a the third member of THE SPRINGFIELDS along with Tom and his sister Dusty. It's probably hard for a lot of young people now to appreciate the difference but however much today might look back at yesterday and perceive THE SPRINGFIELDS as a band, we were really an act. Not in the phoney sense of the word but an act as in the old Variety meaning of the word. I was brought into THE SPRINGFIELDS, I was never really part of the essence. Although the buttons and switches on the machine were controlled by Tom and Dusty, it was Dusty who finally plugged the thing into the mains.

But I watched and listened a lot during the eighteen months I was in THE SPRINGFIELDS. Johnny Franz was our producer for those Phillips tracks and I watched him a lot. For so much of the time he'd appear only to be reading the DAILY TELEGRAPH but he was always listening. He was listening for detail. Whereas most people can only distinguish three separate sounds in a sound spectrum, Johnny had a fabulous capacity to hear everything. He'd pop his head round his paper when necessary and just say: *"Third violin's a bit flat,"* and then go back to reading. I must have absorbed more than I imagined at the time because those times in the studio were later to stand me in very good stead.

After the SPRINGFIELDS, I went into broadcasting for a while and for nine months hosted the BBC's first magazine show for teenagers on radio's The Light Programme called TEENSCENE. That was great fun but it was taking me further away from music.

It was my wife, Marjorie, who suggested one day: *"Why don't you produce records?"* At first I dismissed the idea but as with a lot of off-the-wall notions, this one lingered. I'd met Andrew Loog Oldham when I was in the SPRINGFIELDS. I remember being on tour with Del Shannon when Andrew had bounced into dressing room and asked Del straight out, *"Who does your publicity?"*

So a couple of years later I plucked up courage and I went to see Andrew and he took me on to do all the things he didn't want to do. One of the first bands I produced was the somewhat whimsically nominated GOLDEN APPLES OF THE SUN. Andrew was renowned for whimsicality although the band in question rather sensibly later changed their name to TONY RIVERS AND THE CASTAWAYS.

In 1965, I worked for Mickey Most for a while, again being awarded all the bands and artists that he didn't want to do himself. I was beginning to learn by now that the second fiddle was not

really my instrument so when I saw an ad in the recently repub-
lished SUNDAY TIMES calling for someone to work with the producer of THE BEACH BOYS, I phoned for an interview.

The man I met was Jim Economides. What everyone probably
knows now off the top of their heads, in those days I certainly
didn't immediately spot. Of course, Brian Wilson was THE BEACH
BOYS' producer. Jim Economides was an engineer at Capitol Records
and although had surely worked on the BEACH BOYS sessions, he
was in no way their producer.

But Jim offered me a job and I took it.

Jim Economides was a great talker and Jim had some great
contacts and he set up offices in Albert Gate Court in Kensington
and soon had development deals and other financial arrangements
established with several record companies. We started to interview artists. Mark Bolan who had already recorded THE WIZARD on
Pye, Jim pronounced to be 'crap'. Perhaps that adjudication alone,
quite apart from all the envelopes that weekly winged their way
back to California to settle some rather hiccoughing circumstances
before Jim could return, ought to have warned me. But I stuck with
it.

Jim was out one lunchtime when there was a knock at the door
which I answered.

In the hallway was a young man with a guitar case.

"Is Jim Economides in?"

"No. Sorry. He's at lunch." (God! How often have we all heard
that line?)

"Oh. I wondered if he'd be interested in listening to my songs."

*"He might be. But I'll listen to them now if you like? What's your
name?"*

The young man shuffled and looked somewhat embarrassed.

"They call me ... they call me Cat Stevens," he announced, adding
quickly *"but I'm going to change it. It's just that some girl thought I had
eyes like a cat and so she called me that."*

"Don't!" I said quickly. *"Don't change it!"*

He played me some songs that day and I was knocked out. Jim
HAD to hear them. He HAD to like them.

"Well, bub," Jim said carelessly having just heard I LOVE MY
DOG, *"I think it's shit. You,"* he said to me, *"ain't got no taste and you,
kid,"* he said to Steve, *"you've got nothing."*

Steve was destroyed and so was I because I thought the boy
with eyes like a cat was marvellous.

I don't know what happened to Steve immediately after that but I knew what happened to me. Jim Economides went back to the States taking my unpaid salary with him. Nasty denouements ensued before later in 1965 I took a very nice 'phone call one day. It was a carpet millionaire on the line, one Bert Shalet who was Nat Cohen's son-in-law. How he had got hold of Cat Stevens I have forgotten but got hold of him he had and Steve had very loyally told him about me. AND there was money too, enough to record four tracks. So, Steve and I made SMASH YOUR HEART, HERE COMES MY BABY, COME ON AND DANCE and another one.

Bert Shalet knew Ron Belshay, a big radio noise in the BBC's Light Programme in those days but Bert and Ron could muster no enthusiasm for Steve or his songs. I took the tracks to Pye records and there too, I encountered blanket indifference.

Again, Steve was really disappointed and so was I. It seemed that we were fated to get precisely nowhere.

By 1966, I had become so disillusioned with the music scene in Great Britain that I had at last persuaded my extremely long-suffering and, in this case, extremely reluctant wife to move out to California where I had a job with Vanguard Records. We'd made all the arrangements. We'd put our St John's Wood house on the market (which later sold in turn first to Madeleine Bell and later to John Paul Jones from LED ZEPPELIN) and I'd got all the visa and work papers from the American Embassy.

One Saturday morning, the doorbell rang.

It was Steve.

"Hi. What's happening?" I was very pleased to see him. He, however, was dejected and depressed but he was still in there trying, still determined to win through.

Apparently, absolutely no one was interested in him.

"No one wants to know", he said. "But what about you? Do YOU still want to know?"

I tell you, it takes a very hard heart not to have any reaction to a kindred soul in purgatory. It had happened before and it's happened many times since. If you have any creative sympathy, any artistic empathy at all, you're involved whether you like it or not.

That day Steve played me even more songs. He had about twelve or fifteen at that time. I LOVE MY DOG was still up there as my initial favourite and we all know what later happened to HERE COMES MY BABY but even then, in 1966, there were songs which had that later Stevens trademark although, as was proved, very undeveloped. I was not merely sympathetic but sufficiently persuaded to try just once again.

We had to record and we therefore had to have money.

I'd met Chris Brough some time before; Chris is the son of Peter Brough, whose puppet character ARCHIE ANDREWS had been so successful on radio, television and in live appearance. We'd always been friendly but I wasn't sure if just being friendly was grounds for my question to him: *"Do you want to go into the record business?"* He was still listening. *"I need money, about £350 for the studios and the musicians. Would you like to hear the songs?"*

"No. Don't bother playing me the songs," he said. *"I trust you."* And he added, *"I believe in you."*

I started looking around for studios and went to see Dick Rowe at Decca. The industry was run by people like Dick Rowe then, old-fashioned, old-school, 'gentlemanly' people. I went in and explained that I was just about to emigrate to the United States and that I wanted to make a swan-song record before I left. And I did; that was no lie. I had a song by Mike d'Abo called GOING GOING GONE and I wanted to do it.

Dick Rowe acceded. He gave me three hours in DECCA's Studio two in Broadhurst Gardens. It was all, as I've said, very gentlemanly. Just a handshake. Your word was everything then.

Feeling a little surreptitious bearing on mind my un-revealed background motives of wanting to record Steve's I LOVE MY DOG as well, I now booked musicians and also started work on the arrangement. I knew I wanted something strange, out of the ordinary, weird even. The demo Steve had made himself of the song was like that and I wanted to not only echo but enhance the character of his original demo. Alan Tew appreciated what I had in mind, especially after I indicated that I wanted to do the track without a continuous drum line. A few rolls and some timps but no drum line.

Other than Steve and I that day in Decca Two were John Paul Jones on bass, Andy White from LORD ROCKINGHAM'S ELEVEN on what drums there were, Eric Ford who used to come in on rhythm guitar on SPRINGFIELDS sessions, Vic Smith as engineer (The Vic Smith who later became Vic Coppersmith Heaven after his marriage) and the tape operator, whom we always called 'Lightning'. Lightning's real name was Roy Thomas Baker. (Later to produce

QUEEN.) Didn't he do well later on! In the next door studio, Gus Dudgeon was working, I think, with David Bowie.

When the guys played Alan Tew's arrangement through, I was suddenly filled with dread. It was SO weird and out of the ordinary that I had grave doubts as to what it was I'd done. It's only later that kind people call what you do inventive or innovative. At the time, it's just bloody scary.

You have to remember that it was still the days of four track. Stereo wasn't really much in evidence. I had the rhythm section on one track, the odd-ball items like harps and cellos on another, strings on the third and on the fourth I put Steve's acoustic guitar which I later bounced down to the rhythm track to leave one free for his voice which was the final addition.

I LOVE MY DOG was finished in seven takes and Steve took two to put on his voice. We had just over an hour left to mix and to record the Mike d'Abo song and I thought everything was fine until I remembered we hadn't got a 'B' side. Can you believe that? Nerves? Guilt? Pressure of time? I don't know how I'd overlooked the 'B' side. Anyway, As Steve had PORTOBELLO which was always an acoustic conception, he put that down in two takes with him playing his own guitar.

With no time to spare, we recorded the d'Abo song in two takes and managed to mix all three tracks in the three hours allotted. I was only able to get two acetates cut, Even Steve didn't go away with anything he could play that day. I needed both copies for the next step which was the second meeting with Dick Rowe.

Chris drove me to the meeting which was at the old Decca building on the Embankment. Chris said he'd wait for me in the car outside.

I decided honesty was far the best policy especially considering that word could have easily filtered back from Decca Two to HQ as to who had been the main subject of my session.

When I confessed, Dick was understandably furious. He was both hurt and cross that I had all but deceived him and immediately began threatening all sorts of fates on the only just milder side of blackballing. It was, after all, my well-deserved desserts. In my defence, I begged him at least to listen to the acetate I had brought. Reluctantly, he put it on his turntable.

It didn't stay on there long. Halfway through, he pulled it off the turntable and without saying a word to me, grabbed the 'phone and asked to be put through to Sir Edward Lewis, the chairman of

Decca and the man responsible for selling an enormous amount of recorded product, mostly American, in Great Britain.

"Sir Edward, please come down here at once!"

And still not a word to me. I thought I was in for the roasting of my career and was staring shamefaced at the floor.

Once arrived, Dick sat Sir Edward down and played him I LOVE MY DOG, this time all the way through.

In short, they loved it.

"My boy!" exclaimed Sir Edward, in my direction. *"Did you produce that record?"* he enthused before going on to say the sweetest words I have ever heard either before or since ... *"You're a genius."*

They liked it so much that although they had an artist earmarked to launch their new DERAM label, Cat Stevens with I LOVE MY DOG was immediately scheduled as replacement. Dick and Sir Edward than asked me what I wanted ... What sort of a deal did I want?

With no legal advice on hand and never having had to have recourse to heavy lawyers' weighty deliberations, I mumbled something which they interpreted before announcing that I and Steve would be signed separately to Decca and that for my pains and as an advance against all our royalties, we was given £5000. It was a tidy sum for those days.

I can't remember a thing about getting back to Chris in the car who was both amazed and delighted and we formed our partnership there and then. SMASH Productions was born. And, needless to say, all plans of moving to Los Angeles were shelved immediately.

I LOVE MY DOG went down well with everyone; journalists, BBC radio people, television shows and the pirate stations like Radio Caroline all went with it. Chris and I moved into offices in Kingly Street just next to Carnaby Street and life became tremendously exciting. As it was rush-released with nothing else in the can, Steve's and my first deal with Decca was just for I LOVE MY DOG and PORTOBELLO and the publishing went to Dick James Music. Further recording deals were later finalised with Decca. Steve's was for three years with, I think, no specification of quantity of material to be recorded. The highest chart position the record reached was 24, 'though I believe the general consensus is that it acquitted itself very well at around the twenty eight mark. It did well in Europe too with my wife's dog Shelley featured on the single sleeve in those territories who weren't as mean as the UK and gave the punters fancy record covers. All in all, we suddenly found ourselves at the heart of the happening sixties.

But then, of course, I LOVE MY DOG had to have a follow-up. From Steve's bank of songs there wasn't anything that immediately chirruped: 'Follow up'.

He was a strange mixture of a lad in many many ways. His education had obviously not been the greatest and yet he was such a clever, eager and quick learner. It became clear to me very early on that he was incredibly curious and was like a sponge as far as picking up everything and anything he could was concerned. His continuing education thus progressed not in any structured way and certainly not in a way that he could easily re-iterate and make sense of so that someone else could understand.

Lots of great poets, writers, composers and creative talents in all fields are scavengers and Steve was no exception. He was a great rag-bagger and living in the West End and coming from the family he did, there were certainly rich pickings for the quick, active imagination to filch and process and mix with other ingredients to come up with that special and unique recipe; from his jackdaw hoard of impressions, memories and scraps of knowledge, Steve synthesised his lyric lines. He was, even in those days, without doubt a poet. He wasn't as good a poet as he later became because he was too young and he still had a great deal of growing up to do before being able to find full lyric expression for the images he saw and felt so deeply in his head. It's all there on that early Deram work but it hadn't quite gelled. By growing up, I'm referring to that process where you find yourself in control, complete control of your faculties and your facilities so that what you project in your created work is assured and rings as true as any well-found bell, no cracks, no faults, nothing to make the listener or the reader doubt or question the authenticity of what they are presented with.

Time spent with Steve was never wasted. We would talk about anything and everything including other artists and writers. We both found that we loved the work of Charles Dickens. Steve's interest in the books was re-kindled and he became intrigued by this man who wrote so much about the city with which Steve himself was so intimately familiar. COPPERFIELD, GREAT EXPETATIONS, THE OLD CURIOSITY SHOP ... Out of the huge cata-logue, Steve chose to focus on DOMBEY AND SON and in a flash brought me his synthesised and entirely original version in the form of a song which he'd called MATTHEW AND SON.

And that was the obvious follow up.

Well, it was obvious to me. I set the recording sessions and included GRANNY as the 'B' side. Pre-recording, the way we worked, took the form of Steve first playing me the song after which I would then come in and present my ideas about what it could sound like. Steve and I would discuss and then I would go to Alan Tew who'd translate our joint thoughts - as neither of us could write music in those days - into a communicable arrangement.

We decided to use a harp as one of the distinctive sounds on the track and, having been vindicated by the success of our flirtation with the avant-garde on MATTHEW AND SON, we all really liked what emerged from that session.

There have been many times both in my career and in every other career that's ever been spawned in the music business that the work of the creative teams is met by a total lack of comprehension and acceptability when presented to the record company. It is the most dis-spiriting feeling and, in my view, entirely unnecessary. It hurt then and it hurts today. So often, when presented with product by people whose job it is to make that product, the people whose job it is to sell the product take an immediately negative attitude which turns into a barren and de-constructive stance.

I suppose it's born from fear, being frightened of something they don't understand. I suppose they fear not having a success and that the resulting failure will reflect badly on them. Failure reflects badly on everyone in a team but teams don't go out to bat already believing that they're going to lose. It's the ultimate irony about a business which depends so much on originality and therefore risk and is yet equally seeking similarity to ensure continuity and dead certainties. The record business is a bed which accommodates prickly bedfellows.

When Tony Hall, the head of promotion at Decca heard MATTHEW AND SON he said: *"Oh dear. It's not as good as I LOVE MY DOG."*

When Alan Keene at Radio London heard it, he said: *"I don't think you've got a hope with this one."*

My reaction was: *"Oh God! They've gotta help me!"*

Alan Keene said he'd power-play it for a week but if there was no sales reaction, he would take it off.

After just a week? I was worried. Sales reaction was rarely that quick responsive to the launch of a new single.

As for the pirates, we got a very lukewarm reaction. Radio Caroline said they'd only play it sporadically.

On the third day of that first week, Steve and I were doing a radio performance at the PARIS Cinema in the West End. Steve was miming in front of the PARIS' audience for this appearance on the BBC programme POP INN.

As we were coming out, we saw Tony Hall, the aforesaid promotion manager, hurrying down the stairs waving to us.

"It's fantastic," he exclaimed. *"Fantastic. Forty thousand records before lunch!"*

By the end of that Tuesday, MATTHEW AND SON had sold ninety thousand records in one day.

The record got to number two and to say that we were all more than chuffed would be an understatement. On the strength of the success we moved offices to Townsend House in Dean Street and thought we didn't have a care in the world.

Until the 'phone rang one day and on the line this time was a lawyer.

"Hello, is that Mr. Hurst?"

"Yes," I replied.

"Is that your real name?" enquired the lawyer.

"Yes," I said, *"as real as it needs to be. Why?"*

"I have to know the name you want to be sued under," he said.

Sued? By whom? Why? For what? The lawyer was representing an Indian writer and singer who had recorded a song entitled, as I remember, ROSE PETAL TIME. The lawyer sent round a copy. The lyrics might have been in Hindi but the melody was unmistakeable. I called Steve and told him to get his ass round to Dean Street pronto. I didn't have to say anything. I played him the Hindi song and his face drained of colour.

"Oh," he muttered sheepishly, *"I didn't think anyone would know."*

Swearing he would never do anything like it again and swearing that nothing else existed in his catalogue for which he wasn't totally responsible, I was able to settle the matter and we split royalties on the song.

I remember saying somewhere once that a record producer not only has to be a musician, but they must also be a politician and a nanny. It's what you do. You encourage, you cajole, you guide, you advise, you educate ... You do everything for a child at the top end of childhood that a nanny does for a child at the bottom. Not only was I Steve's producer, I was also Steve's manager. I'd set everything up for him. Keith Goodwin had rung me and asked if he could do Steve's publicity which was great as Keith had looked after me in THE SPRINGFIELDS and had Mike Gill working with him. There was nothing I wouldn't do for my charge.

I was so convinced that Steve was the greatest thing since sliced bread that, in retrospect, as far as the management side of our relationship was concerned, I think I probably boxed him in too much. In fact, I know I did. I so wanted him to be the star I knew he was that I engineered keeping him apart and made sure he inhabited the world I wanted him to live in, on top of the pedestal that I was erecting for him.

Steve resented this. He hated being fenced in anywhere. He was a party animal in those days. He liked going to all the clubs, he liked a good time and he was determined to have it. I remember many instances where I acted sufficiently overbearingly to ensure his displeasure. Once, someone called to say Steve was in a club called THE BAG OF NAILS behaving badly and I drove over there and physically yanked him out of the place.

Sadly, not only did our personal relationship start to slip but so did our professional one. I'm a very definite person and so was, and presumably is, Steve. This deterioration in our association was so ironic when I think that our records were hits in every country of the world ... except America where London Records had not done the greatest job of promoting them and Decca refused to let me take the material elsewhere. As things turned out, when Steve finally did hit America it was pretty much with musical virginity intact and so discoverable as a 'new' talent.

Artistically, our differences hinged on the fact that Steve was finding that my approach was too over-the-top musically to suit his developing perspectives in that he wanted to substitute a more folksy and simple style and progress in that direction.

I had my way and Steve had his but the two weren't destined to move forward in synch.

Before KITTY and BAD NIGHT were issued in 1968, Steve and I had already resolved our differences by going to law. It's always a sad recourse. He had already acquired a lawyer in the person of

Oscar Beuselinck of the Soho Square firm Wright and Webb as his success was engendering the need for other structures in his business life other than just my management company. Cat Music had been formed to look after his catalogue after the debacle with the Dick James-published I LOVE MY DOG. Steve's brother David had also been brought into to deal with the everyday aspects of the career. The juggernaut was rolling.

Our agreements were dissolved on the basis that as an eighteen year old, he had been too young to sign his management and record production contracts himself and that his parents, who had signed on his behalf, had not realised the nature of the documents they were signing. The family was a very strong element in Steve's life and in this event, they closed ranks.

Effectively, we had drifted so far apart by the middle of 1968 that when Steve had been taken ill and was in the clinic I wasn't aware for some weeks of the seriousness of the situation. I regret not having gone to see him but at the time, I suppose it would have seemed an ill-conceived notion. It seems that no one other than his family saw him.

By the time he had convalesced and was ready to get on with his life, I was onto other things. Steve however was still contracted to Decca.

In order to extricate himself, he informed me that he wanted to do one more single, two more sides and so Mel Collins, who had come to work for me as my business manager, arranged contracts for us to do one more single which was WHERE ARE YOU?, a plaintive title for a song which in spirit was not unlike MORNING HAS BROKEN.

In the event, it did nothing. I'm sure Steve wasn't too upset for at least he had achieved the freedom to manoeuvre he wanted, having discharged his obligations to Decca records.

I think of him fondly. I wish him well and I'm so pleased to have been part of his life and career. I shall always champion his work. I loved his music and his lyrics and am often moved to righteous indignation when I think of how little significance seems to be ascribed to someone who was a true original, a musical trendsetter and a bright star in the pantheon of British musical history."

The pattern of great closeness followed by a detente far from cordial is one which characterises many of Steve's relationships as his life and career progressed. He seems to have been able to walk away from people with surprising, even calculating, ease. However, such unhappiness was surely absent in those months of 1967 and 1968 when his records were hardly ever out of the UK charts. 1967 saw a total of twenty nine weeks in which Cat Stevens records figured. Both the concept and the reality of family was very much used by Steve as a convenience. However, although they were conveniently around to bail him out in the late sixties, they were to be found wanting when he really needed them as he floundered in the confusion which true superstardom brought.

He must have been very petulant in those days and given his volatile character, he must have hated being told what to do by Mike Hurst, loathed being 'taken care of' and mortally insulted when Mike had occasion to remonstrate and censure him. And yet, how easily he seemed to have plagiarised the Indian writer's melody hiding behind the lame excuse that he didn't think anyone would find out. Interesting way of conducting oneself on a moral basis; the code seems to say do anything as long as you can get away with it and if found out, shrug and blame it all on the post-pubescent hiccough of a callow youth.

There was a season in the British music business which vaguely corresponded to puberty; a sort of late spring ... It started somewhere around 1963 and went on until around 1968. Pappy pop was beginning to lose its puppy fat and hair was beginning to grow in all sorts of previously smooth places. Moodiness and displays of temperament began to creep in to mar the sanitized edges of teenage and adolescence. Real, proper, hands-on sex began to rear its head and the hands-off, all-go but no-come teenage pastimes of snogging, partying sans alcohol and chevying to the levee which had previously been reported quite innocently became redolent with rudery. Clothes worn by the previously be-suited, mop-topped boys next door were generally being scrapped. Trousers got tighter and leatherier and were worn to be not merely suggestive but downright dirty and men, especially men, began to reveal in their lyrics and in suggestive gestures as they bumped and ground their way round the monitors and microphones that lurve an' kissin' wasn't all they'd been a-missin'. Girls, it has to be said, were still singing of loves lost and loves true and loves singularly lacking in anything approximating to an orgasm.

This was rock 'n' roll's spring, just as confusing as puberty and the era, as far as music journalism in England is concerned, should be more properly re-labelled the Penny Valentine era.

Penny was one of the first music journalists who helped the punters make some sense out of the plethora of confusion which bore some good music, some bad and a hell of a lot of mediocre. Penny knew about music. I can hear her being hotly embarrassed but she both did and does know about music and wrote about it superbly to the edification of record makers and record buyers alike. Everyone I speak to in connection with this book mentions her name.

She has taken a break from writing recently to work for a degree and to produce a rather fabulous young person called Daniel.

PENNY VALENTINE: "I started work on DISC in about 1964 after I'd worked on BOYFRIEND Magazine. IPC owned both DISC and MELODY MAKER which always considered itself far superior and infinitely more serious than DISC whose employees were thought to be rather frivolous. But we WERE Fleet Street and we WERE journalists.

Ray Coleman was my editor and I remember my counterpart singles reviewer on MELODY MAKER in those days was Chris Welch. It hardly needs saying but people should be aware that music journalism in those days was barely out of its infancy. The genre really had two lines of pedigree, one being the fanzine sort of publication which the cinema, both the Hollywood and the Pinewood/Shepperton varieties, had spawned and the other, more intelligent parent being jazz journalism which had established a credible history. JAZZ NEWS was just one magazine in which serious musicians could be read about in pieces submitted by lovers of the music who almost incidentally happened to be writers. Jazz was certainly part of my growing up; I was raised on a mix of Gigli and Rosemary Clooney, Johnny Ray and Guy Mitchell. One of the first singles I owned was actually STELLA BY STARLIGHT by Bud Powell although when I first bought it I never thought of it as jazz. Later came SWEET SMELL OF SUCCESS, the film sound track by the MJQ with Milt Jackson.

You will have gathered that what substantive musical education I picked up was at best stumbled upon and only intuitively recognised.

I would have to be arguably convinced that the main qualification for music journalism in 1964 was that you were passionate about the music. Put most politely, the quality of the writing itself was at best variable, both in the pages of the magazines and in the lyrics of the songs the magazines were discussing. The stuff you read and were reading about was often excruciating. It was all incredibly naive because there was so little tradition of pop/rock music. Even the distinction between pop and rock was only just being made and there would have been few people who would have appreciated the need for any distinction at all. Though we didn't appreciate it at the time, we were trail blazers.

I must also point out that people all over the sharp end of the business, artists and journalists alike, felt very much that they were equally part of the cutting edge. I'm talking about the days before there arose any sense of 'us and them', before journalists started to have 'side', before they started to write things which would alienate the artists and the work they were writing about. In those days, the stars came to us or we went to the stars. There was no power play going on where he/she who succumbs to doing the visiting is seen by he/she who is being visited to have in some sense lost ... People were very flexible and very understanding; if times and dates were not convenient for either party, you accommodated. The artists didn't immediately feel that all journalists were hatcheteers.

The market for recorded product in those days was primarily oriented to singles and I became the singles reviewer on DISC and I must say, I did the job pretty assiduously. I listened to everything that came in, often ninety records at a sitting. I will admit to a bias and confess to going through the weekly stack of records to initially pull out sleeves I immediately recognised ... The way the M and the T of MOTOWN were combined in the logo was distinctive and the Stax label and sleeve always drew me. The only time I remember making a major boo-boo was one of the Pet Clark records. I put it on and because it started a bit slowly, I immediately took it off, flung it aside and dismissed it entirely. It became, of course, a number one.

But what was a solitary piece of humble pie when faced with accolades of the sort that Mick Jagger once sent in to DISC, acclaiming me (and I paraphrase) 'the best singles reviewer in the world'? On the strength of that one piece of applause which I stupidly squealed across the office, the DISC management decided to promote the paper by promoting me. My photograph and the

Jagger accolade appeared on massive posters. My 'blown-up' face appeared giant-size plastered on walls all over London. It was decided to turn me at a stroke from being a solid, sensible citizen into a celebrity! For a year afterwards, people would say: *'Oh! You're MUCH smaller than we expected!'*

I have to say I was initially horrified at being so singled out and I was embarrassed beyond belief but after this initial 'yuk' response abated, I sneakily rather enjoyed the acclaim. Never knowingly overlooked by record companies, I found myself pursued. I appeared on JUKE BOX JURY three or four times. It was the first experience I had had of the cult of the personality and I was entirely unprepared for it as were, obviously, most of the people I found myself interviewing and writing about. From just doing a job of work and being part of a bunch of people in an office, life suddenly assumed a very singular aspect and I had to recognise ... an ego! It made me feel both rather isolated yet somehow special. With no initial desire on my part, I found that I'd become a celebrity in a world of celebrities. It was exciting, but looking back, a very odd time in my life. I was twenty-one and felt about thirteen, a bit like Shirley Temple but without the curls!

I'd always liked DERAM, the label that Decca had developed to carry bands like PROCUL HARUM so it wasn't a particular surprise when I liked what I heard from a new DERAM signing who went by the name of Cat Stevens. I never used to make a particular point of reading the biographies and press details that accompanied the singles which the record companies sent us and so I knew very little about the singer. It didn't particularly register that he'd written the song. It wasn't something a singles reviewer especially looked for in those days unless it was a Holland Dozier Holland composition on a new MOTOWN release because I was besotted by their work.

I LOVE MY DOG caught my attention from its opening. It started in a very weird way ... a strange chord and then it went on not predictably but jerkily with odd, jarring bits prodding your interest all the time, making you look forward to what was going to happen next in the song. I thought the lyrics were fairly silly but eminently memorable ... I mean, just repeat them: *"I love my dog as much as I love you ..."* Please.

There are so many ingredients that go to make a hit song and so many of them depend on time and place. Having said that, ascending chords seem to be a fairly common ingredient as do key changes. Whatever ... The time and the place were right for Cat

Stevens and I remember giving I LOVE MY DOG one of the prominent reviews that week.

Then, of course, I interviewed him because it was 'de rigueur' to work on pushing your favourite single. A bit like backing the horses. You became very involved in publicising your favourite artists. You thought it was totally on your own terms. No wonder in those days there was a very obvious symbiotic relationship between journalists and record companies which continued for years.

But before talking about that first interview, I have to mention my own background which turned out to be not unlike Steve's. I too had been born and brought up in the West End. My parents lived and still live in Tottenham Court Road and my grandparents lived in Bury Place, a turning just off New Oxford Street. Whilst his parents were Greek, my family was of Italian origin. My grandfather had also been in catering. He worked at Braganza's, the Cafe de Paris and many other celebrated West End restaurants.

I'd gone to school first at Marylebone Primary School and then to Maida Vale High which was a single sex grammar school for girls. I studied journalism at the Regent Street Polytechnic (The Poly) for a year before working on a local suburban newspaper and then landing the job on BOYFRIEND. My whole life had been the West End.

I remember taking rather than being allowed liberty as a kid - God, I hope Danny doesn't read this - and this liberty I spent basically lounging around coffee bars drinking frothy coffee and listening to records on the juke boxes. Such was the corrupt life of a West End teenager in the nineteen fifties! Coffee bars were rated for their juke boxes. Perhaps because it was the West End of London, we always got to hear new releases very quickly. I don't remember going to the TWO I's but there was one very good one at the side of the Dominion Theatre, there was a very good one in Tottenham Court Road which had THE PLATTERS and a lot of early soul music and then of course there was the MACABRE in Meard Street where you sat around tables made like coffins. Lovely stuff. If I went to listen to live music there was THE MARQUEE as well as KEN and to be really up to date, in Soho there was a coffee bar which had a juke box which showed films of the singles it was playing. You could actually see your favourite artist performing and this was a hell of a long time before video.

It was exactly the same playground that Steve had known.

I was surprised, when I finally met up with him at his parents' cafe in New Oxford Street, that we didn't have more in common. But I suppose I shouldn't have been ... Apart from our sexes being different, he was four years younger than me and, well ... Four years when you're that age is a huge gap. Anyway we decided immediately that we'd never met before and there was certainly no question on my part of a women-to-man attraction. I just didn't react to him in that way but then women journalists were thin on the ground and I was determined to be 'professional' and to be thought of as the equal of the men.

I only remember that first meeting. I'm sure I must have talked to him many times but it's only that first meeting I remember. As we talked, his father would interrupt by shouting things from across the room and Steve would break off what he was saying and shout back to his father in Greek. I certainly guided the conversation. Being me and being then, I know I would have written down my questions in advance. Being a woman journalist later became not the greatest fun and men you were interviewing would invariably think of you as some kind of groupie. Professionalism helped to ward off such unwelcome interpretations and I pre-armed myself for this development by being thoroughly prepared for any assignment from the earliest point in my career.

Steve, I must add, was not of the macho persuasion and he was perfectly sweet to me and very friendly. However, his replies were very difficult. I found him, strangely, not articulate at all in those days. His sentences were very short and then he would frequently wander off on some tangent. Whenever I see him being interviewed on television or talking on radio now I find him so impressively articulate that I wonder if my memory isn't playing tricks on me.

So much else has changed too. The business for one. It was such an evolving thing then. You could almost see it growing ... changing. It wasn't considered art of any description and there was absolutely no cultural or sociological aspect to be considered. It was just pop music ... Pop. Even the business aspect of it felt disorganised and haphazard. I remember being very surprised, nay shocked when I first went to America and finding myself going into record and management and PR companies that were run like real corporations. It was all proper grown up stuff, quite alienating and a far cry from the home grown variety I was used to."

I like Penny's story about Stavros shouting at Steve whilst he was being interviewed. Was whatever it was so important that an interview with the most prestigious music journalist in London needed to be interrupted? Steve was invariably interviewed like this on home territory. In his later career, he granted few interviews and Barry carefully filtered those he did accept from the plethora the long-suffering Tony Brainsby relayed. Being interviewed on home turf obviously provided a fundamental confidence and Stavros' interruptions credited as providing grass roots local colour. Steve was an exceedingly charming person. He knew he had the quality and could turn it on at will. The recipients of the charm offensive invariably melted. His relations with the press always continued to be good. He was never at that time pilloried for anything. Even today, the press interest in him and his current Islamic career appears undiminished.

CHAPTER FIVE

DOG DAYS, CAT NIGHTS

Other than John Gee and Mike Hurst as well as all the people at Decca and Deram records, Steve's early career naturally touched many other music business lives. The social life surrounding the business when you're a beginner is like that surrounding many other professions. Like clings to like. Ostensibly, a fellow performer, another professional in the same work has more to offer in common as a companion.

Although Steve undoubtedly was a very social animal, this next testament gives an idea of how isolated he was even in those seemingly carefree early days. However close his friends may have thought they were, it was a closeness which Steve controlled, always prepared to shut off relations if times got rough. Ultimately, in all his relationships, there was an area of himself which Steve never disclosed, discussed or even acknowledged. When he became ill and was forced into hospital, who, I wonder did he tell? Was it only his family and, more likely, his mother who noticed just how ill he was becoming?

Amongst Steve's friends in the DOG days of 1966 and 1967 was the young Mike Gill. Mike and Steve were incredibly young to have so much responsibility. Not only were many of the artists themselves in those days technically minors - for these were the days before majority had been established at age eighteen - so were the people who worked incredibly hard promoting and supporting them. Mike was one of them.

MIKE GILL: "I met Steve in 1966, just before I LOVE MY DOG

came out. I was working for Keith Goodwin Publicity in those days in Monmouth Street, not a stone's throw as it turned out from Steve's father's cafe in Shaftesbury Avenue. It was only my second job. I'd left school at sixteen and I'd worked for a year on BOYFRIEND magazine before joining Keith who'd built up a well-respected and established Publicity and PR business having handled some of the major stars of the sixties. He'd had THE SPRINGFIELDS who, other than Dusty and her brother Tom of course, included Mike Hurst who was now, unbeknownst to him, to play a big part in my life.

I was very much into music and hung around a lot at the Marquee in Wardour Street both for pleasure and as part of my work looking after AMEN CORNER, THE MOVE and the many name bands of the sixties whose publicity I managed. Of course, I knew John Gee, the manager of the Marquee, very well and it was with John one night at The Marquee that I first heard Steve Giorgiou as he was called in those days singing I LOVE MY DOG. It was John Gee who told me that Mike Hurst was managing and recording Steve for Decca.

I went back to the office and raved about Steve to Keith who merely called up Mike, an old friend and former client, and asked who was doing the PR on his new act, Cat Stevens. As no one was, that's how Keith Goodwin Publicity got Steve as a client and that's how we became friends.

I really knew Steve well between 1966 when I LOVE MY DOG came out and late 1968. To say we were best friends wouldn't be true, not because we didn't see a great deal of each other and spend a lot of time together but because Steve was essentially a loner. There was always that ultimate barrier. I don't remember him having loads of acquaintances either. There was no one mate he'd had for ages and ages, no one even from his more recent art school days. He was always very insular, very separate and ... well, self-sufficient.

I know we were probably scheduled to spend time together but I know at the same time that we definitely were mates. Although he was a client of the company, I never felt in awe of him; I never felt I had to watch what I said or anything like that. With someone like Dusty, someone who I also admired and respected a great deal, it was different. I always felt that she was the client and I was the company representative doing my job, however close we got to be. Obviously I wasn't the only person Steve would go out in the evenings with. I remember his spending quite a bit of time with Scott Walker from the WALKER BROTHERS, another act whose publicity we handled.

The sixties were a truly amazing decade. I was born in Dulwich although by the time I was seventeen and working for Keith, my mother and I had moved to St Paul's Cray. I was the archetypal mod, dressed up in my parka and riding around London on my incredibly souped-up, bored-out 225 cc, hundred-and-five mile an hour Lambretta scooter which had all the radio aerials, flying fur tails and banks of lights as well as extremely desirable chromed side panels which had cost me a fortune. Mind you, I suppose I was earning a fortune in those days compared to say Terry, my friend from school who I still see to this day and the other guys. However flush, I was still gutted the night the chrome side-panels were nicked and replaced - yes, thieves were thoughtful in those days - by ordinary green and white-painted ones!

But back to work ... and play ... and Steve. That sounds glib but it's a way of saying that life then was all one. There were no boundaries. Work for me was also play. I socialised with a lot of the people I worked with and when I wasn't socialising I was going to concerts and other gigs at, for example, the Marquee.

Perhaps it was because we were the same age, perhaps it was that we discovered that we were both mad about cars ... Whatever the reason, we started to hang around together outside office hours, going out to clubs and places where, basically, we knew we'd get rip-roaring, rat-arsed drunk. Yes. Strange, isn't it, but the Cat Stevens of those days was well-known for ending up the evening legless. Looking back on it, I also find it hard to believe but legless we certainly got. Don't ask me what we talked about. I really can't remember. I just know that when Steve called up to ask me what I was doing, I went knowing I was in for a really great evening.

If Steve and I had made a definite date to go out, I'd usually meet him at his father's cafe and we'd have something to eat there. Steve was incredibly meticulous about every aspect of personal hygiene. He'd take great care getting ready to go out. His hands and nails were always immaculate and his hair never betrayed the slightest hint of neglect. If we were going out together, we'd obviously head off wherever in a taxi and take a taxi home although sometimes I'd go on my lambretta if I knew I had to either get back home or go on somewhere else afterwards. I can't remember Steve ever riding on the back, though!

Despite my having quite enough money of my own, I can remember Steve being insistent that I never pay. Steve was incredibly generous and it was a 'thing' of his. Try as I may to pay, he never allowed me put my hand in my pocket for anything. I suppose all this sounds a little odd but he was being incredibly successful by the standards of the time. Halfway through 1967 he'd already had three hit records yet, on the other hand, he still lived at home, he wasn't acquiring vast possessions and despite his passion for cars, I can't remember him having one at the time we were close. I think he wanted to be generous with money almost as a witness to this success because he certainly wasn't greedy or acquisitive for anything else.

The Cromwellian was a favourite haunt, the club on the corner of Exhibition Road and Cromwell Road by the Victoria and Albert Museum. It was run by Les and his wife and, co-incidentally, the club itself was a client of the Goodwin organisation, Les, the owner, sensing that the more his club's name appeared in the press in connection with its famous clientele, the greater would be his customer base. Anyway, I was a life member of the club and therefore Steve and I never paid when we were there together.

It was a very red sort of place, smothered with plush and flock wallpaper and low red lighting. It was to pop and rock 'n' roll what Stella Richman's WHITE ELEPHANT CLUB in Curzon Street was to the theatre and movie business. There were two levels to THE CROMWELLIAN, other than the casino, of course; there was a downstairs where all the younger crowd went and the upstairs where the Tom Joneses and THE BACHELORS and others of that age group used to hang out. It would be to the downstairs that Steve and I would gravitate with people like Twinkle, Adrienne Posta, Peter Noone, Eric Burdon even ... I remember one night the above mentioned Burdon at our table with me and Terry whilst Steve held forth for ages on the subject of house-bricks ... Yes. That does sound odd in retrospect but it happened.

I can't emphasise enough how hedonistic Steve was in those days. When he and I went out it was in the unerring search for the pleasuredrome. Ultimately, the search also encompassed the Speakeasy, the club that opened to cater mainly for rock and pop's heavier party-goers and it was at the opening of the Speakeasy that Steve and I spent an evening which, for me at least, was a turning point.

Steve and I arrived and of course soon made our way through

the packed celebrants and celebrities to the bar. On the bar was a parrot ... This sounds like the start of a long shaggy dog story but it's long only in hindsight as I can't remember much of what happened afterwards. The parrot, as Steve and I very quickly discovered and as you've guessed, was not real but a plastic one which actually talked back to you if you spoke into it's beak. This must have been a pretty advanced piece of technology for 1966 but, sadly, it wasn't advanced enough to withstand two hours of Steve and I, yelling into the poor thing's beak just to hear it talk back to us. We became more than hysterical and eventually the parrot blew up ... it conked out never to pretty polly again.

Robbed of our toy, I was later told that we spent the remainder of the evening wandering about the club holding hands, holding each other up, giggling and laughing crazily at our huge private joke. Apparently, we even embraced, hugged. And then ... blotto. Oblivion. I can't think I was able to go home and so we must have collapsed back at Steve's and spent the night there.

When you're eighteen, you recover so much more quickly after such nights than later on in life and I didn't reflect at all on the events at the Speakasy. Steve also never talked about what we had done or where we'd been the previous night. He wasn't the sort to get on the 'phone the day after for a post-mortem or an analysis about who'd said what and who'd done that and discuss other people's or one's own loves and lusts and, usually, rejections.

I trundled down to Monmouth Street to work but when I got in Keith asked to see me. Although he was some sixteen years older than me, I was more of a partner than an employee and he'd never given me a 'wigging' for anything. That morning he hauled me thoroughly over the coals as 'word' had got back to him about Steve's and my behaviour the previous night at the Speakeasy. I don't think it was the dead parrot which had anything to do with it but it was the fact that people were 'talking' ... Did I know how we'd behaved? Didn't I realise that above all else, Steve was the company's client?

If there remained even a millilitre of active alcohol in my bloodstream, Keith's admonishment instantly sobered me. I was also very confused as our behaviour had been so innocuous, so innocently high-spirited, I couldn't understand why anyone should want to 'tell tales' to Keith.

Keith spelled out in no uncertain fashion that it would be better for all concerned to allow Steve's and my relationship to become one more relevant to the representative/client association on which it was founded. Basically, I went along with it. I didn't stop seeing Steve but the closeness of our relationship cooled. It wasn't difficult for me to immerse myself in work. There was a lot of it, especially with the release of Dusty's MEMPHIS album in 1968 and Dusty became my preoccupation. You mustn't forget, either, that at that point Steve was still only a singles artist, a teen star, a pop idol.

Dusty was an institution.

I felt that Steve too was doing some backing off. Although it was mutual, I definitely felt him withdrawing from me although whether that was because of any pressure from other sources, I don't know. I do know he went on carousing. He'd still come to the office to meet journalists for interviews and he'd still be friendly but there was something odd about him. There was certainly something wrong with his health. He looked terrible. Terrible skin colour and thin ... I know he's naturally skinny but I'm talking thin.

The withdrawal I sensed was also because he was beginning to gather a ring of protection round him. I remember his elder brother, David, starting to make more of Steve's arrangements both with Mike Hurst's office and with ours whereas earlier in the year, Steve would make his own directly.

Steve's 1968 single KITTY wasn't at all successful when compared with 1967's list. I don't know why Steve's absence from my life didn't register sooner but Steve had apparently already been in hospital for four weeks before I got to know about his having succumbed to tuberculosis. It wasn't a situation that required publicity. Quite the reverse. To both media and public alike, it must have seemed from the non-information pouring out of our office that Steve had simply slipped un-witnessed off the edge of the world into indefinite limbo.

What the public and we saw as a limbo must have been pure hell for him. I can't pretend to understand what he must have gone through. There was no communication between us whilst he was in the sanatorium. I never went to visit or even had a call. Other than his family, he must have been even more alone than usual. It's terrifying to think that TB, once thought banished, is now becoming prevalent again with those whose constitutions have taken a bashing either from poverty, abuse, neglect or disease.

What Steve went through obviously had a devastating effect because after he'd recovered, it was obvious he was a completely changed man. Sober, introvert.... all the things that the old hell-raiser I'd known never was. I never saw him much but his changed nature shouted from every aspect of his new work. When I heard the 1970 MONA BONE JAKON album, I instantly realised it displayed all the hallmarks of a deeply sensitived creativity of which I'd never been aware. That he had written his own material before, I obviously knew but there the awareness stopped. When we knew each other we were both seventeen, hardly out of short pants and, as he said in one of his songs, *"I was a pop star then..."*

I became steeped in my own career. I was aware of the renaissance of Steve's but we all had our way to make. I regret never having seen him perform live. I've been told that some of the concerts were magical.

The last time I saw him was when I was working with Billy Gaff. It was in the sitting-room of a hotel suite in New York with Billy, Barry Krost, Barry's partner Doug Chapin and Steve. Billy and I had been invited in for a drink.

Steve was very awkward, ill at ease... I suppose I was as well We relaxed a little but I said goodbye that day, thankful that I'd known him at an easier time."

CHAPTER SIX

WIZARDS IN WEST ONE

In Steve's case, the difference between being poetic and being a poet was surely the period covered by his illness and convalescence. The songs on the DERAM albums, NEW MASTERS and THE WORLD OF CAT STEVENS clearly point the way but both his art and his craft benefited enormously from the enforced hiccough his life and career endured through the breakdown of his health.

John Gee has intimated that he felt that Steve wasn't entirely happy being a pop star despite the facade of the madcap, devil-may-care pretence whose shallow veneer indeed concealed a more than troubled state of mind. I don't know how long Steve was in hospital nor do I know how long he lay in bed at home looking out at the Shaftesbury Theatre as HAIR! conquered London and pioneered the way to new forms of musical theatre.

HAIR! was merely deceptively anarchic. Its hippy clothes were worn over a skeleton of solid steel construction, its limbs, lungs and larynx were given form and voice by some of the best young actors and singers in the land. Oliver Tobias, Paul Nicholas, Peter Straker, Annabel Leventon, Tim Curry ... the talent which emerged in the course of the various productions of HAIR! is still there in the West End today and as I write is enjoying a production at the Old Vic. At the heart of HAIR! is a basic theme of the purest grand opera. Love, friendship and death ... Struggle, collapse and tragedy. HAIR! embraces all the concerns which touch us most deeply and which operettists had been manipulating for two centuries. The peg of the Viet Nam war on which it was hung was a concern which motivated not only Americans but which touched hearts and minds throughout the Western World. War may have been a go-situation with politicians and militarists but with the people it was definitely a no-situation.

I don't know how often Tim Rice and Andrew Lloyd Webber saw HAIR! and nor do I know how many times THE WHO went to see it but as well as the aforementioned teams who were very soon after HAIR! appeared in London in 1968 to write and produce, respectively, both JOSEPH AND THE AMAZING TECHNICOLOUR DREAMCOAT and TOMMY, there was another, an individual sitting hunched over his guitar not a hundred yards from the Shaftesbury Theatre. Steve was hatching a giant plan which would ultimately enable him to make a return to work less as a pop star but more of a legitimate, substantial talent. Steve was generating his own theatrical musical. He called it REVOLUSSIA.

To a child of the 60's who was to come of age in the 70's, anything was possible and for this particular child, blessed with visual imagination and talent as well, his native intelligence and instinct were easily primed. Steve was multi-talented and he knew it. For many people, this can be a confusing and distracting condition, dissipating energy in several directions which deserves to be channelled only in one. For Steve, choosing to focus himself with the help of REVOLUSSIA, his multi-faceted talent was never a problem.

Steve took as his inspiration the last days of the Romanovs, Tsar Nicholas II and the Tsarina Alexandra in the early years of the century when the Tsarist regime first lurched then shuddered and then finally fell to the communist ideals of Lenin. The idea of REVOLUSSIA was to remain with Steve for at least three years and he wrote many, many songs for the musical which he insisted was credited on the first albums which Island records issued.

REVOLUSSIA was also important because it introduced Steve to a world which once he had come upon it he instinctively realised was the right one to support the sort of career he wanted. The new songs he was writing brought him to Island Records, Island records brought him to Paul and Rosie Samwell-Smith and his musical brought him to the most important person he was to meet, his second manager Barry Krost.

That was the order in which correct chronology applies. To better appreciate the situation in which Steve found himself, I have chosen to look at these three key areas in a rearranged order.

First, Barry Krost ... I feel I can best describe him by recalling my personal memories.

He was a short, tubby, ebullient, irrepressible Jewish ex-hairdresser in his early thirties who had infinite charm and plausibility. Barry was a sort of wunderkind, I suppose, and surely a close relation of Sammy Glick, the Sammy in Bud Schulberg's WHAT MAKES SAMMY RUN? The late Harold Fielding was once heard sagely to remark about Barry and, presumably, for the edification of all who dealt with him: *"You wanna watch that boy!"*

Barry had been a child star, in Hollywood even, but his thespian career had proved a non-transferrable asset as child grew to man. Presumably his lustrous and plentiful hair had been a good advertisement for his trade as hairdresser but it was as an artists' agent that he finally found his niche. He could perform, toss that magnificent mane which topped his leonine head and indulge his manipulative and persuasive skills all at once. He found that the actor in him could be applauded, the ego in him could be assuaged and the need for money rewarded simultaneously. When I met him, he was just extricating himself from a financial backer's arrangement for his Barry Krost Management Ltd agency business with William Piggott-Brown and about to enter a similar one with Michael Medwin and Albery Finney's Memorial Enterprises. He was like a little boy with an excessively sweet tooth to whom an infatuated benefactor had bequeathed a chain of sweet shops. I always felt sorry for William Piggot-Brown who quit the arena just as the fanfare heralded the biggest crowd-puller ever and I rather think that Michael and Albert and Memorial Enterprises didn't benefit as much as Barry.

As far as I was concerned, Barry's major qualification as a potential employer was that he was gay. In fact, Barry was riven through and through with the predilection, shamelessly, openly and extremely publicly. Barry was, in his way, a pioneer. He was relentlessly gay. From the moment he woke up in the morning to the second he lost consciousness in sleep at night, Barry was unmistakeably not merely homosexual but gay, gay, gay.

And so too, although perhaps a little more shyly due only to the tenderness of my years, was I, all but fresh out of University and still very wet behind the ears as far as the ways of the world were concerned. I must have been instinctively drawn to Barry. Instinct must have been the only reason for I can truthfully say that we had nothing else in common whatsoever. Not that I didn't like him. I, like many others, came to love him and that was my undoing. Barry had a huge talent for making people first fall in love with him and then, completely hooked and unable to let go, care for him. We might often not like the people we love; we might even go so far as hating them on occasion but we never stop loving them.

Anyway, his immediate offer of a job certainly was a relief in that summer of 1970. It was surely one I knew I couldn't refuse and I could not wait to follow the unravelled skein of glittering thread that led through the secret caverns of my future. Contrary to many perceptions, there are not hordes of gays running show-business. Certainly there are probably a few more than there are in chemical engineering but not, I hazard, that many more. Showbiz ones are just a bit more vocal, a teensy bit more obvious and perhaps not quite as married as those in chemical engineering. It might sound strange but it is most definitely true that Barry's exhibitionist nature coupled with his tireless flaunting of his gayness was not only generally deemed acceptable but also considered charming. Its very destabilising effect also proved shockingly potent in his business dealings. It had been so for years.

I rather think that in the company of a majority of gays, such behaviour would have self-marginalised in five minutes flat and Barry relegated to the theatrical end of the bar to rehearse a more appropriate script.

No. In those days, it was the straight, heterosexual man, (usually plain, often as aesthetic as a pound of ground beef and staunchly homophobic behind the usurer's smile) who was irredeemably in control of the asylum and as far as I can see, despite feminism and all the other emancipation and social enfranchisement of the past twenty years, he still is.

REVOLUSSIA brought Steve and Barry together. It was through Oscar Beuselinck at Wright and Webb, co-incidentally the father of Paul Nicholas, one of the emerging new talents in HAIR! Barry must have had many dealings with this powerhouse of a show-biz lawyer who operated out of Soho Square, hardly a stone's throw from Steve's parents' cafe.

At the time they met, both Barry and Steve were bearded, both dark and although one was taller and thinner and the other shorter and fatter, they could have been brothers. They certainly both shared a street-wise intelligence which unerringly led them to the nearest, easiest and fastest buck. They both had the spiv's attitude to money. It was there to be used, preferably spent and spent in order both to impress and also if necessary to buy the people they wanted to impress. As Mike Gill pointed out, when he and Steve went out drinking, Steve always paid. When out with Barry, Barry always paid. When Steve and Barry went out together, I wonder if they took it in turns or if they went Dutch? Steve was later to be as generous to Barry as he was to his own family.

Before going further with the flame of Steve's relationship with Barry which was to burn so brightly for the few years that it was alight, REVOLUSSIA deserves a greater mention.

The dramatist and lyricist Robin Miller, responsible for the book and lyrics for DAMES AT SEA remembers Barry Krost introducing him to Cat Stevens sometime in 1969. I can't recall if there was ever a complete book for the musical but I cannot help thinking that Barry, having met Robin several times, must have taken Steve along to check Robin out as a possible writer. DAMES had just proved a great success all over the world and Robin was hot theatrical property. Robin does not remember the subject of the show being raised although he confirms that Barry and Steve came to his Islington home twice.

He remembers Steve as being very serious, not shy but not talkative and sitting cross-legged on the floor most of the evening. As Robin had no knowledge that Steve had written a musical and only Yusuf or Barry Krost could reveal whether or not they were scouting for a writer for REVOLUSSIA for which role Robin would have been perfect. Anyway, although REVOLUSSIA was credited on a couple of albums, the project never grew. Perhaps Steve developed the idea only so far before being sidetracked by the time and energy-consuming demands of his recording and touring success. I'm sure that REVOLUSSIA wasn't abandoned because Steve didn't need the experience. I'm pretty sure it was because there wasn't time. To have songs already well-known to the audience when they heard them again in the context of the show is a marketing ploy now used everywhere, notably by Andrew Lloyd-Webber.

Two songs, certainly which had been earmarked for REVOLUSSIA were re-cycled and appeared with slight changes to the lyrics one on TEA FOR THE TILLERMAN and the other on MONA BONE JAKON. I have a tape of what music existed for the musical. It's a five inch, seven and a half IPS, EMI tape and it's in a white box and the track list, written in biro on the exterior of the box runs thus: IT'S NOT TIME TO MAKE A CHANGE; HIM, YOU & ME; LITTLE DADDY-O; RASSIA; GOD SAVE THE TSAR; STICK TOGETHER and MAYBE YOU'RE RIGHT, MAYBE YOU'RE WRONG. The first became FATHER AND SON and the last stayed the same, included on MONA BONE JAKON. There were at least three more songs written for the musical, THE RAVEN, THE DAY THEY MAKE ME TSAR and REVOLUSSIA.

I have a feeling that the idea for the musical was current very early and I have an inkling that its existence was more than one of the reasons why Steve felt that a man like Barry Krost with his wealth of theatrical experience and contacts was the man to manage him. I feel these things because unless Yusuf contradicts me, the musical fund which kept the Cat Stevens career so well-supplied between 1969 and 1973 was virtually intact by 1969.

I imagine that the REVOLUSSIA demos were recorded in a studio. The sound quality is frighteningly good and playing it through decent speakers gives the impression that the recordings were made yesterday. Steve is in clear, full voice slightly lower pitched than usual and yet sings other 'parts' in either deeper voice or comic falsetto.

I'll give a musical context to the best of my ability. IT'S NOT TIME TO MAKE A CHANGE (Sung in a very deep voice) The song is Russian-ised. It has that central-European marching, dancing flavour which is a little Russian and a little Jewish. There are obviously at least three characters singing here. Who they are can only be conjectured. Steve handled the factional rivalry between interested parties in the Revolution with dramatic effect by giving each faction a Talking Head, not to mention the woolly-thinking brother. There is guitar and piano on this track and more than a hint of humour, like the three commissars in NINOTCHKA which became, of course, SILK STOCKINGS.

There's a touch of cathedral Orthodox in the music for LITTLE DADDY-O on which Steve accompanies himself on guitar, adding his own voice as harmony at certain points. He sings some lyrics in a comic vocal tone obviously indicating the presence of a chorus. Whether the Daddy in question is the Tsar, as Father of All the Russias, or one of the Party Grandees I don't know but the rapacious nature of the subject is obviously indulged by the fawning or terrified chorus. And only Cat Stevens could have rhymed 'jewels' with 'roubles'.

RASSIA; There is a very definite Greek feeling to this song of which the lyrics in the main are unintelligible. Steve plays guitar and there is a piano accompaniment. Other voices are important to the structure of the song which has a supplicant atmosphere as though a congregation is praying for benefit. Why Rassia and not Russia? I don't know.

GOD SAVE THE TSAR; This is short and to the point, obviously a company piece which could obviously be expanded or merely be repeated. The guitar and piano accompaniment ends with chords which signify the pealing of many carillons of steeple bells.

STICK TOGETHER; is a song sung alternately by the Romanoff family and, presumably, their guards perhaps, when the Royal Family had been taken into captivity? It's a dance-y melody, quite up-tempo, guitar and piano accompaniment. It would seem by the la la-ing at the end that more lyrics were to be written.

MAYBE YOU'RE RIGHT, MAYBE YOU'RE WRONG ... Steve sings and plays here in demo form what appeared on the MONA BONE JAKON album and what arguably must be a perfect song either in the demo form or the finally produced version. I know there are zillions of perfect songs but if I'd been Steve and I'd have known I'd written this song, it would have made me heart proud to know that at least I'd written one perfect song. I happen to believe he wrote many perfect songs. Who are the two parties in the song? Nicholas and Alexandra perhaps, before they go to their deaths?

The quality and character of the lyrics of these songs have a maturity and an awareness which simply was not present on the material recorded by Mike Hurst. Steve was patently in full command of the faculties which were about to be so widely recognised. It is fairly obvious that he knew exactly the kind of sound he wanted to achieve in studio recording and understood both the nature of clarity as well as the importance of simplicity and stillness. So much of rock and roll had had to do with physical movement. Now it was the turn of stillness, quietness and introspection.

Steve must have decided to sign management contracts with Barry Krost in 1970 and, by doing so, realised he was throwing in his lot with a thriving theatrical agency. Barry's office hummed with activity. The switchboard was always fully used, the waiting rooms always full of clients or would-be clients waiting to see either Barry, Sara Randall or Gordon Black, the three active agents in the company. Barry's client list when Steve joined was impressive. The late Peter Collinson, director of many films including the legendary ITALIAN JOB, playwright John Osborne and his actress wife Jill Bennett, Charles Laurence who was to score such a success with his plays MY FAT FRIEND and SNAP!, the young Maureen Lipman, the young Michael Cashman, Fenella Fielding, actress Jane Asher, director Mike Hodges. Writers, actors, actresses, directors and producers. The staff in Barry's office were always kept very busy and usually kept very late at work. Overtime didn't exist and even Saturdays were fair game if Barry wanted to push you the extra mile.

Steve himself too was very much hands-on in those early days. If there was something to be done, he would do it himself. He didn't have a secretary or any one employed by him until Di Hughes arrived some time after we had moved offices from Davies Street to Curzon Street in the winter of 1970. The two floors which BKM (Personal Agency) Ltd occupied were at the top of the premises at 27 Curzon Street. They had been Barry's apartment which he shared with his longtime lover, the actor Tony Beckley. Tony and Barry moved first to Jill Bennett's flat in Mount Street whilst the house they had bought in Walham Grove, Fulham was being prepared.

A long three flights of stairs led to the inauspicious doorway to the attic premises, which, once accessed proved to be light and spacious. One floor of the apartments was a through-room separated by dividing doors, the rear room being occupied by Sara Randall with, later, Richard Eastham and Norman Boyack, and the front room with the view over Curzon Street which was only used by Barry. After a while actress turned decorator Jill Melford was brought in to choose some furniture for this first floor and advise on some oh-so-tasteful blinds and suitable colour schemes. We upstairs, being merely heard and not seen, were left to fend with no interior decorator to soothe our fevered way until Steve took the building over and clouds appeared on the ceilings in 1976. By that time I had sadly left. Sally Moore who did the agency's accounts in those early years likened our working under the coved-ceiling beneath the roof to being in cages.

'S'pose you've come to rattle MY cage now?' she would ask when we went into her office with our queries about the clients' monies.

After a while, even I could tell life was getting better for all of us when Barry, due to pressure of all the rooms at Curzon Street being used and needing a secretarial assistant's services fairly constantly, excused me from part of the personal services section of my job specification in that he allowed me to take his laundry to the dry cleaners a little way down Curzon Street instead of insisting on my ironing it myself!

For a while, 1971 and 1972, Barry seemed jollier and happier than he had ever been. The realisation that Steve's career had taken off came very quickly after that first appearance of Steve's at The Troubadour in LA in 1970. The implications of Steve's career launch, however, took longer to be revealed.

Steve's career up to that time in America had been fairly parochial; it had had to do with his potential rather than the reality of any success. Whatever high-flying talks Barry may have had with Chris Blackwell and the others at Island records meant a 'phone call between Curzon Street and Hammersmith. It was hardly transatlantic and it was all very much between chums. The people at Island sat at large round tables in open offices where everyone knew a lot about most company matters. It was all very ... comprehensive? Steve's American success made the transatlantic phone lines start jumping, activity which of course didn't start for us until six in the evening because Los Angeles was eight hours behind us in time.

As TILLERMAN and TEASER successively established Steve's record selling status all over the known world, the calls also started flooding in with offers from all over the world for him to tour. The overseas record companies were frequent callers. Promoters both from the UK and Europe were forever on the line and of course there soon started those almost nightly calls to CMA (as ICM was once called) in New York where Vincent Romeo handled all the live performance enquiries regarding Steve's career.

Barry's office really started to hum as Carl Miller began to assemble the road crew and other touring personnel to accompany Steve on his conquering sorties. As Barry became involved in the careers of other artists like Colin Blunstone on CBS and Mike d'Abo on A and M Records both of whom maintained working bands for quite some time, the number of road crew and band members passing through the office ensured a constant whirligig of activity.

It goes without saying that Barry learned fast. It therefore follows that his staff did too. It was a very good thing we were capable of learning for there was no hint of any constructive, structured training at BKM. We were there to work and to work for as little money as Barry could get away with. To Louis XIV was ascribed the saying: '*L'Etat, c'est moi.*' Exactly the same summation could be applied to the way Barry saw his company. It was him. Without him, it was nothing and nothing therefore needs no one to run it and so no one had any significance other than the pragmatic, the functional and inevitably, the dispensible.

But there were several years to run before my turn came in that inevitable round and in the meantime not only myself but all those who worked at Curzon Street set to with a will.

Barry employed several women and girls and towards them he feigned a rather theatrical misogyny. There were many occasions on which he would send himself up, making a joke out of pretending to lash some poor woman as a slave-driver might abuse his charges. He often boasted that he'd taught one particular member of the staff how to fellate her partner by showing her how to employ a Coca cola bottle as an appropriate tool for experiment. Perhaps his misogynist displays were not quite so theatrical as I fondly imagine although he always was most courteous with women in general, whoever they might be, when they called at the office.

In this context, I hasten to mention two ladies of Steve's early acquaintance, the fabled Patti d'Arbanville and the equally advertised, at the time because of PEYTON PLACE, Barbara Parkin. I know not of the closeness of Steve's relationship with Miss Parkin except that I was told she had 'appeared' one day at the studios Steve was using at that time in the country attired entirely in white, as might have befitted some southern belle, reading from a book of poetry. Perhaps she thought this image was appropriate to what poetic rock stars found appealing. However, Barbara's appeal had to be pitted against the tireless Patti's prior claim and one day, perhaps invoking the necessity for some cosmic resolution of this unsatisfactory amorous situation, both arrived at Curzon Street at the same time.

Barbara was already at the top of the stairs whilst Patti was coming up them. Barry acted with a marvellous spontaneity (perhaps reacting to a life time of sitting through bedroom farces). He instructed us to bundle Barb into the bathroom whilst he and Steve ushered Patti through to his office at the front of the building. When storm doors were firmly shut and no bulkheads breachable, we had to hurry Barbara downstairs. None of us ever saw her again.

After Patti, there wasn't really anyone significant in Steve's life other than Maggie Gill in the early years of the seventies and Avril Meyer in the United States. There were other women who occasionally appeared with him but no sooner than our 'Hi's' and the 'Hello's' and the initial politesse had been overcome than they were gone. They were rarely introduced and always looked as though they felt very awkward as they waited for Steve to conclude his business.

Steve certainly spent a great deal of social time with the people he worked with especially Paul Samwell-Smith and his family and Alun Davies and his family; this took care of love but what Steve did for more intimate companionship was never discussed. Later we had our ideas but ... well, he was Cat Stevens, after all.

Steve's renaissance was obviously as much to do with Island records as it was with himself or with Barry Krost. As I've mentioned, the staff at Island were incredibly well-integrated. They all seemed to know exactly what was going on in most departments and with most of their artists. Chris Blackwell had certainly developed a highly professional organisation. David Betteridge was Managing Director of Island Records at the time Steve joined. David Betteridge is a most honourable man as his life spent in the record industry lends testament. Other than his time spent at Island, David has also run CBS and been associated with RCA, Virgin (with his SIREN label) as well as MCA with whom he is now associated with his own independent company.

DAVID BETTERIDGE: "I'm really not sure how much I can tell you , but ...

I was Managing Director of Island at the time Steve was introduced to the company and to be truthful, I really can't say exactly how Steve came to Island. Maybe Muff Winwood ... you'd have to ask Chris Blackwell or Muff about that. It was certainly via Muff (the brother of Stevie Winwood of TRAFFIC and solo fame) that Steve got together with Paul Samwell-Smith.

Barry and Steve? I honestly don't know how they met or were introduced but I have a feeling that the name Mel Collins features somewhere. He was a manager ... Although now you mention the name of Wright and Webb and Oscar Beuselinck, maybe that was the connection. Only Steve or Barry, I'd think, could answer that.

From my point of view, Steve was the perfect artist to have. He was creative from every point of view, from his artistic input into the album design and illustration to the writing of the songs; he sang well, he was a decent musician and he looked like a Greek god! Today? With what he and the industry have learned in the last twenty years, he'd be so much bigger.

If anything, perhaps his management wasn't quite the right

one. That is a big if. The music business is a delicate system of checks and balances and to succeed, every component, every tooth of every cog has to be in the right place at the right time so that when the public presses its 'Play' button, the machine effortlessly provides the career that is wanted and by 1970, the record buying public was looking not for just then latest catchy single to latch on to; pop music had come of age and the public wanted to discover artists whose 33 rpm careers they could adopt and grow with as they themselves grew. They wanted their chosen and anointed favourites to have careers for these favourites became in a surrogate way, best friends, brothers, sisters ... Your day's gone badly, get home and play a Cat Stevens record. Life, as the songs say, doesn't always go right, even for pop stars and that's a kind of good, comforting feeling.

Careers ... yes. Management. I liked Barry immensely. I think we all did. It obviously worked for Steve and Barry for a long time although I feel things were a little ad hoc. When Barry's outfit had really learned their trade and had come of age, it was sadly too late. Steve and Barry had become distanced; the magic had faded. At the time it was needed, there wasn't too much forward planning, I felt, although I am talking as a representative of the record company and don't appreciate the finer points of what was going on in the intimate regions of the artist's life.

And perhaps this sense of pragmatism that came through to us was in no small way due to Steve's huge output. He really did whack out some product between 1970 and 1974, almost too much I felt and of course no sooner than the last fader had been tinkered with in the studio than Steve wanted his product out there. He was, as is well known, a perfectionist. As soon as the product was perfect he started on the artwork.

Tim Clarke and I had charge of the artwork for album sleeves and I remember Steve calling up one day and giving me a tremendous bawling out when he felt that the yellow line surrounding the proofed cover artwork for CATCH BULL AT FOUR had been printed an infinitesimal tone yellower than the original. I believe he asked me if I realised that I was ruining his career ... Happily, I don't think I was but equally happily, I suppose, I happened to be the one on whom all that pent-up frustration and tense anticipation that many artists experience just before launching their latest product was out-poured. Record company executives fulfil many functions ...

In many ways he was a paradox. And, before I forget, speaking of artwork, it always amused me that he never charged us for the designing and illustration work he created for the sleeves and inserts. He could have done and charged what he liked.

But back to paradox. I think his work was superb. I also think it was influenced very much by his illness, by the TB. Anyone who faces death automatically realigns their thoughts of mortality and therefore their own lives and what matters most. I do think in Steve's case, the poet was a very different bag to the poem and I say this in no way wanting to take away from the work, to detract from the poem because you can't. It's there and it stands. However, I do think Steve was a very clever man, in many ways very astute and he calculated the future of Cat Stevens vis a vis the record business extremely well. The over-seriousness of MONA BONE JAKON was certainly tempered in the product that followed it.

I think he chose well with Island. I think we were a company that was always evolving. Open. Organic. We had no blanket policy that covered all artists or all product. Every one of Island's artists was treated on their individual merits and needs.

Steve, post-convalescent in 1969, had a career that was basically floating down the tubes. Island stuck with MONA BONE JAKON for a long time, over eighteen months and it only made money after TEASER and TILLERMAN, the seminal Cat Stevens albums, had come out and had sold; then people went back to rediscover and found MONA BONE JAKON.

Contractually, when he first came to Island from Decca, the terms were almost laughable. They were so much to our favour that when TEASER and TILLERMAN proved so successful, we upped the royalty rates voluntarily. There was no over-ride paying any Decca interest off. He just got himself out and came on board. His publishing too was free and that helped a great deal. Of course, there was no resolved contractual situation after the expiry of his first contract with us. All the product after 1974-75 was supplied ad hoc. He did of course make an enormous amount of money despite royalty rates which now would be considered miserable. Vast sums because he did it all himself. Apart from Paul Samwell-Smith, everyone else to do with him other than, I presume, Barry was either on a retainer or on salary.

He was of course never as big at home as he was abroad. In France and Germany for example, he was a huge star. I remember having to exert a fairly strong pressure via, I hasten to add, Barry for Steve to tour and in those days an act had to tour to promote the work. It was the pre-video era and the only way to build and then sustain success was to schedule released product carefully and back this with tours which one could then amplify by orchestrated press and photo coverage.

Though, obviously, we would have liked to have had him on Island in the USA, had things been that way, maybe his career wouldn't have been quite so enormous over there. I think A and M did a pretty good job although I do feel that the haggling and the bidding when it came time to renew contracts (and after album four when A and M tried to sign Steve for the world), especially with Atlantic also muddying the waters, didn't do Steve any favours. There was a bit of a falling out between Jerry Moss and Chris Blackwell from what I can remember and THAT also added to the heap. Things between Barry and Steve can't have been that great then because there was a lack of direction about what they, about what Steve wanted.

I always say that you can tell when an artist has become truly successful when you can only get to talk to them via their lawyer - or their manager. I think this probably characterises all relationships between artist and record company. Steve certainly started out ery closely involved with us - Chris, me, Muff, Tom Hayes, Tim Clarke, Lionel Conway - and used to come to Hammersmith a lot but then things tailed off. You got to see him on tour, of course and on other work occasions but that initial closeness goes. So, when situations like contract renewals come up unless you have a very straight-talking manager who balances up all interests - financial, the artist, the work, the commission - no one will really know how best to proceed for all interests to be satisfied. Obviously you can't give away negotiating hands with so much money involved but things can be determined in ways that aren't necessarily messy.

I think by that time Steve had realised just how huge a business Cat Stevens was in financial terms. It was a heavy burden to carry and an added one to the existing one he'd always carried around - that of himself. All those advisers and lawyers and consultants and accountants.

I honestly think he found it hugely off-putting. That and the aftermath of such an enormous output brought about a dilution of the energy after about 1975. In a way, I think Steve was written out, sung out and starting to look elsewhere for the assuaging of his creative urges. He had to seek elsewhere, really. The songs and the work didn't do it for him after that. IZITSO was the last album and it had lost the gloss. Sort of co-incided with my leaving Island. I remember the date exactly. September 4th 1977. I honestly feel Steve never really knew how good he was. I think he'd been so clever with his work that he somehow missed how REALLY good it was. I think maybe he achieved seventy five percent of what he could have done, all things being equal and with the wonderful benefit of hindsight but despite his sales, over twenty four million album units, I feel he never got to be the top-flight artist he deserved to be."

The messiness that shrouded the end of Steve's close relationship with Island was underpinned by a certain amount of bitterness. Understandable, I suppose, if out of the kindness of their hearts Island had so substantially upped Steve's royalty rates when they really had had no legal need. It was obviously politically motivated as much as good-heartedly for they wanted relations between themselves and the artist to remain sweet, to say nothing of their relationship with the manager.

On the subject of REVOLUSSIA ... I can remember a sort of sigh of relief when the project faded in importance on Steve's priority list. The people at Island were not only not keen on it - I think they found it distracting and they understood nothing of theatre - they were openly derisory.

Overall, however, Steve's relationship with Island was more than mutually rewarding. MONA BONE JAKON had cost some £1500, TILLERMAN and TEASER had each come in for not a great deal more than £7000 AND they'd had free art work! Many people have done very well out of Island Records and the record company, however generous and altruistic, ALWAYS does better than the artist which makes them. But that is capitalism.

CHAPTER SEVEN

THE INSIDE OUTSIDER

I'm sitting at my screen pretending to write but, instead, listening to The Suite from Steve's FOREIGNER album which came out in 1973. I'm thinking how grandiose Steve's conception was. I'm also thinking how I thought it did not succeed in 1973 and how it continues, sadly, to fall short in 1993. Of course, it didn't have Paul Samwell-Smith on it and it had none of the usual 'in-house' band. FOREIGNER, therefore, very little objective input.

Of course, I'm now feeling awful for even thinking such a cruel and horrid thing because, thinking back, I'm trying to pin-point that person or those people who were Steve's objective input, his touchstones, those human points he came to for a frank and unbiased opinion of what he was doing, especially work-wise. We all need those people. They're called friends and they tell you things like: *"The novel stinks, old dear. Sorry"*. You hear that, get stunned by it but realise that there must be something in what they say. Then you go and, first, find what's really wrong and finally fix it.

Then you say thank you.

I don't remember there being anyone like that for Steve although there must have been. Personally, I know I would never have thought of saying: *"Well, er ... If you really want to know what I think, it IS a bit long, Steve and there actually isn't much structure to it other than it all segues together and starts at A and finishes at Z"*. Unlike Freddie Mercury's BOHEMIAN RHAPSODY, you can see the joins in the FOREIGNER SUITE and I wish now he would have written the four or five individual songs separately which, instead, cobbled together make up the whole suite.

But ... back to who told Steve the way it was. I suppose it's true that stars surround themselves, or become surrounded, with syco- phancy and that stardom and sycophancy are as inevitable as peaches and cream, as indivisible as de Sade and von Masoch. The only times one could come out and be on one side or another vis a vis Steve was when his particular current balloon went up. Then you knew how he wanted you to think. Other than that, in the management company, I honestly think he only ever received praise; eulogistic, arse-licking, grovelling plaudits.

I firmly believe that although he could have done with some sharper input, Steve was only too well aware when he had fallen short. Criticism can be made about the amount of product he put out in those early seventies. If you take away FOREIGNER on the basis that it was followed with BUDDHA AND THE CHOCOLATE BOX, a tender album packed with relevant, optimistic simplicity not over- ambitious self-indulgence, I think the balance of this work is corrected. Steve knew what bummers were - and I'm not merely talking commercially - and I'm sure he recognised his own only too painfully. But he did have friends. He might not have known it and as later events were to prove, he didn't do very well by them. But he surely had friends.

Having written and then rewritten the previous piece about FOREIGNER and wondering what right I had to do so and even whether it was fair to even begin to criticise another person's work and what the point of having opinions about such a tiddly thing as rock 'n' roll was anyway, the 'phone rang.

It was Yusuf Islam, ex-Cat Stevens, ex-Steve Giorgiou reply- ing to my letter to him informing him that I was embarking on this project.

I was so pleased to hear from him and at the same time horribly guilty that I'd been sitting there thinking about him and saying not too complimentary things about his FOREIGNER album about which he must have been once very proud! As we talked, I heard myself rabbitting on and now, of course, I can't remember a thing I said. I was just absolutely knocked out that talking to him was as though we had not spoken for two or three days. I had in fact last spoken to him fifteen years ago.

By the end of our conversation, I was reminded that if we ever met again, I probably wouldn't agree with many of his views or current opinions but just from that telephone call, I know that I think I would have understood him.

I think I can understand a little bit ...

Yusuf loves his God as I love my friends and family and the whole of life; by that, I am of course not implying that he doesn't love his friends and family. I'm just trying to find words ... Unlike him, I cannot even conceptualise God except by superimposing the faces of people I have loved, whom I love and, as some of them are dead, those whose love is rendered immutable and eternal. If I force myself to reify Him (or Her), I cannot help thinking of a force which is not benign and which cannot have a conscience, at least as I understand the word.

I understand religious rapture, I feel religious magnetism, I can recognise good and evil, temptation, strength and weakness and I see it all around me in my fellow creatures ... But God? God I've never recognised, never felt, never understood in this life. And if I did, I'm not sure at this point in my own life how much we'd have to say to each other.

Leaving God on one side for a moment but returning to Steve's friends, I spent an afternoon with Rosie Samwell-Smith in Hampstead. Rosie's a major player in the league of our lives. Now divorced from Paul, Steve's producer for so long, Rosie lives in the latest of a succession of beautiful Hampstead houses with her children and her mother, Sheila.

Could women be somehow much more equipped to achieve? They do, after all, build things of progressive, enduring significance called children. They care and nurture and equip and launch. Men, it so often seems, only really need occupations to keep them out of mischief while they build for the next orgasm or, more germanely, search for the next breast to lean their wounded and weary cheek on.

Of course, I'm generalising but ...

Having seen her family, Nicholas her son and Katharine her daughter, on the road to adulthood, Rosie went back to university and having gained a law degree then pushed on to study for the bar. She became a barrister and after some time practising as counsel in family-oriented matters, she now spends the majority of her time teaching trainee barristers their art and craft. They're very lucky to have her on their side. So, it turns out, was Cat Stevens.

ROSIE SAMWELL-SMITH: "I suppose I've always been a career

woman. God! I've been at it long enough. I started as Vicki Wickham's assistant on READY STEADY GO! in 1965, the very trendy music programme made by Rediffusion. It was my first job and, as it turned out, the jumping off point for the rest of my life. Not only did I first meet my first husband Paul whilst working on it, I also first met Steve. That must have been 1966 because the song he'd come on the show to sing was I LOVE MY DOG.

Actually, at the time, I didn't immediately take to Steve but ... Remember that I was nineteen and he was nineteen and there was no way I was going to be that easily impressed by anyone! Of course, though it'd never have entered my mind to have demonstrated such thoughts, I did also think him tremendously beautiful and extremely glamourous. I wanted to touch his skin, that sort of feeling. Tactile perhaps but purely aesthetic. Not sexual at all. I also, privately, thought he was very talented and his work was very different, a refreshing change from all that SEARCHERS sort of stuff and the band sounds that were popular then.

I'd met Paul whilst he was in THE YARDBIRDS in 1965 when I first went to work on READY, STEADY GO! I remember so well. He pinched my bottom as he walked behind me going up the stairs at the studio. *"Cheeky little bugger!"*. I thought. READY, STEADY GO! was about to get some kind of gong and the award was going to be handed over at a party at the AD LIB CLUB. Paulie came as my date and we were together from that time on. Funny to think that when Steve performed on RSG!, Paul was probably there listening, watching and yet they weren't to get together for another few years.

I left Rediffusion in 1966 and went to work for the BBC. I shared a flat in West Hampstead in those days with Fran Knight, now the gracious Lady Wedderburn of Charlton and Paul was still living with his parents in Teddington. He left THE YARDBIRDS, I think in 1968 and had started working in record production. In 1968 he went down very badly with pancreatitis. Not pleasant. People die from it. He spent weeks in the West Middlesex hospital and then took months to recover. He convalesced very slowly. I know the sixties were the glory days and all that but I know how tough it was to be in those big name bands so young. The life really took a great deal out of the musicians and the toll that high living took too turned up a lot of casualties. Peoples' constitutions weren't made for it.

By 1969, Paul had been in to Island records and had met Chris

Blackwell and for Island had produced two albums for a band called AMAZING BLONDEL. Minstrelly, troubadourish stuff as their name would imply.

It was Chris Blackwell who put Paul and Steve together. Steve, also just out of hospital, had arrived at Island's threshold and Chris, on hearing the newly written work tied it up immediately with the material that Blondel had been doing, realised the direction it could go and called Paul to arrange a meeting. Chris Blackwell was a very caring man. He adored both Paul and Steve. He must have known too that they would get on. Just playing and liking the same sort of music isn't enough to transfer what sounds great when played live simply on a guitar into a record that will sell well in the market place.

The appointment having been made by Chris Blackwell, Paul had one initial meeting with Steve. That meeting alone convinced him. Later, Steve came to see Paul and I at my little flat, four flights up. Knock at the door and there was Steve lugging his guitar. He sat down cross-legged on the floor and played the songs that later were to comprise MONA BONE JAKON. I remember being very touched, very moved. I was quite shocked, really surprised by how good and new and, again, how different they were. I immediately said Paul should do it, work with Steve.

Well, of course, they got on like a house on fire. There was an instant chemistry between Paul and Steve. You could feel it ... I could feel it. They were soul mates. Neither was nor is a particularly clear communicator on a banal, day-to-day level but on the level of the work, their cerebral rapport was immediate, intense and could be somewhat exclusive. I was once again impressed by Steve's creative musical talent. I thought he played both guitar and piano really well and his new songs were deeper and more substantial than the pop singles and I'd liked those a lot too.

As far as I can remember, MONA BONE JAKON was recorded at Olympic Studios in Barnes in 1969 although the later ones were done at Morgan Studios. Though the sessions weren't particularly private and certainly not secret, I never went in unless I was specifically invited. Being a BBC staffer, I knew the significance of studio work and could never abide those hangers on who have always 'ligged' I believe is the expression, hanging around the people who are really doing the work, never really understanding how serious it all is. But, as I say, there were exceptions, one being when the string section was being recorded for INTO WHITE. It was via Paul that Alun Davies was introduced to the proceedings. I believe Alun was working with Jeremy Taylor, the anglicised South African singer/guitarist on a documentary programme at BBC Television.

Both Steve and Paul were very well ordered. They always knew what they were going to record when they began their series of sessions for an album recording. Recording was always as least unprepared as possible.

MONA BONE JAKON must have been finished about the beginning of 1970. The people at Island raved about it and both Steve and Paul were obviously very pleased too. What happened next is, in retrospect, pretty unbelievable. The story concerns America. Either there wasn't an Island records in America ... who knows. Whatever the background, Chris gave Paul and I the go-ahead to try and place the album in America. With no funding from Island, Paul and I drew out every last penny we had and flew to New York to try and sell MONA BONE JAKON. To whom? At that time, I thought, to anyone!

No one wanted to know.

There's nothing worse than New York when no one wants to know.

In the spirit of those wretched dolls that just won't lie down however hard you buffet them, we picked ourselves up, dusted ourselves off and started out for California. We were due to stay with our friends Larry and Carol Peters in Los Angeles. Although both have now long seen sense and retrenched well behind the lines in the comparative safety of the groves of academe, Larry in those days worked in the record business and Carole, I had last heard, was working at Elektra Records. Of course we also knew Peter and Betsy Asher very well. Peter and Paul had known each other from the PETER AND GORDON and YARDBIRDS days respectively and they had stayed friends. They were both highly intelligent, very bright and very talented and of course Peter had teamed up with James Taylor. I remember him coming to see us in my flat in London with the, I think, as yet un-released JAMES TAYLOR first album. Peter and Paul now had even more in common for Paul had now found his own James Taylor in Steve. The careers of both artists and producers were in many ways uncannily comparable. Peter of course added management to his bow. That was all so long ago and life is greatly changed. Betsy is now, sadly, dead. Never-to-be-forgotten, she is greatly missed.

When Paul and I arrived in Los Angeles that year, we found that Carol Peters was still with Elektra but that her husband Larry was working for A and M records, the company which Jerry Moss and Herb Alpert had started after Herb's band success. Capitol Records may have had a building designed by Frank Lloyd Wright but Jerry and Herb's company occupied one of the really glamourous sites in Hollywood, the old Charlie Chaplin Studio complex, much refurbished of course, on La Brea Avenue. Instead of going to an office, it was like going onto a lot, into a film studio.

Obviously Carole and Larry knew why we'd trailed all the way out to the coast and naturally insisted that Larry make arrangements to take the album into A and M and play it to the A and R people. How open and helpful and friendly things were in those days. Especially in America. People really wanted you to succeed. People like Lance Freed, Gil Friesen.

Ultimately, when the album reached him, highly praised, Jerry went potty. He loved the album, understood what it and Steve were all about immediately and after making all the necessary telephone calls and business arrangements with Steve and with Island in London, signed MONA BONE JAKON and Steve for the USA.

Joy, shall I say, was un-confined! I can still feel how excited I was.

I can still sense the buzz of enthusiasm and excitement which rippled round the lot as more and more people heard Steve and Paul's album and joined in the groundswell of support for A and M's new signing.

I remember it like yesterday. A Joe Cocker tour was about to go out and the trucks and buses were leaving the A and M lot, people hanging out of the doors and windows ... waving goodbye, waving to us, wishing us well, congratulating Paul. There were the A and M people too as well as wives and girlfriends waving the tour goodbye, wishing Joe and the band and the road crew 'Good Luck!'. Like carnival.

I shall never forget it. God! Rock 'n' roll was wonderful then.

Also wonderful was the five thousand pounds advance Jerry gave Paul and I. We returned to England not unlike Francis Drake who very foolishly forgot to claim California for Britain when he sailed the Golden Hind past Marina del Rey in fifteen hundred and something or Walter Raleigh who of course brought his own brand of goodies back from the New World. We got married on the strength of that five thousand pounds in July 1970; July 4th to be precise. Did we choose the date in honour of America? It was certainly thanks to America that we at last felt ready to marry because we could afford our first home together, a house which we bought in Steeles Mews in Hampstead where our son Nicholas was born on 28th March 1971.

Barry Krost docked at Steve's port in 1970. Both bearded and with their magnificent manes of hair, Barry and Steve could have almost been taken for twins; well, brothers at least. Barry was very quick to take on board the new potential that his signing of Steve for management had opened up. Record producers also earn a good whack if things go well and it wasn't long before Barry, rapidly being schooled by several eager West End law firms in 'signing' not as a form of communication with the deaf but as a form of leading the blind, was after Paul's signature on a management contract too. Paul's caution had been noted and no sooner had I become a mother than Barry had invited me out alone, with my baby in a basket, for a sprauncey restaurant meeting to persuade me to persuade my husband to 'sign'.

I continued to work at the BBC throughout my pregnancy which co-incided with the gestation and recording of TEA FOR THE TILLERMAN and TEASER AND THE FIRECAT, Steve's second and third albums. I think the recording had started before I got pregnant because I remember joking to someone that it amazed me that I ever got pregnant at all. I was alone throughout the night on many occasions as Paul seemed to be in the studio so much. As Paul's and my baby grew to its full term, so did Paul's other baby, the album he was making with Steve. Just a few days away from my due date, I happened to joke to Steve that if I went into labour, he would find himself without Paul. Though it was on the surface good-natured, Steve's riposte was *"Never!"* And I sensed immediately that he meant it. Never has 'Never!' been said with such a carelessly-disguised depth of feeling. As far as Steve was concerned, there was no question where Paul's first loyalties lay!

Ultimate conflict of interest never arose, thankfully. Paul came home from the studio at about seven on the morning of 27th March 1971 and announced tiredly but proudly that the TEASER album was finished. Four hours later I went into labour walking round Sainsbury's in Marylebone and the following day, Nicholas was born. Steve sent flowers and on the card was the message: 'Thanks for Waiting.' Later, he gave Nicholas the illustration he'd done for the TILLERMAN album cover. Was it just a co-incidence that the completion of that crucial third album and the arrival of our son occurred within twenty four hours? Certainly Steve's life was never to be the same after TILLERMAN and TEASER and our family's certainly wasn't. At last, when TILLERMAN began to sell, we started to earn some reasonable money and we moved into Gayton Road in July 1971. I never returned to the BBC although it wasn't long into Nicholas's infancy that I started my own film production company.

I must mention Steve's talent as an artist/designer here for I pass the said TILLERMAN album cover illustration every time I go up and down my stairs. Steve was most private about his drawing and painting, so much so that I never realised he painted until he brought in the MONA BONE JAKON illustration one day. I must say, I was rather shocked that it was going to be an album cover. The way I reacted to it lead me to interpret it on a very overtly sexual level, that cylindrical dustbin gobbiting out that glob of goo. Phallic symbolism epitomised, I thought. Later album covers were duly modified as TILLERMAN and TEASER testified. The branded childlikeness replaced the more radical poeticism of MONA BONE JAKON and I think Steve picked up immediately on how successful this approach was and pushed it as much as possible as the immediately remarkable vein running throughout his work which people felt comfortable with. Everyone, after all, sometimes wants to recapture childhood which is seen as a golden, unsullied age.

Both Steve and Paul had their royalties upped after TILLERMAN and TEASER sold so well. These albums were so successful that I always laugh when I remember the time Chris Blackwell took Paul out for a ride in the car to some airport not far from London and gave him a less than gratuitous wigging about having gone over budget on the TILLERMAN recording. Admittedly, Paul was over-spent by £2000 although the album's budget was only £5000! I think it remained in charts throughout the world for three years. The costs of albums in those days were almost trifling when compared to the huge sums incurred by later recording schedules.

I'm going to say something now that might sound over the top but I've thought about it and I really believe it. I've met some pretty bright people in my time and although I'd have to reserve a couple of places above him, I don't think I've ever met, apart from said two, a more fundamentally intelligent person than Steve. In comparable terms, he was uneducated, un-crafted and un-channelled but without a shadow of a doubt, he was very, very bright. I think he was so bright that there were things about himself even he couldn't understand and which he certainly couldn't communicate even if he'd wanted to. I see very intelligent people struggling every day with their own intellects but Steve's struggle stood out as exceptional.

He had so many problems within his soul. He was tortured, in my opinion. It's not too strong a word and it was this very tortured quality that I sensed made me realise very quickly that apart from the success he pursued in music, Steve would do something else with his life. There was still something to come. He was a man with a mission and even though events have proved me right, I knew then that however he saw his career, the one way it was definitely developing was as some sort of evangelical stepping stone.

Steve was on a perpetual quest for something. The quest for whatever grail he was after to fill that inner lack, to slake that gnawing, nagging emptiness which also urged him onwards became accelerated as he grew more successful. He was almost in a wilderness, like he was crossing a desert. He was also very much alone, however surrounded he may have appeared to be by friends, family and fans.

We saw a great deal of him. Of course he had girlfriends. Patti had been the most significant, I feel. She was around for a couple of years from 1969 onwards and, in my opinion, I think Steve treated her pretty badly. There was an equally significant falling off in his involvement with partners, companions ... girlfriends, call them what you want and this deceleration in his interest in regular partners co-incided with the acceleration in his religious searching. The dictionary definition of religious is interesting because it starts off with: 'imbued with religion', then 'pious, god-fearing, devout' and finally 'of, belonging to, a monastic order'.

He seemed to pass through what appeared to us as fads. Faddish he obviously wasn't but he was like a ravenous wandering spirit, desperate for reincarnation and eagerly assumed and inhabited, almost parasitically, a likely host incarnation of any new philosophy or religion that entered his orbit. With his acute intelligence and knowing what it was that he didn't want, Steve would very quickly suck the essence of the current phenomenon dry before finding that it would not sustain the sort of life that he wanted. Still yearning, he would move on to another host.

The more hardship or deprivation a new religious path de-manded, the better Steve liked it. It was almost a flagellation, a punishment for a mortally, temporally comfortable life. Whilst his bank accounts snored on a bed of many zeros, Steve's soul slept on a bed of nails. No sooner comfortable than he would have to move, only then to be reminded of his pain. The search was the only hope for an anaesthetic.

Yoga was one of the disciplines he embraced after a transitory espousal of Buddhism. When we went to Jamaica for a holiday in 1973, Steve came with us. Not only Steve but Charles and Caroline Levison, my mother Sheila and my old friend Nicholas Ferguson.

Nicholas, our son, was two. I remember standing by the house we had rented looking down across the grass which lead down to the sea as Steve tried to teach my baby son some of the principles of yoga. I have to say, he adored children and was tirelessly patient with them; he really talked to children as equals and would converse with Nicholas for hours. Nicholas would understand probably but one word in ten and very little of the sense but I can still see them now, that tiny blond-haired baby and that beautiful, bronzed-bodied man sitting side by side after doing head stands and hand stands.

Steve was very vulnerable at the beginning when he and Paul started to work together although the vulnerability went very quickly and the soft spots in Steve's life rather healed over. That initial reticence, that somewhat wounded quality partly vanished because of Paul. Theirs was such a strong relationship, definitely a deep love although totally non-physical. After all, like or loathe the result, they were making art together, pooling creative genes just as two people get together to create a fresh and original batch of blended DNA to make new life in the form of a baby.

Things started to go wrong for them when Steve wanted to do FOREIGNER. Paul was not happy with the work and told Steve so. It must have been an awful time for Paul, realising that what he was doing was something he wasn't going to be proud of and knowing it wasn't going to be good. Then, of course, that battle with himself about what to say to Steve, how to tell Steve and then the final moment when it all blurts out, probably, rotten communicators that they both were in those personal areas, in a way that was immediately taken by Steve as a mortal wound ...

Thereafter, when they worked together, their albums were specified co-productions. I think that Steve allowed a lot of his relationships to fall down about that time. I say 'Steve allowed ...' because relationships have to be two-way. Steve's rather stopped being so. His 'In' and 'Out' channels got very confused. I think he was so concerned with searching for God that the ready existence and importance of man (and certainly woman) had become rather obscured. Other people still wanted their relationships to continue; Steve saw only obstacles. If only he could have seen the obstacles for what they were - people, humanity, human nature and frailty - and thus made them part of his path instead of barriers to be removed.

The more successful he became, the more his temper shortened. The early concerts were often very moving. Brilliant. They made me cry. Then came the big shows, the huge productions and although the audiences enjoyed them, backstage there was a lot of tension and tantrum. Steve wasn't happy but he seemed not to want to create the conditions in which he could be happy. The house he bought in Fulham, and spent more time than you and I could afford in setting it up 'just so', was the most un-homely home I've ever seen. I see it as painfully ironic that when he had the money to create what anyone else would have deemed a paradise, he made a hell-hole.

What do I think as a woman? Well, of course, that's the sixty four thousand dollar one as far as I'm concerned. As anyone who knows me will agree, I've always asked questions. Perhaps that's why I ended up a barrister. Back at the beginning, although it was always like pulling teeth trying to get anything out of Steve, I asked questions. Very direct ones. I know he found this difficult, not only the questioning but also that I was a woman asking questions. I don't think he ever considered that women would be other than like his immediate family members; his sister Anita and, of course, his mother. Both of them worshipped him, never seemed to say 'boo' to him, always gave in to him, acceded to him. Most of the other women he'd come across were, frankly, groupies who, although perhaps not directly to blame, didn't have much of a brain rattling round in there. I was in neither of these categories. I had a brain, I had an insatiably hungry intellect and I think I frightened him. I was also a girlfriend, later a wife and finally a mother and as such made demands which he interpreted as encroaching on his turf. I know that he saw Paul as his territory and

I was often an unwelcome interloper. I know this because there were times I felt unwelcome and there's often no greater revelation of truth than what you feel.

However, I think he was pleased to have me as his friend and I think he was grateful to have me to talk to and he did talk to me about his problems, not only then but also more recently after I had qualified. I knew he even valued my opinions about his work and I have to confess that I am one of the world's most un-musical people. However, I have a lingering doubt whether it was my opinion as a woman that he was after. He could at times be most un-lovingly undemonstrative to adults and yet to children he would invariably be tactile and loving and open. Children of course didn't demand, question or threaten him in the way that grown-ups obviously did. I honestly think he lacked the ability then to give anything that was really personal that would have made you feel vindicated as his friend. I think he rarely honoured you with intimacy or made you feel privileged by knowing you were loved back, in return. Steve could accept very easily. It was, for him, easier to receive and to some this may have appeared tyrannical. Power never ebbed for Steve. It always seemed to flow.

One rarely has more than one person like Steve enter and leave one's life. Such people are special, extraordinary and they have a commensurate effect on your soul and your senses. The scars of the cuts and abrasions take longer to heal and are ones you always notice, like little lines on one's face which can never be ignored for they are revealed each time they're shown a mirror. Similarly, the memories of the good times, the great times linger longer for their roots have reached to the very wellspring of your life. One can accept with a lot of past friendships that their intensity wanes as mutual circumstances change. I've seen many friend-ships float gently away, secure in their bubbles of time. But in the main, I always know how to find them again and very few have burst other than through death. Somehow, when a period of your life of such core importance seems to have drifted just that little bit too far out of reach that you can't easily pluck it back again for that necessary once-a-year reunion and reminiscence, you feel rather robbed. Like something's died that's left un-buried. It makes for unquiet spirits."

There are some things that divorce cannot separate or divide and certain times in previously married people's lives fall into that indestructible category. What Paul and Rosie went through for Steve was pure friendship. Of course the cynical might say that it was to do with careers but knowing all protagonists, what they shared was faith in each other and the certain knowledge that once on board, the train had to be ridden to where-so-e'er.

Paul Samwell-Smith intensely dislikes what he calls 'interviews'. He is a savagely private man, almost awkward in person in social situations and I can therefore well understand his natural reticence which, thankfully, he decided to eschew for me. In the studio, he is a different man, unchained, unleashed, he flies free.

Of all the links in the artistic chain, of all the members of the creative 'committee' which has to be correctly constituted before achieving anywhere near-decent recorded results, record producers, as Mike Hurst has pointed out, are very difficult people to provide with a job specification. Guitarists play guitar, singers sing, engineers know all about the state of the art electronics hidden deep beneath the recording desk ... Record producers do all the above and then some. The job is more of a role and the role of a record producer changes not only with each day working with an artist but with each successive artist and often with each track. Sometimes, the record producer is expected to contribute opinions, judgements and to make decisions, at other times merely to patiently await the arrival of the muse on the other side of the glass of the control box. George Martin, Paul told us, finally gave up talking in interview at all.

The Typical Question - *'What was it like working with the Beatles, Mr. Martin.?'*

The Only Answer - *'Great.'*

So ... I didn't ask Paul what it was like working with Cat Stevens! Illumination can be achieved as much by a candle at dusk as by the sun at midday. It all depends what needs to be seen.

Paul remembers leaving THE YARDBIRDS on the night of a May Ball in Oxford where he'd been playing at one of the colleges. He'd always produced with THE YARDBIRDS and knew that production was what he wanted to do. Dates are a bit hazy with him but he acknowledges doing quite a bit of work before the excesses of life he'd indulged in whilst with THE YARDBIRDS caught up with him. He went down badly with a case of pancreatitis.

Before meeting Cat Stevens, he'd worked with Paul McCartney

and THE SCAFFOLD and had done an album for Jac Holzman at Elektra, a band called RENAISSANCE. It was this album which led him to Island Records. Chris Blackwell seemed to like what he was doing and offered him work. At Island, as well as mixing a couple of albums for BRONCO and JIMMY CLIFF, Paul worked with AMAZING BLONDEL.

He admits to not knowing how Steve got to Island. Paul thinks perhaps Muff Winwood would know but is definite that it was Chris Blackwell who thought that he and Steve might get on. Before the time he met up with Steve, Paul had been listening to a lot of Bob Dylan, Simon and Garfunkel and Joni Mitchell. Lately, Van Morrison's ASTRAL WEEKS had been very influential, especially the song MADAME GEORGE.

Paul first met Steve at Steve's parents' cafe in New Oxford Street. They sat and talked in Steve's room upstairs. He'd got several taped demos and the rest of his material he just sat and played on acoustic guitar. He had a huge fund of songs and Paul still remembers their urgency. Paul feels that Steve always had a purpose, a sense of something that was greater than himself ... That he'd been put here for something. The day Paul met him started one of the most intense periods in his life for between January 1970 and March 1971, they made three albums together. But, first things first.

They felt their way by going into a little three-track studio at Pye near Marble Arch and made some more demos before selecting the songs that were to be included on MONA BONE JAKON. Paul believes that the first three Cat Stevens albums are the most important and seminal. That they are each so different one from the other is something he says he can't explain. What the reasons were for our selecting the songs which went onto MONA BONE JAKON, Paul doesn't know but he confirms my view that the album does have a character all its own. Paul points out that when listening to it now that Steve, via his vocal delivery, is so much in evidence; his very essence is so ... close to the microphone. Paul emphasises that there was that same quality all through those first three albums even though TILLERMAN and TEASER were so different. After CATCH BULL AT FOUR, Steve seemed to get further and further away. His body got tighter and the voice seemed almost constricted and removed.

MONA BONE JAKON was recorded between December 1969 and January 1970 at Olympic Studios in arnes on a sixteen track desk. Other than Alun Davies, Paul singles out John Ryan as having played bass and Harvey Burns playing drums. Those three, with Steve of course, were the core. Paul remembers that Peter Gabriel came in to play flute on KATMANDU.

Paul tells me that he always knows when he's done good work. He admits that he is the sort of person who leaves the studio and immediately wants to play the work to someone. In those days, the first person to listen to it was Rosie, his girlfriend and with the finished album, Rosie and Paul went off to New York in early 1970 to both master the album and, because they were there, to try and place it with a record company in the States. Paul mastered the album, as he did with all the work he did with Steve, at Sterling Sound in New York. MONA BONE JAKON Paul did with Bob Ludwig although the successive ones were done with Lee Hulko.

Chris Blackwell was all for the idea behind Rosie and Paul going to the States and Chris completely agreed with Paul's desire to take the mastered MONA BONE JAKON to Jac Holzman at Elektra. Precise memory again eludes Paul but either Jac was away or on vacation but for whatever reason they drew a blank at Elektra and went on to CBS.

The person they got to see at CBS received them whilst talking to someone else on the telephone. They went in to the office, sat down and the guy just kept talking. He took the album, put it on the turntable and played just two tracks before taking it off, handing it back and mouthing "No" whilst ALL THE TIME talking to this other person on the 'phone. Rosie and Paul couldn't believe it. Paul was really crushed and nominates the rejection as one of the most hurtful experiences he's ever been through.

They decided to stay on but to try California instead. Paul had known Carol Peters whilst she'd been doing A and R for Elektra in Britain and so Paul and Rosie went to stay with her and her husband Larry who worked at A & M Records, not on the creative side but, Paul believes, in a sales capacity. Larry took the album in and played it to someone in the A and R department. They liked it and it went on to someone else and they liked it and then it came to Lance Freed who more than anyone else Paul confirms is responsible for MONA BONE JAKON and thus Cat Stevens being signed to A and M. Chris Blackwell was quite agreeable and Steve was more than amenable and suddenly they all had a US record company.

Steve also had a manager. Paul first remembers meeting Barry

Krost whilst they were recording MONA BONE JAKON. He came to Olympic Studios whilst they were working. Paul can't remember discussing Steve's decision to go with Barry particularly but Steve was famous for his instincts.

Whereas recording MONA BONE JAKON had been relatively easy, TEA FOR THE TILLERMAN was quite laboured. It took five months to complete. It was recorded at Morgan Studios in Willesden on a sixteen track desk. Paul still has the track sheet for it which he painstakingly wrote out using different coloured pens to show just how complicated all the track listings are. The album was mixed at Island Studios at Basing Street in Notting Hill Gate. In addition to the album, they were also working on incidental music for Jerzy Skolimowski's film DEEP END which used the song BUT I MIGHT DIE TONIGHT from TILLERMAN, a song which Steve wrote specifically for the film. Paul remembers once working for twenty-six hours at a stretch as there was a deadline for the delivery of the film's music.

Different musicians arrived in Steve's life when they did TILLERMAN. Paul had worked with drummer Gerry Conway when he'd been doing something with Ian Matthews and Sandy Denny in FAIRPORT but it was Steve who brought in Larry Steele who played bass, Alun James who also played bass, Bruce Lynch and Jean Roussel the keyboard player.

That line-up remained pretty constant for a while, certainly through TEASER AND THE FIRECAT which of course set the seal on the Cat Stevens success story. TEASER was recorded too at Morgan and it was mixed it as they went along. Although he isn't credited for it, the piano on MORNING HAS BROKEN is played by Rick Wakeman, a classically-trained musician who was introduced to them by Carl Miller who had known Rick since working with the STRAWBS. The whole song was recorded in a day and mixed before nine o'clock the same evening. Paul remembers staying behind and mixing whilst the others went to the bar. When they came back it was done. MOONSHADOW too was recorded very quickly in an afternoon and Paul remembers engineering that particular track.

Paul is fulsome in recounting their enjoyment in working on Colin Higgins' and Hal Ashby's HAROLD AND MAUDE. In addition to the music that Steve permitted the film makers to use from MONA BONE JAKON and TILLERMAN, he wrote IF YOU WANNA SING OUT and DON'T BE SHY, neither of which songs ever appeared on any other Cat Stevens recorded work except, Paul believes, in Germany. Steve went out to LA himself and played piano on set for a schedule of filming which was instituted after he agreed to participate in the film. Where Ruth Gordon sings in the film, it's Steve accompanying her on piano. Paul went out to Los Angeles a month later and worked with Hal Ashby on the soundtrack.

CATCH BULL AT FOUR, Steve's fourth album, was recorded at the Chateau d'Herouville in France and also at the Manor studios in Oxfordshire. By the time they'd finished CATCH BULL, the Cat Stevens edifice was becoming monolithic. The success was taking up more and more of Steve's waking time and Paul also fancies that Steve had naturally become distanced from the man who had produced that body of work he'd listened to originally. There is no law in heaven or on earth, Paul points out, to say that just because someone has done three brilliant things that he or she can and should therefore go on to do thirty more brilliant things. Creative people become tired and drained just like anyone else and to just go on and on is an impossibility.

Paul reluctantly admits that what he is also trying to say is that Steve and he had become distanced too. By the time CATCH BULL was finished, Paul admits to being convinced by the substance of what he was intending to do next. Perhaps, he reflects, he should have been more forthright when expressing his opinions at the time but sensibly adds that it is all such a long time ago that feelings and motives and thoughts are impossible to recall with any reasonable accuracy to be repeated and rehashed and to try and do it would serve no purpose. Paul is quite right ...

Paul insists that Steve was surely a poet and that he was incredibly bright. Paul thinks he was a genius and feels that his seeming lack of formal education must have been a great help for there was never anything to stand in the way of the received natural education which he was able to afford himself, culling musical inspiration from any source which caught his ear, often directly from other songs. Paul remembers being on holiday with Steve in Jamaica where they heard a traditional Greek song. Steve hardly had need to tell Paul that he had used the song as the source of inspiration for MOONSHADOW.

Lyrically, of course, Steve's images were deeply attractive and mysterious. Paul illustrates that it wasn't as though Steve had to try and be original; he was original and unique and his talents took him in many directions. Paul describes how Steve certainly covered virtually all of the performing arts. He made records, he created a book, he was responsible for a film and of course there was REVOLUSSIA, his idea for a stage musical which, bearing in mind the date of 1970-71, was a pioneering project. Paul regrets that Steve never finished REVOLUSSIA and believes that certain of the musical material he later used as the basis for other songs. It was, as we know its name would imply, set in Russia. The song he wrote called THE DAY THEY MAKE ME TSAR Paul remembers well.

Steve went off and did FOREIGNER all by himself using none of the old team. Paul has his own assessment of the work: FOREIGNER is what it is and for his next album, BUDDHA AND THE CHOCOLATE BOX, Steve chose to return to more seminal roots. Paul points out that much of the apocryphal inevitably creeps in to sourcing creative inspiration but as so many people seem to think OH VERY YOUNG was written about his young son Nicholas, perhaps the impression should be left like that. Suffice to say Paul very much liked all the songs on BUDDHA. He didn't start out working with Steve on BUDDHA. Another producer, Paul heard, had been ear-marked to do the job and, indeed, had already started work. Steve merely asked him to come along one day and so along to the studio he went. He ended up staying.

But Paul pulled out of working on NUMBERS at the last moment; as a lot of people will know, this album was recorded at Le Studio at Morin Heights in Montreal, Quebec. Neither did he work on IZITSO and so it is BACK TO EARTH, again recorded at Morin Heights in Canada which stands as Steve's and Paul's last collaboration to date.

CHAPTER EIGHT

SCRATCHES ON
THE FACE OF TIME

I suppose it's enough just to think something is good. There is obviously no requirement that weighs upon us to justify any of our likes or dislikes in the area of entertainment to anyone. But I've never been satisfied with the 'Don't-know-anything-about-art-but-I-know what-I-like' school of appreciation because if I really thought like that, I know that a great deal would pass me by. I know, for example, that opera passes me by. I am very conscious of my ignorance of opera and my lack of interest in wanting to find out more about it and I regard both shortcomings as nothing less than vices. I don't want to just think something is good, I want to know it's good and believe it.

I want, therefore, to be able to explain what I like and why I like it if anyone should ask me the question: 'What and why?'.

The truthful answer would have to be that I cannot be alone in admitting that, of course, I can never explain; not properly except in terms of something else which is why I have included this next passage. Anyone who reads it and understands it will also have been or could be a fan of Cat Stevens or Dusty Springfield or Edith Piaf or James Taylor or Rod Stewart or Maria Callas ... The passage which follows is my abominable precis, with additions, of a lecture given many times by the Spanish poet, dramatist, graphicist and musician Federico Garcia Lorca in the nineteen twenties and thirties both in Spain, in America and in South America. Lorca, born in 1898, was murdered by the Fascists in Granada in 1936, just as his fame and celebrity were beginning to precede his prodigious talent.

As with all the music people I mentioned, Lorca was a performer/writer/artist, feted by his public and lauded with plaudits by the cognoscenti in his time just as indulgently as Steve or Dusty or Paul Robeson or whoever have been lauded in theirs. Lorca too needed to show off and was as greedy for celebrity and success as any of those I have mentioned. But, like them, he soon found himself compromised by his own ambitions almost as soon as they were achieved. The publicity he needed in order for him to be famous in order that he be able to exercise his talent ultimately killed not only his career but ended his life.

Lorca's original lecture is very florid and very Spanish as he dramatically performs his text to illustrate that most constant of his motivation which he knew as 'Duende'. Lorca characterises 'Duende' as that quality of artistic creativity and/or the art of performance, 'the hidden spirit of suffering Spain'.

What Lorca is trying to identify and describe and make real is that quality in vocal, instrumental or Terpsichorean performance which makes an audience hold its breath, which spellbinds, which raises the hairs on the back of the neck and the arms, which sends waves of shivering goose bumps shuddering over the body, which brings the lump to the throat and tears to the eyes. The 'Duende' is the Spanish word depicting that Spirit.

Only certain artists have the ability and the facilities for 'Duende' to manifest itself. Steve had the ability ... So did and do all the others I mentioned and so do many, many more. Some try to fake it with a crack in the voice, a well-rehearsed pause, a lot of sweated energy. Those sorts of ploys, as Lorca points out, aren't necessary. You've either got it or you ain't and if you've got it, it's not necessarily an easy thing to get along with. Living with the knowledge that you can raise this Spirit can be cruel, painful and, often, enough of a reason as any to want to quit. In Steve's case, I have a feeling that he recognised his 'Duende' very well. Whether or not he called it his Moonshadow, I don't know. But I can call it that and I know Steve fought his battle for a time with as much determination as any artist.

As you read this next bit, try and keep in mind that the Giorgious are as Mediterranean as any Andalucian or any Moor and that buried millennia-deep in their genes is the subconscious memory that for centuries in ages past, the young men and women of the family fought with bulls, in front of cheering crowds whilst poets eulogised and harpists played and the crowds applauded their heroes and booed the fainthearts and wept over the dead whilst all the while feeling gut-wrenching fear.

FEDERICO GARCIA LORCA: "... What is 'duende'? Though I could tell you that 'duende' is pure spirit, that it is enlightenment, that it might even be God, those words are not enough for they imprison what can only be both free and as difficult to capture as a single raindrop or a particular grain of sand or a cloud.

Manuel Torres, a great Andalucian artist, once said to someone who he had come to hear singing: *'You have a voice, you have style but you will never be a great success because you have no 'duende'.' On listening to the composer Manuel de Falla playing 'Nights in the Gardens of Spain', Torres further observed: 'All that has dark sounds has 'duende'.*

These dark sounds Torres speaks of are the mysterious roots through which 'duende' pushes up out of the depths of the very earth for it is from the earth that everything comes that is real in our creative life and which many of us, inevitably, ignore. 'Duende' is what makes art real, true and credible and, for that tiny moment, tangible, visible and appreciable. 'Duende' is that mysterious power which everyone can feel and yet which cannot be explained.

Every creative person, sort of like Nietszche might say, climbs each stair in the tower of their own perfection at a rate equal to the success they have had not in the struggle with their guiding, guardian angels or their butterfly muses but with the search for and ultimate struggle with their 'duende'.

We all have guardian angels. They operate high over our heads, guiding us blithely and presenting us with opportunities which we can either take or ignore ... meaning that for the most part we stroll through our lives with little struggle. The muses feed us with our lines and sometimes even inspire us although you can hear their voices without knowing anything about them and, as a result, remain ignorant of any meaning. Muses spur the intellect but then that function is often the enemy of poetry because it facilitates and encourages the temptation to imitate to make one's work far too derivative and then to claim such work to be our own, original, to cheat ... to pretend. Such false poets set themselves up on very shaky pedestals from which they forget they can only fall when the muse deserts them.

The Angel and the Muses exist outside the artist, the angel providing the light for the artist to work and the muses giving the ability for the artist to give structure and then shape to their work.

The 'duende', however, draws its life from the deepest depths of our very blood and bone. It is composed of our very essence and it is with the 'duende' that the artist has the most important relationship for that relationship is a battle.

It is not like finding God. The ways we can find God are comparatively easy. These ways are known because they have been thoroughly explored and documented and in the end God provides us with the light to guide those who seek. For God is also outside us.

The great artists of Southern Spain, gypsy performers of flamenco, know as they sing and dance and play that it is impossible to convey emotion without the presence of their 'duende'. Some may try to deceive their audience by giving an impression of the presence of 'duende' when it isn't there. Many do it successfully, every day. But if you pay attention, listen and look very hard you will soon come to realise the abscence of 'duende' and the clumsy fraud will be obvious.

Once, the Andalucian singer Pastora Pavon, 'The Girl with the Combs', was singing in a bar in Cadiz. Her voice was all shadows; it sounded like melted tin, looked and felt as though it was covered in moss, tangled in her very hair, lost in deep, far-away woods and drowned in manzanilla (heavy wine)... But it was just not quite right. It was, therefore, useless. The audience remained unmoved and Pastora finished her song to the sound of silence.

Then she suddenly jumped up like madwoman. Bent over and panting like a religious penitent, she downed a large glass of cazalla and with her throat on fire, sat down to sing with absolutely no hint of control but with ... at last, her 'duende'. She had torn down structure, ripped through the outer fabric of the song to release her furious and blazing 'duende'. She had to wrench her voice because she knew that her knowing audience didn't want the form and the fabric of the song but the essence of that form, the soul of the song, released through her singing, pure music held up as though invisibly, floating, swooping and soaring. She had to weaken her own skills and safeguards, to escape from her imprisoning muse and reveal herself defenceless, threatening her own security by tempting her 'duende' to come out and fight, to struggle with her until the end of her song. And how she sang! Her voice was like a jet of her life's blood, a torrent of rage and grief, howling with that sincerity and truth which knows no bounds. Pure meaning for that moment.

By inducing an almost religious fervour, 'duende' brings its own miracle ... that of new creation, as perfect as a newly-opened rose, creation which, like God, demands not only our attention but our worship and our reverence.

In all Arabic music dance or elegy, the arrival of 'duende' is greeted with fervent cries of: *'Allah! Allah!'*, very similar to our bullfighters' cries of *'Ole! Ole!'*. In southern Spain, the emergence of 'duende' is greeted by the audience's cries of: 'Long live God!', a deep passionate human acknowledgement of what they believe is a physical communication with God through their five senses, ears eyes, smell, taste and touch which the 'duende' has enabled them to achieve.

Spain is a land of death, a land open to death. It has always been and will always be so and 'duende' will simply not appear where there is no possibility of death. In fact, 'duende' only appears with death at its elbow, prepared to enter into the ring with the one who is due to fight that day. The 'duende' is looking for a straight, fair, one-on-one fight. The angel and the muse will both flee, safe behind their shields, the Angel's emblazoned with a compass, the Muse's with a violin. The 'duende' will remain, it will never run away, it will never duck or be beaten until it has inflicted that particular wound which, although not necessarily mortal, will nonetheless never heal.

It is the way that the artist and the audience experience and then deal with this wounding which is the litmus test for the presence of 'duende' and the true test of the power and quality of the artist ..."

The last time I spoke to him, Yusuf told me that what he was striving for in the Cat Stevens years was to make music for God. He had a name for it, an Arabic name.

So now, both out of and yet amongst those dark sounds, listen to MOONSHADOW again. I've never been to a bullfight but I've cried at a good many concerts and blubbed shamelessly whilst listening to TEASER AND THE FIRECAT in my car. I can also say that, without exception, everyone quoted in this book would recognise 'duende'. They recognised Steve's.

Alun Davies certainly did.

It is entirely logical to me that Alun should now be a landscape gardener. If Steve was the exotic, the rare azalea that blazed with vivid blossom, Alun was the very earth in which the shrub was planted and which nourished it season after season. Any more horticultural analogies would be wasted and banal but suffice to say that Alun cared, nurtured and supported Steve through many years of professional musical association and even more years of deep friendship. Great men are only as great as their friends and family and associates enable them to be. It surely follows that the friends of great men and women must be pretty great too so if having great friends makes great men then Alun Davies was as fundamental to Cat Stevens and is as essential to understanding those years as light, air and water are to life itself. And, if that's true which we believe it to be, then what of Val Davies, for she bears equal honours?

I could also think of no more patient, understanding and tolerant a man than Alun and if I had to think of a perfect friend for Steve, someone who was strong enough to share the limelight as well as knowing the moment when to retire, that friend would have to have been Alun.

Alun and Val have been married for twenty nine years. They have two wonderful children, Rebecca and Abigail now in their twenties. Rebecca wants to be a singer ... I suppose that genes must out. Together Rebecca and Alun play in GOOD MEN IN THE JUNGLE. If a human face had to be grafted onto the king of trees, the true keeper of that glade where we were all either seedlings or saplings, the face could well belong to Alun Davies.

ALUN DAVIES: "I don't know if you remember but I started off as a gardener working in Cannizaro Park in Wimbledon. You learned a lot in those days from the older gardeners. Things like pleaching ... Pleaching limes, planes; trees like that. Pleaching is basically pollarding except you remove all the upward-shooting growth the tree has made in the previous season and just retain wands that you can bend and shape horizontally, running them into similar growth which you've trained from a neighbouring tree to make a walkway, an umbrella ... Make them look as though they're growing seamlessly into each other.

Then I started to train to be a teacher. Val and I got married and had Rebecca. She must have been about two and a half and Abigail only just about to be born when I first met Steve.

I was still at college but doing the odd session when I found myself at the BBC working on a programme with Jeremy Taylor, the South African singer and guitarist. The programme's music was being overseen by Paul Samwell-Smith. He told me that he'd got a meeting set up with Cat Stevens which Chris Blackwell at Island had suggested. Would I like to come along?

The meeting was to be at Rosie's, Paul's girlfriend's, flat in West Hampstead and so I went along. I have to say that I wasn't entirely happy. All I remembered of Steve was of him as the pop star and the only visual images I retained, which made me shudder when I thought of them, were of him in some terrible white suit singing I'M GONNA GET ME A GUN and then another daft press story where he's driving round the West End in a sports car with a dolly bird on the bonnet drinking champagne.

I suppose I must have taken my guitar along to the meeting although I can't remember playing anything. All I can remember is having every illusion shattered about the man about whom I'd been so badly predisposed. Steve played dozens of songs that day, wonderful songs. He must have written his heart out in that year whilst he was both ill and convalescing and they just flowed out of him in, one huge outpouring of deeply felt poetry.

I heard songs that day that I would be hearing for the next four years. All the songs on those first four albums were contained in that mini-concert Steve gave that afternoon in Rosie's flat. It was a huge pool of material and everyone of them a winner. It was as though Steve had stumbled out of a long lightless tunnel and emerged having come across a treasure trove, almost a bequest from destiny.

I can honestly say that I never had any doubt from that moment on, especially when we started recording the songs Steve and Paul had selected to be included on MONA BONE JAKON, that he was going to be anything else but enormously successful. You get to be able to recognise that something special and Steve had it. I have to say that I also got the feeling that not everybody shared my faith. I felt distinctly that there were many people at Island, Steve's record company, who thought that Steve was a lightweight and many of them, despite hearing the new material, had their perception tainted by the 'pop star' image of the early days. I think a lot of people didn't think that Steve was what Island was really all about, far too commercial.

We recorded MONA BONE JAKON during the later months of 1969 and by June 1970 when the album was released, I graduated from teacher training college. Faced with a further year of teaching practice which I would have had to have done in order to qualify fully, I'm afraid there was no contest when Steve suggested that we do some gigs, try the stuff out live. Val still has a piece of paper at home on which Steve originally scribbled out the suggestions for my retainer salary. It didn't stay as low as it was originally for long, I have to say but even low, there was no question but that I would join up with Steve. I'm not suggesting that it was an easy decision by any means. The girls were now only three and one, something like that, and Val had always rather fancied me as a teacher. But ... We made the decision.

One of the first dates we played was at the Redcar Jazz Festival in late summer of 1970. No back-up at all, just the two of us. I remember we hired some ORANGE PA from a shop in Charing Cross Road. It was just four channel stuff. It was way before the days of specialist companies providing road and equipment services at the end of a telephone and with no track record in his new guise, Steve had to get down to the dirty work himself. We were just two guitars, two voices ... No road crew either, just the two of us! I remember going up to Yorkshire on the train and loading all the gear into the luggage van of the train. We were supporting LINDISFARNE.

Whether we'd started to record TILLERMAN by that time, I don't remember, but I do remember going to the States for the first time later in 1970. Same scenario as for the Redcar gig. No back-up, no road crew. We just went. Someone from Island, I think, was on the road with us occasionally but mostly we got around by ourselves.

We were due to be away for some six weeks and I took the incredibly extravagant sum of forty pounds. Steve was Rockefeller by comparison. He had almost two hundred pounds! I know the value of money has changed but even so, it seems laughably little to survive for so long. Anyway, off we went, a guitar and one bag each with Val waving us goodbye at the airport. It felt strange but it also felt tremendously exciting.

I must say A and M were very good to us when we arrived in New York where we were due to support TRAFFIC at the FILMORE EAST. TRAFFIC were huge at the time and were promoting JOHN BARLEYCORN. After the Filmore, the razzmatazz was swiftly withdrawn as we were due to play a club called THE GASLIGHT on McDougall and Bleeker Streets in New York's west village. It was a tiny club no more than seventy five or a hundred punters a show and we were booked to play there for five nights. It was a paradox of a place. There were absolutely no frills ... The artists had to get changed for the set in the kitchens but, on the other hand, you'd go out and play and in that seventy five person audience would be all the musical cognoscenti, rock journalists and social illustriosi you would ever need to ensure you favourable reviews ... IF they liked your set! A lot of careers have foundered on that big 'IF'.

We did six more dates across America supporting TRAFFIC after that, starting off in Florida. Then we arrived in Los Angeles. Carly Simon's first album had also just come out and she had met with a lot of success. However, she wasn't that keen on live performance. In fact she wasn't keen at all but Elektra, her record company, got her to agree to a week at Doug Weston's TROUBADOUR in Los Angeles if Cat Stevens would support her. She must have heard MONA BONE JAKON and liked it.

There's not a lot more I can say about the week at the TROUBADOUR except that our performances obviously generated a great deal of critical praise. Remember, the way that other people have seen things in hindsight and the importance which has been attributed to certain events at certain times in the Cat Stevens calendar often goes way over my head. I realise that a lot of what I say sounds almost understated, almost as though they're throw away observations but being at the epicentre at the time that such remarkable future circumstances were being set in train, all I can remember is our last night at the TROUBADOUR and how unre-markable it was. We were due to fly on to Chicago that same night on a twelve o'clock flight and we got incredibly tiddled on a bottle of tequila before my friend John Mark took us to the airport. It wasn't at all an auspicious, tickertape, frenziedly adulatory occa-sion at all. We didn't even go back to our hotel after the set. We each had that poor little travelling bag all packed at the edge of the stage and off we went. Did we think we'd ever return? I'm sure the possibility never crossed our minds and if it had, the negative would never have been voiced.

Obviously, looking back it was an all-important time. Had we gone down with merely mediocre critical response, Steve's American future would have been very much more difficult. The reviews as we all know were very good and, basically, radio airplay did the rest. Steve's popularity spread like a bushfire from then on. The next time we came back to the States, it was as a big success with a full band. However, it has to be said that it would have been nothing without those two initial acoustic bookings in New York and Los Angeles.

We returned to England in early December and almost immediately played the Fairfield Hall. I will always remember Penny Valentine's review. To paraphrase her - and with apologies, Penny - she said that although it was just Steve and I, she sat there and closed her eyes and heard all the arrangements and accompanying instruments just like on the record even though they weren't there. Thanks, Penny.

Thereafter, the huge success that Steve became is well-documented. Though he didn't substantially write anything new, TILLERMAN, TEASER and BUDDHA used all the best of the songs from the fund, re-written, re-arranged and constantly worked on by Steve as each album passed. As one was done, so Steve and Paul and the band as it ultimately shaped up (especially Gerry Conway) just got better and better. Studio techniques improved and we got to know each other's musicianship almost instinctively.

For four years we really had a wonderful time. Val and I have so many great memories. Steve came with us on holiday after the 1972 American Tour. We flew straight to Jamaica and had a marvellous time. 1973, we went to Greece and were royally treated by friends of Steve's who entertained us to a very bibulous dinner in Athens on our first night. He was carefree, happy, ebullient and far, far away from the morose, serious, introverted person that a lot of people seem to have known and remembered from that time. Throughout that holiday we played games, silly, wonderful and totally inventive games that Steve thought up. He had a tape recorder, a sort of early walkman and we would play consequences on it. Steve'd start things off by putting down the first bit ... "There was an old lady and she went to the woods one day." ... that kind of thing. Then the next person would add what the old lady was wearing etc... etc... and the consequence was ... The consequence was we laughed our way through that entire holiday.

When we arrived on Kos for a few days, we hired bicycles and went off to the Temple of Hippocrates. The bikes were all equipped with hand operated bells which we rang furiously each time we passed a house or went through a small village. Steve was very quick to work out that each bell emitted one note on the inswing of the lever and another on the outswing. As there were three bells, there were obviously six available notes. Needless to say that in five minutes he'd composed a melody line and each time we went past an audience even of three goats, we'd start this bicycle carillon.

He was so up and so full of fun and didn't seem at all constricted. He was the first to abandon his swim-shorts on the beach at Mykonos and on Kos, when someone recognised him, he and I were persuaded into performing a short, half-hour set in a rather empty local amphitheatre. He was really happy then and it's strange to reflect that in the course of a few all-too-short years, Greece was to be the scene of a period of obvious unhappiness for him and the venue for the last gig of the last Cat Stevens tour.

But before we got there, there was a lot more work. FOREIGNER was the fourth album and I and the rest of the band didn't work on that one much. It was Steve trying to be different. He used many of the heavyweight American musicians who were so prominent at the time. I'm aware that there are people who don't like FOREIGNER and indeed, as it's name would imply, it's something of an interloper in what is otherwise a pretty seamless canon of work. I personally like it very much although I would probably have to concede that thereafter, something uneasy settled onto the Cat Stevens edifice.

Steve himself started to exude a feeling of being embattled. The mysticism which had always been with him and to which he was inevitably drawn, accelerated and he seemed to pass himself on from the attraction of one quasi-religious source to the next. He certainly seemed to enjoy touring less and less. We had moved out of the more intimate two and three thousand seat auditoria and into arenas and venues that were just enormous. The shows too got bigger and bigger and I remember remarking to myself how dwarfed Steve appeared, backed by the billowing parachute silk set of the forty five date BAMBOOZLE tour. It was as though he was being overwhelmed by props, overburdened by an extraneous, even artificial context which had developed around him.

Obviously no one had imprisoned him, no one had foisted this upon him. The situation was born of his phenomenal success and was entirely born out of his own volition. It was just the same with the proliferation of his business activities. Princes from huge merchant banks in the city, grey suited high-powered lawyers and accountants from Dickensianly named partnerships started to arrive for seemingly endless meetings about figures, tax breaks, money-saving schemes for Steve and money-earning schemes for the gray suits. Just like the stage sets, Steve had okayed all of it, had asked for it to happen, insisted initially that his interests be protected by X by Y and by Z just as he wanted the most up-to-date, state-of-the-art lighting and sound systems on the road ... It's all very well to see it, like a holiday photo in a brochure and ask for it but another thing to realise that after you've booked it and you've got there, the photo has shall we say, misrepresented. You try and keep afloat and stay under way but you find that you're gradually sinking like an over-refitted ocean liner beneath the weight of a superstructure which your hull was never designed to support. Even decisions about where we recorded were taken according to financial and tax advice. Something to do with where the work was done ...

I begged him to stick in future to the smaller auditoria. To an extent, he did and by the final tour, the MAJICAT tour, he was playing places that certainly no other headlining band would at that time be thinking of playing. The magic act, in one sense, turned out to the disappearing act.

We started in October 1975, rehearsing for three weeks somewhere outside Frankfurt in Germany, more than likely because of a 'gray suit' decision. By the time we'd been all the way round the world and eight months later, we'd arrived at Thessaloniki in Greece. How we got there at all was a minor miracle.

Steve had fractured his leg in Spain, jumping down some steps. Rather than cancel or postpone which would have happened nowadays, we went on, Steve encased in a specially designed and commissioned plaster cast which sort of hinged and after hingeing was altogether removable. Steve became the embodiment of 'The Show Must Go On' ethic. Oh, how we begged him not to keep taking off the plaster but he took no notice as he was in the grip of a current notion that if he bathed his leg in the sea, the powers inherent in the salt water would aid the healing process. All well and good except that one day he went into the sea and someone had forgotten to tell a swarm of miniature jellyfish that the Cat Stevens leg was really not for biting. It sounds mildly amusing other than it was painful for him and as an instance it was almost nothing but it was just one example of a trail of growing annoyance and cumulative frustration that had brought us to Thessaloniki.

That suddenly sounds like the climax of some ancient Greek myth ... the arrival of the ragged army at Thermopylae with one more battle to fight and in a way that's what it was. That's how we felt.

Rock 'n' roll tours bring together a very motly collection of people in a brew which is inherently immiscible. Musicians, road crew, humpers, truck drivers, riggers ... they're all of them rampant individuals whom real life is unable to contain. They've each of them turned their backs on anything approaching a nine to five.

How anyone could even imagine that an eight month non-stop tour of the world is likely to contain those rabid egos as well as the bristlingly homesick and the dangerously exhausted in any happier state than real life would have otherwise provided is a scenario that to my certain knowledge hasn't yet been written.

Without wives and girlfriends for most of the tour, at least so close to home, at the start of a European summer, with our kids available and not having to go to school, those of us with families were at least able to be reunited. But however much the two week lay-over between arriving in Greece and the Thessaloniki gig had sounded wonderful, in reality it became even worse than being without our families.

The hotel we were staying in was unconnected to anything. It was not close to a town where we could take our kids when sunburn and swimming got too much for them. We were none of us in a mood to heed Steve's calls for rehearsals. His suggestions that he'd *"got an idea of how we could change"* such and such fell on more than deaf ears. We didn't want to change anything. We just wanted the last two dates to be over and to get back home. This more than infuriated Steve who hated seeing people idle.

Worse conspired. The day of the gig dawned and it was then made apparent that the promoter had set up the date on the eve of the Greek education system's most important public examination and that ticket sales had suffered accordingly. The arrival in Thessaloniki of Zeus himself it seemed wouldn't have kept the Greek school-kids from an early night. Their futures depended on their passing exams, not listening to Cat Stevens.

The PA whistled ominously during the set and I think we got through no more than three quarters of it before Steve announced, *"That's it. I've had enough,"* and peglegged off the stage. He'd just sung FATHER AND SON and that was the last song he ever sang on a tour of his own creation.

There was due to be another gig in Athens but when we got there, we found that the promoter had chosen an equally unhelpful date which conflicted in proximity with an England versus Greece football international. Ticket sales had been disappointing and so he and Steve decided to pull out of the promotion.

And that was that.

At the time, though he might not have told us, I for one felt like we were at the end of something. Like Buddy Bolden once sang: *"Open up the window, let the bad air out ..."* The only other date Steve played subsequently was a concert in aid of UNICEF at Wembley Arena celebrating the UNICEF Year Of The Child. We played with WISHBONE ASH, GARY NUMAN, DAVID ESSEX.

And that really was that.

After Greece and the end of the MAJICAT Tour, having got back home and returned to what passes for normality in the music business, it gradually became very clear that Steve wasn't going to be touring any more and that his recording work would be more than limited, I felt very directionless. I can remember coming up to town and meeting Gerry Conway in various pubs and always lamenting what was going on. We felt rudderless, as though we'd been bereaved. Of course Gerry's proved the opposite most successfully, but at that time when we were bemoaning our fate, he couldn't see himself ever playing for anyone else. He saw himself as entirely attuned to only being able to play with Steve.

It had been an amazing few years and at least we'd survived. Somehow, we'd been able to get through it. There'd been incredible highs and of course there had been horrible lows. I prefer to remember the former and to know with a certainty that I had worked with an immensely, hugely talented man on the best work that I could have ever done. I wish there could have been more of the same.

There has, of course been more, albeit a different more. The Alphabet Song which Steve, in his new life as Yusuf, made with just the aid of a drum accompaniment was so charming ... It confirmed my thinking that the magic hasn't disappeared at all. It has just quietly slipped into another room."

If Paul had been Steve's teenage sidekick and tower of strength, protection and support, Steve found as a young man that Alun played the same role. Steve's career is unthinkable without Alun's permanent, solid presence.

Alun's confirmation that Steve had already composed all the legendary songs on the first four albums by 1969 is, to me, fascinating and lends more credence to those who believe that it was his enforced aloneness after his brush with TB which focused Steve's mind and creativity into writing. The pool of songs could certainly be thought of as heaven-sent and when it had been exhausted it is also interesting to note that it was the beginning of Steve's redoubled efforts in his search for a divinity and his withdrawal from the world. Some even believe that when the pool ran dry, he began to doubt his ability to produce any further meaningful work.

FOREIGNER was that turning point. Followed though it was by BUDDHA, an enchanting album, FOREIGNER had proved to everyone closely involved that Steve was quite prepared to dump people in order to pursue what he wanted. That they were all still around to work in BUDDHA is perhaps not so much a testament to friendship but to the fact that they were again employed. When musicians, even a producer, are so closely allied to working with one artist, as Gerry Conway told Alun, not only they but the music business in general tends not to want to see them in any other association and that's a tricky situation for a working person to sort out when there are mortgages to be paid and children to bring up.

Without wanting to labour the point, it has to be realised how much rock 'n' roll has been, is and looks like staying very much a male preserve. However true the observation is, it makes for an erroneous perception of the whole-and-nothing-but-the truth. It doesn't account for the sexual overlap ...

After all, where do they go to, these rock 'n' roll legends when they're not strutting and peacocking and voguing in the limelight, when all the applause has died away? Like all the rest of us, they go home.

And what makes a home? For a lot of people, it helps to have a partner and under those circumstances, it will be two people who make the home just as it takes two people to make the babies to put into the home. And, sure, we understand that if there are babies in a home and there are two parents, the babies have to be clothed and fed as well as being looked after minute to minute. It should all be very equal but as we are all only too well aware, it's at this point that the equality can come to an abrupt halt because it's crunch time ... Who stays at home and does the looking after and who goes out and earns the living? Here on in, homes can begin to look suspiciously like traps and going out to work masquerades as an excuse for escaping.

The way things work out for most people, the lady gets to stay at home and the man gets to earn the money. Equality? With a great deal of love and the perfect woman and the perfect man and enormous understanding and no moodiness, with great neighbours and close supportive families, no temperament, no illness, no crises and two point four perfect children... with all that, it could still just be a home on equal terms. In rock 'n' roll homes, the man in the model doesn't just get to go out to work for eight or nine or ten hours; he gets to go out to work for weeks, maybe months on end. He often works in recording studios at night when most other people, wives and mothers are asleep, ladies who have been working all day long from the first to the last murmur from the nursery.

In rock 'n' roll, these women wait, almost like in a Greek tragedy, waiting to see who comes back from the wars, waiting to see if it has been the turn of their man to fall victim to The Harpies, to The Gorgon, to Medusa and The Sirens ...

Men going off to war... It's the oldest story. For war substitute rock 'n' roll and for all those Greek myths, substitute rock 'n' roll misses. Val Davies has been with Alun for over thirty three years, married for twenty nine. She has survived many campaigns.

VAL DAVIES: "I remember when I was very young standing on the train every morning between Clapham Junction and Central London, squashed and breathed-on and jostled and looking around me at everyone in that state of early-morning or early-evening suspended animation and thinking, *'One day, something wonderful is going to happen in my life. Something really special is going to happen to me.'*

I had the same feeling the other day, umpitty-ump years later. I had some reason or the other to go up to town on the train, a rare journey for me these days and I stood and I looked around and I thought to myself, *'Something really wonderful happened to me. I've had a very special life.'*

I suppose it's full circle, isn't it? As though you've been round the world, which of course, we have, several times. The difference between that young girl of then and the woman of now, other than age, is that the girl was restless, the woman is calm. Well, calmer.

There comes a point in your life when you realise you've done it, you've discovered the secret, you've seen the magic, you've braved the perils, you've beaten the dragon and you've returned to the place you started for no other reason than to realise all this and to be able to be grateful. Standing on that train, I reminded myself that I haven't brought back any great treasure unless you count some wonderful memories and some pretty livid regrets but I suppose what I have brought back, other than the scars, is wisdom. Understanding. Greater tolerance, maybe?

These are the things that, if you let it, life brings you. You understand that it would have been impossible to start off life with them for with them, we would have been hampered and shackled and we might never have moved because we could have been too put off. If we'd understood what lay ahead, the effort might not have seemed worth the pains.

I met Alun on September 11th 1960 in Ravensby Park in Mitcham. I was sixteen and still at school. Alun was eighteen and was a picture restorer then although that didn't last long. He went through lots of things including learning gardening in Cannizaro Park. We got married in 1964.

With hindsight, a luxury we might all have wished for at the time, I now see that for those first years of our relationship and our marriage, I looked on myself as merely an extension of Alun. I couldn't conceive of myself as a separate entity. As a result, I was completely dependent on him. I'd lie awake at night until I knew he was home. As a woman of the nineteen sixties and as Alun's wife, I not only considered my role as one of giving Alun a stable home and a regular background but I actually wanted to play that role more than anything else. And I played it bloody well too, although, as one is now aware, in doing so, I, like millions of other women in that first flush of newly-wedded euphoria who did the same thing, allowed myself to become only fulfillable and only wholly vindicated with my husband's blessing. And, believe me, there's nothing wrong with that, nothing more rewarding than being appreciated and loved back, nothing wrong at all as long as those 'perfect' conditions of marriage or partnership continued to apply.

Of course, Alun always played the guitar and of course I was always fiercely proud and protective of his playing basically because he was my boyfriend. Music and the company of other musicians was always a part of our lives although it figured only on the sidelines of the basic game which was always how we were going to earn our livings. By the end of the sixties, we had Rebecca, our first child, and Alun had completed a three year teacher training which we had thought would stand us in very good stead.

And it probably would have done had that 'special' thing not happened.

Alun's great friend was John Mark and they played together as well as socialised. In fact I can remember going up to The Speakeasy in the West End with John Mark and as we were going into the club, Cat Stevens was coming out dressed in a brilliant white suit and looking just tremendous. I was thrilled to have seen him although Alun was very sneery.

Male friendships are not something that young women of twenty think of as a particular irritant in a happy marriage but, again, as with thousands, millions of other women, I hate to admit that I found Alun's friendship with John Mark often infuriating. They would do things together, talk about things, plan things and go places which inherently excluded me and I often got very cross about that, mostly inside myself. Rather than blaming your partner, it is most natural to blame the one who you feel is really to blame ... the friend. I often got to the pitch where I would wish that Alun could be best mates with ANYONE as long as it wasn't John Mark. Of course this is all so silly now, looking back, as the situation had nothing to do with Alun and John Mark but a lot to do with me and my own insecurities and vulnerability.

But, given the circumstances, I was not at all displeased when Steve first came into our lives. As soon as he heard the music that Steve intended to record with Paul Samwell-Smith, Alun's initial misgivings about Steve evaporated. Alun was still at college for the first year they knew each other and so our basic plan was still going ahead. Alun was set to become a teacher.

I don't think I was particularly surprised when Alun came back one day in the summer of 1970 and told me that Steve wanted Alun to join with him full time. In fact, I was very pleased Steve had asked.

Alun and Steve got on very, very well together and Steve was very different from John Mark. I found that I got on very well with him too. I've never been one for hanging around in the music business ... I hate going to recording studios or being on tours if it isn't for something really specific. For example, when the strings were dubbed onto SAD LISA I went along to Olympic Studios in Barnes and I have on occasion flown out to visit Alun on a tour just for a few days. So, for the limited contact in those days I'd had with Steve, I think he liked me too so at least I felt a degree of mutuality.

Obviously Alun had to make a decision which affected not

only me but also Rebecca and our second child Abigail who was barely a year old. Always bearing in mind that ventures such as this one could easily turn out to be a flash in the pan, I agreed wholeheartedly. Until he met Steve, I hadn't actually realised just how good Alun was both on guitar and vocally. A door had been opened and I was sure he had to go through it.

Success takes musicians onto a very different plane of living from the rest of us very quickly. The difference is indefinable except by quoting examples like not having to lug your own equipment about, like not having to worry about travel arrangements and catching planes and getting up on time. It's essentially the difference which existed in the olden days in big houses, the difference between 'them' upstairs and 'us' downstairs. When you're successful you get looked after. When you're not, you look after yourself.

Rock 'n' roll is the perfect environment for a man. It's birthdays, christmases and every school holiday rolled into one. It's a never-never land holding out it's arms welcoming any one of millions of eager Peter Pans ... and all of them, bar very few exceptions, men. Women don't make very good Peter Pans as, indeed, the story told us. I suppose it's why Wendy houses are called Wendy houses and not Peter houses.

However, there were a few dues to pay before the good times really rolled. I first remember waving Steve and Alun goodbye at London Airport in the autumn of 1970 when they set off for their first tour of America. It was all so human-scale then, like two young boys going off to scout camp. They were away not more than four weeks but it was the first lesson in a long course of learning and I remember it very well.

Abi, our second baby, was a cryer. She refused to settle and would be awake and active for seemingly most of the twenty four long hours that made up each day. It was therefore only after a very short time that I began to miss Alun. I'm not saying he was a new man or anything like that. He wasn't one for getting up in the night to the children but I so missed him not being there. I missed not being able to just complain and moan and get sympathy and support from him. It is truly a rare talent that some women have if they manage to bring up more than one child on their own. It is incredibly difficult. I began to get very depressed and feel very alone. Of course I had neighbours, wonderful neighbours and we would pop back and forth even leaving our keys in our front doors; but the breaks were only momentary. I never went out socially, to a pub or a club as such and staying at home for that length of time breeds a sense of isolation which sort of eats at you. It was way before easy transatlantic international dialling so telephoning was a very rare event. I relied on postcards and letters to let me know how things were going and, most important of all, when Alun would be coming back.

Well, of course, he did come back and as it was just before Christmas that year, the homecoming was all the more special.

But abscence does very strange things to a relationship and my reactions to Alun being at home again were often involuntary and sometimes confusing. After two or three tours and realising I was having similar reactions, I started to work out that the isolation breeds a kind of resentment. Quite uninvited, life has bestowed on you your own form of freedom in that you do chores and set up your routine just as you want to with no interference or input from anyone else. When your partner returns, the resentment you had previously been able to shrug off emerges when your own routine is upset and you find yourself having to accommodate the needs of your partner in a life which has run on just fine without him! It's almost as though in a way you resent him coming back at all even though it's the very thing you want most! Very confusing.

I have noticed that because men are both visibly and tangibly cyclical in their emotions and you often feel a man drifting away from you temporarily, women are always afraid of being left, abandoned. I suppose that was all part of my 'give him the best home ever' philosophy for I have noticed that men find it infinitely more difficult to leave their wives than wives find leaving their husbands. It stands to reason too ... It's a relief to leave a trap, it's hard to leave a nest; inconvenient, annoying and in the end a great bother. Men hate bother.

I remember quite a few rows before Alun went away on successive tours. Just knowing the loneliness and the slowness of passing time that lay ahead was enough to make me tense and I suppose, in the way that one does, one takes the tension out on the nearest and dearest.

And of course, it has to be said that our lives under the rock 'n' roll microscope were not always pretty. I know for a fact that if Steve had carried on being Cat Stevens and Alun had remained with him, the likelihood of Alun and I being together today is pretty slim. Stories and tittle tattle about bad behaviour abound and, waiting at home, you get rattled by them.

I remember once being so furious and helpless that on the spur of the moment I bought myself a ticket and flew out to Atlanta to sort out a particular crisis and didn't tell Alun I was coming. After I'd made my point in, as you might imagine, a somewhat dramatic way and let off all the furious steam I'd been building up, I was left wondering what the hell I was going to do. Steve was absolutely sweet to me. He hated things going wrong with his friends' relationships. It was one of the ways his simplicity came out and a very endearing way it was. If you were married, you were somehow inviolable. A married lady was a very special thing, an object of a sort of veneration. I'm not sure he treated unmarried women particularly well as many of his girlfriends would probably tell you, but me ... As soon as he found out I had arrived in Atlanta, he immediately sought me out, took my side and, sensing that I must have felt very much out of depth, offered to be my date to go to the show the following night. He was wonderful. As I said, that righteous indignation was very vivid and he saved no invective when dressing down the 'guilty party'. He was a strange mixture. He could be the worst bully, really quite a tyrant, and yet the best and most supportive friend. If he thought someone was in the wrong, he'd tell them in no uncertain fashion.

As the children started at school, I became involved with Steve's fan club. There had never been a fan club as such despite the thousands of letters that were sent via Island and A and M and which ended up at Barry's office at Curzon Street. When Sarah Harrison started to work for Steve, she and I made a start on sorting something out. Never one for the ordinary, Steve wanted it to be a 'special' fan club and finally suggested it should be called THE FANTASY RING and symbolised what he envisaged in a drawing he did in 1974 of a circle of flying birds, a circular formation instead of a v-shape or just a massed jumble. His Confucian interests were apparent in the poem he asked us to reproduce in the first and only fan club magazine. The poem is by the Chinese poet/philosopher Lao Tsu:

> *Knowing others is wisdom*
> *Knowing the self is enlightenment*
> *Mastering others requires force*
> *Mastering the self requires strength*

> *He who knows he has enough is rich*
> *Perseverance is a sign of willpower*
> *He who stays where he is endures*
> *To die but not to perish is to be eternally present*

Of course, as we all know, Steve ultimately embraced Islam, not Buddhism but Lao Tsu's lines when applied to the Steve I knew are more than prophetic.

I have to add a personal postscript. In 1974, after the Madison Square Garden gig, Alun and I and our children flew to Vancouver and thence drove in a hired car all the way down the Pacific Coast to Los Angeles and ended up staying at the Chateau Marmont Hotel on Sunset. We stayed in a bungalow in back of the hotel and had a marvellous time. Tim Curry, another one of Barry Krost's clients was staying at the hotel whilst he was appearing in THE ROCKY HORROR SHOW at the Roxy, further along The Strip and we spent a lot of time with him by the pool. We had a marvellous holiday. I can't believe now that our children were so young. The postscript concerns Rebecca, our eldest daughter and her boyfriend Jim Moncur. Becca remembered what a wonderful holiday she'd had at the Chateau Marmont and so she and Jim also stayed there many years later. On going up to the reception, Rebecca was handed an envelope by the desk clerk. In it, there was a note from Jim which read: *"Will you marry me?"*

She said yes."

CHAPTER NINE

MATES AND MECHANICALS

There are few music people who have had the benefit of training in their arts and subtle craft. Linda Lewis is one of them. She comes from a very talented family and after going to stage school, she appeared in several films and on television as an actress. As a singer and writer, her career began whilst singing with John Lee Hooker when she was spotted by record producer Ian Samwell. Her hits are legion - ROCK-A-DOODLE-DOO, IT'S IN HIS KISS, DAYS OF THE OLD SCHOOLYARD and her albums adventurous and memorable. She lived in America during the eighties where she had so successfully toured. She now lives in Surrey with her young son, Jesse. She is, grace à Dieu, as irrepressible as ever.

LINDA LEWIS: "I suppose I must be pretty unique in all this because I knew Steve both personally and professionally. I hadn't been aware of him in his MATTHEW AND SON pop star phase and when I first ran into him in 1969, I was living in a house in Hampstead with some other friends. It was Kelvin and Cheryl who introduced him to our house, I think. Everyone seemed to be into something special in those days and I remember that Kelvin and Cheryl had already discovered Islam. But my meeting with Steve had nothing to do with religion.

We were all musicians, singers ... I suppose we all wanted to make it and it didn't seem to matter in those days about writing your own stuff. I was just happy to sing. When I first started, I was managed by Don Arden and I used to cover American songs. I'd make up the words and just sing rubbish if I couldn't decipher the American pronunciation. I remember Don Arden gave me an awful telling off for that! No one made that big a deal out of being the singer-songwriter although that was just about to change as the decade drew to a close.

One of my first memories of Steve is him coming into our house and sitting cross-legged on the floor with his guitar and playing a song he'd just written. It was MOONSHADOW. I can certainly remember feeling that he thought he was something special. There was definitely that feeling of: *"Oh, oh ... Cat Stevens has just come into the room!"*

He didn't mention having been in hospital. I didn't even know anything about that. He didn't talk either then or later about his personal, inner feelings. He wasn't really a good communicator on a personal level. He liked talking about anything around a point but never on the point.

Later, I went out with him ... Like on a date! I remember going back after going to the Speakeasy or wherever to his parents' place above the cafe in Shaftesbury Avenue and nothing happening! He'd talk and talk and I'd just get sleepier and sleepier. I had the distinct impression that he wanted to put women on a pedestal. His mother was certainly very beautiful and a lovely person and in one way I think he saw all women like that. Our little affair didn't last long.

I didn't see him then until we started to work together in 1974. I have to say that professionally, he was a very helpful person. In that area he did give, generously. If he liked your music and respected you as an artist, he would go out of his way to give you a hand. He asked me to support him on the BAMBOOZLE Tour of England and Europe and later the tour went on to America. Strangely, I didn't open the show. Steve did and then went off, having mumblingly introduced me and left me to get on with it. I did my set with his band still on-stage and then he would come back and finish off with me transferred into backing vocalist.

I remember it as being a pretty good experience on the whole, except in Paris where the audience, not comprehending Steve's mumbling introduction of my set decided that Cat Stevens had left the stage never to return and started to boo me off. That was a horrible experience!

But horrible experiences often have antidotes and in Paris, we all went to see HAROLD AND MAUDE, now firmly one of my favourite films. As he hadn't even hinted that he had been involved with the movie and I had no idea that Steve's music had been used in the film, I found the whole thing a great surprise and terrifically emotional. I was never one to go overboard in praising Steve. There were enough other people around him who did that well and willingly. However, on this occasion, I needed no urging to express my admiration for his work. I sometimes wonder now if he ever identified with the troubled and painfully shy Harold?

The American end of the BAMBOOZLE tour was a strange experience. The show reverted to an 'as per normal'; I would open for him with no preamble so the reaction I got from the audience was all mine and I knew that if they clapped it was because they liked me not because they were already applauding the imminent return of the headliner. Everything on that tour went smoothly. There were no hitches, no particular problems.

It was therefore more than strange that the atmosphere both backstage and on-stage deteriorated progressively as the tour ground on. Some very black looks got thrown around on-stage and the bonhomie level sank to all-time lows. By the time New York and the last date was over, people's stress levels were at volcano point and at the party given to celebrate the end of the tour, there were a lot of hard words spoken, lot of tempers lost including Steve's.

We did have completely different opinions as far as music was concerned and this, coupled with his difficulty in communicating, made the experience of being produced by him in the studio sometimes frustrating. I remember doing BONFIRE, a song he'd written. He made me sing it again and again, trying to explain what he wanted but ... maybe we were both bad at communicating. Anyway, finally it dawned that what he wanted me to do was to sing the song to sound the way it would have sounded had he been singing it. When I'd worked that one out, everything went fine.

And that sums up a lot about Steve really. He wanted to be in charge. Wanted to be in control of people. You almost felt that he thought he owned you. I really don't think that his religious evolution was only spiritual although I respect him for whatever he believes. He's still a star, after all. He's still a soothsayer though he's listened to now by not quite so broad an audience.

This is odd, isn't it? We're talking like he's passed away when he hasn't? He's still there and yet he isn't.

But he was always not quite there ... Always apart. We all noticed it before his behaviour started to set him apart. I'm thinking of things like the stick he carried around all through that tour.

Like a prophet's staff. He came across it walking through a forest near Frankfurt and it never left his hand. I remember when he started to unfold prayer mats. I walked in on him one day as he was genuflecting and I apologised. I felt I'd intruded. He gave me a copy of the Qur'an to read. That must have been around 1975. I felt he was beginning to lose real contact with people, that he was retreating somewhere ... withdrawing. He was never naturally affectionate and I remember when I went out with him that he obviously couldn't cope with instant intimacy.

It's strange, thinking back all those years. When I first met him I sensed he worked on a very short fuse, even to the point of there being something of the hooligan in him; something almost violent. He was like a spring. Always thin, very thin like a sinew. I think he was rather spoiled from very early on. I never got the feeling he had to struggle for things. His family were always there for whatever he wanted and always over-praised him so I don't feel he was ever the victim of much objectivity.

He told me once when we were talking about favourite things, that his favourite fairy story was Robinson Crusoe and ... well, it's him, isn't it? The man alone. Waiting to be rescued. Finding a friend in a total stranger who devotes himself entirely to our hero's well-being. Robinson of course took Friday over completely, assumed complete 'droit de seigneur'. I was almost married to Jim Cregan in 1974 who played both in my band and also for Steve in this combined show thing he called BAMBOOZLE. Odd name; I always thought to bamboozle someone was to fool them ... Anyway. Jim, for whatever his reasons, got very close to Steve and Steve seemed to take a great liking to Jim. They spent a lot of time together even to the extent where I felt more than a little excluded, that I was in an area where I had no rights, where only Steve had rights.

He was very black and white. Life and opinions were always one thing or another and if the opinions of others were different from Steve's ... Watch out.

Whatever personal problems he may have had, you have to admire him as an artist. He was a great risk-taker. He was a first in many respects, especially the tours he did. Great events, very avant-garde. And, as I've said, he was always only ever helpful to me. I suppose that of all those people in our house in Hampstead twenty five years ago, Steve became the most successful in terms of fame and money. Shame they proved to be such empty vessels for him. Steve certainly felt that money provided nothing per se in the terms of achievement. He used it, sure, but it never turned out to be anything but hollow.

I have a regret. It's to do with the last time I spoke to him. He called me up one day when, I think I'm right, he was spending some time with Kelvin and Cheryl, my and his Muslim friends from the old days.

I was smack bang in the middle of a humdinging row with my then husband and I asked to be excused and said I'd call back as soon as I could. In the way of things, I forgot and when I remembered that I'd promised to call back and made a call, it was too late. Steve had sort of ... disappeared."

Stars, big stars, aren't like people. That they are people is self-evident but that they conform to the predictable, assessable, forecastable mores shared by the rest of us is outside the remit of being a star.

I honestly don't think that stars really care who they go to bed with and the fact that they might sleep with one partner whilst having another is not a matter of great moment or significance. And far more important than who is going to do what to who with whomsoever's dangly bit is who is going to be best at massaging the star ego. Rather than considering sexuality as self-limiting, I think stars and such distrait creative spirits as are called stars consider sexuality as all things and any things as long as at the end of the necessary physical procedure they have a shoulder to cry on, their back is scratched and the right sweet nothings have been whispered in their ear. If all those conditions are met then the baby will have been comforted, will have stopped crying, is replete and now wants to go to sleep.

Thank you and good night.

Steve was indubitably a very attractive man to both sexes and he knew it. I can agree with all those who proclaim his humility but I also know that he knew he was good-looking and well-put together and quite prepared to advertise all his charms. He also knew full well that the camera lens processed his image superbly. As he knew he had to pose to have his photograph taken, he did so as a professional and he had his photograph taken in the best way he could achieve. Photographs of him betray that wry quality of cynical contrivance ultimately displayed by all who know that the lens can be made to love them and that they're having their photograph taken only for a very good professional reason to achieve some specified aim. Such knowledge does not deny humility nor does it proclaim vanity.

Although Steve looked to be a very sexual person, I am convinced that a large portion of his sexuality was devoted to his creativity and his ambition. Even being the slightest bit creative seems to make me horny. What the head-scratching, pencil-biting, irritating process did to Cat Stevens makes the mind boggle.

I do believe that women are more interested in what goes on behind bedroom doors than men. I do believe that women always like to think that, '... it SHOULD (could) have been me!'

Doing sex with no post-mortems and no morning-after agonising is, shall we say, a more Mediterranean trait than could be ascribed to many Northern Europeans. What is considered mentionable by Greek men is bragged about, what is not is usually ignored. Sex and emotion don't necessarily go together. Talking about sex makes who you do it with significant. Merely doing sex does not. More significantly, sex can just as much mirror power as it can love.

Steve knew a great deal about love. You can't write the wonderful love songs he wrote and not know about love. 'How can I tell you that I love you when I can't think of right words to say?' 'My Lady d'Arbanville ...', 'What makes me me, what makes you you?'. But Steve usually kept love separate from sex. If you have multiple partners, that's how it often is.

That love, separated from sex, can sometimes also mirror power cannot be ruled out of the equation. That love can also breed obligation is a factor, necessarily, that stars do not need to cope with. The obligations are necessarily one-way. If one is not adored, one is not a star and without adoration, self-doubt can destroy in an instant what a star has taken years to construct.

But that's enough about sex.

So, sorry girls and those guys who feel robbed of revelations, all I can tell you is what I can guess at as equally as you. Steve's mona bone jakons were certainly never lonely for long and when they did get seen to, I'd like to bet that the relief, just as with us mere mortals, was mostly self-administered.

The smallness of the music world is underlined by the following co-incidence. Carl Miller, Steve's Tour Manager and confidante for so many years, is now handling some of Linda Lewis's business affairs. Twenty years ago, Linda was the support act on

Steve's current tour and as such under Carl's supervision. It seems that past lives are often re-lived.

Since he left working for Steve, Carl has worked on a host of projects including concerts for UNICEF, television specials for MTV by artists such as Tina Turner, Barbara Dickson and Iron Maiden, tours of classical companies such as THE KIROV BALLET, THE RED ARMY ENSEMBLE and THE PHILADELPHIA ORCHESTRA and it is into the classical arena he seems to be moving with his latest projects of the Christmas Carol Concert by THE ROYAL CHORAL SOCIETY and the recently issued re-mastered MESSIAH by Handel, conducted by Sir Malcolm Sargent. He has also produced five albums. It's a long way from a Ford Transit and the Blue Boar truck-stop on the M1.

CARL MILLER: "So much time has gone by ... It's odd, thinking back about a guy I spent the best part of seven years with, living cheek by jowl. We were so close and yet I always basically knew he was so far away.

I was his tour manager and all that entailed and I started work for him in winter. The winter I remember. The year? It was either 1970 or 1971. Two years, same winter.

First of all, you get to know the job before you start to get to know the guy you're working for. Work-wise, there's a lot that has to be said about Steve. Technically, working with his producer Paul Samwell-Smith, he was great. Always ready to explore and keen to learn. What they could have done together now, twenty years later with the technology that exists today ...

Musically, he was always, can I say eccentric? Unconventional, perhaps is a better word. He was very inventive and very creative but his musicality was so specific, so particular to him, that it was often very difficult for his fellow musicians to pick up on. And Steve had the greatest difficulty explaining. His rhythms were so broken up and often so difficult to follow that even a drummer of the talent and professionalism of Gerry Conway could easily slip. Steve's formats were very very tight. There was absolutely no room for improvisation. If anyone did, or slipped their concentration even the least bit, it would often throw the whole song. It was why the shows were like they were ... You'd never see a Cat Stevens show where he departed from the exact routine we'd rehearsed. He could never just put down his guitar, pick up a hand mike and stroll across the stage singing. The songs surely communicated with the audience but as far as Steve communicating ... he really did have great difficulty even with the members of the band and the crew and we were the closest people to him on a day to day basis other than Barry Krost, of course. He was highly intelligent, that's obvious, and it was a real mystery about the communication thing because it ran through his whole life. Perhaps it's carrying so much on your own shoulders, or, at least, feeling that you carry so much yourself. He wasn't ever interested in what the other musicians had to say or contribute. Steve obviously knew exactly what he wanted and just expected everyone else to do it, to go along with it. He was of course a perfectionist not only about standards but also about ideas too. If other people's ideas fell outside the boundaries of his own, they were not only not considered but immediately ignored. It was as if he hadn't heard you, sometimes; when you voiced an opinion that differed from his own he sort of glazed over. Steve was sealed very tightly inside Cat Stevens and must have been for many years, ages before Cat Stevens was invented.

This tightness and restriction which he alone imposed on himself sort of created it's own tension and it was this tension Steve seemed to be able to communicate with no difficulty whatsoever. Life with him would have been so different if there'd been anything of a sense of humour to temper it. But there wasn't. I remember Paul McCartney coming in to some place we were at and asking, cheerfully with that Scouse tease in his voice: "*Is that Greek about?*" Steve did not find it funny. Not at all. Other times, yes ... of course he laughed. We had lots of laughs, couldn't help it with people like Barry about and the guys in the band but I'm talking about a sense of humour ... that encompasses a lot of things. Cynicism for example. Me, I'm really cynical I know, but it helps you to get through things, get over situations which you've half seen coming. If you can't and you're hit by them, you're left flattened, disappointed, let down. But to allow yourself to be cynical, or ironic or even sarcastic, you have to have an appreciation of where the other people in your life are at or where they're coming from and Steve wasn't able to do this easily. I should be surprised if it ever crossed his mind that he should even be supposed to think in that way. The ego was, of course, huge.

Funny thing, ego ... I know we've all got one but stars have a different kind of a one, almost uncontrollable, following no rules or predictable behaviour that we, the non stars, share and run our lives by. Odd too, that such a strict, almost repressed personality can be ruled by such an unruly, volatile thing as an ego. But it's like that; the star puts him or herself at the centre of everything over and above anyone else. When that sort of isolation happens, of course there's going to be a few explosions when orbits collide.

I suppose I saw more of the explosions than anyone else. Exalted position though mine as tour manager might have been, I was nonetheless the whipping boy. Everyone has to have someone to take out and often aim their fustrations on and in Steve's case, I was the prime, though not the only candidate. It often seemed that if there wasn't a problem in Steve's life, he would make one. Cruelty might spur someone else to observe that such behaviour is surely to ensure that our hero remained firmly centre stage of other people's attention. Kindliness and intimacy might add that people like Steve need volcanic outlets, naturally, and if no active crater exists, they'll take any old hole. It's almost as though they need to be evacuated of tension; gut-bursting, groin-crunching, head-banging, eye-popping tension - it has to be assuaged, exorcised, in order that they be able to remain on a keel even enough to carry on.

I remember one of the more public occasions of Steve-in-eruption was at the end of tour party for our 1974-5 American tour. It was at JP's in New York and we were all relieved. The tour had gone very smoothly but the tension and the aggro that had built up, most of it emanating from Steve, was mystifying in its intensity. Pure pent-up frustration which bred, like an alien life form in a space movie, bubbling and seething just beneath a paper thin surface.

The guest list for the party had been, as everything always was, compiled by Steve and I was given charge of the door - like, who comes in and who doesn't. Steve gave me strictest instructions not to depart from the list in any way. Like NO ONE was to be allowed in if their name wasn't on his list. No one!

So, party goes on - champagne is downed and everyone's having a pretty excessive time whether upstairs or down. Until John Lennon arrives ...

His name is not on the guest list.

Even though I'd worked for Steve four years, there were still dilemmas, occasions when I just didn't know what to do. Usually I could pick a right time to tell him something, break a piece of not-so-good news which Barry, his manager, wasn't around to impart but about which he needed a reaction. Muggins, me. At first I didn't recognise Lennon who was wearing a very short haircut but Muggins mumblingly explained to John, one of my heroes and one of rock's nicer guys what the situation was and John was great. Even offered to leave but I asked him not to and that I would go immediately and check with 'my guv'nor'.

Steve exploded first in the opposite way when bearing in mind his original instructions - Of course I was to let John Lennon in! Back I go but JL is nowhere to be found. Back I go to Steve who explodes again, grabs a bottle of champagne breaks it and stands there facing me with the jagged thing in his hand. Other people were horrified ... I was scared and I'm afraid my temper then snapped. Of course, it was all over in moments and it was the final eruption ...

I suppose for Steve that was it, over and done with. He'd had his long awaited release and he was spent. Yes, spent. It was almost as though the tension he relieved by losing his rag, working himself almost to a point of being physically violent was the equivalent of a sexual release of energy. Tension, after all, is only energy and stars are well-known to be people of extremes, more prone to radical behaviour than we mere mortals.

As a person, a personality? Obviously, after the work thing had been established when I first arrived at the beginning of that crazy decade, life in the Cat Stevens caravan went on. A lot of aspects of relationships just become accepted. You don't spend every waking moment of your day at the time wondering why, analysing, speculating what kind of a childhood people have had. Life just goes on. Steve was Steve, a feature of my every day just like lunch or going to the bathroom. Now, looking back, one's had a lot of years to think and ponder and to tie up your memory with specific events. I think Steve was a very clever and talented songwriter. I think a lot of his work was poetry, creativity on a very elevated level, far far set apart from most other writers and per-formers. Having said that, I also feel that the work was very cerebral. It came from the brain and not necessarily from the heart. I'm not saying Steve didn't feel. That'd be daft but I do believe that his work had nothing to do with his life, his inner life which I'm convinced was in a turmoil from a very early age and in every aspect. Sexually, creatively, regarding friends and family but most of all his relationship with himself. Initially, I reckon he found it really difficult coping with Steve Giorgiou and then Steve Giorgiou had difficulty in coping with Cat Stevens and then Cat Stevens had difficulty in coping with Cat Stevens and then Cat Stevens had difficulty in coping with Yusuf Islam and then Yusuf Islam found that he didn't need Cat Stevens at all. I hope that Yusuf is now happy in all his relationships.

I find the childlikeness as well as the childishness in his character and therefore his work interesting because they're obviously linked. I can find huge parallels between Steve and what is publicised about Michael Jackson, for example. Both have enormous affinities with childhood, children and animals. Steve's last tour in 1976 was full of bloody animals!

Of course, I knew them as individuals but I still don't really know a lot about Steve's family or that background. His dad was pretty strict, I know and his mum was always a lovely lady. Mind you, being brought up in a society based paternally on Greek culture and Greek orthodoxy is often, to British eyes, somewhat hypocritical. The men often conform to double standards. If this was the case in Steve's upbringing, with his sensitivity and tendency to see everything in black and white, such conflicts would have left him very confused, wondering which was the right thing or the wrong thing to commit to. To do one thing but to be SEEN to do another. Amazing how easily children learn that to be political means being deceitful and that you have to be political to survive. Perhaps Steve worked out in the end it was better to commit to nothing, say nothing, keep yourself and your thoughts to yourself.

He was spoiled by his family. That's for sure. He was the baby boy, after all. He never had to struggle in his life for anything like a Robert Plant or any other of the working class pop stars. He wanted a new guitar. He got it. He was pampered in every way. Pampered people get used to not needing to give. They just expect things to happen, to be done nicely to by the world in general and when that doesn't happen ... One howling baby.

Growing older for Steve certainly wasn't growing up. Like the child understandably sees him or herself as the centre of the world, so did Steve as he grew older. The only way the world has worked out to make that trait acceptable behaviour rather than committable lunacy is for the subject to become a star, to become someone who people still willy nilly dance attention on. Stars, just like baby boys, can be forgiven anything.

But, in going that route, the child runs the risk of cutting itself off from ordinariness, from ordinary peers and, later, ordinary grown-ups to the point where when the child finds that he's at last ready to join the adult world, he can't 'cos he's just never learned or been taught how to.

But what it was that made Steve so private so early on, I shall never know. He had buddies when he was young but no real friends. I remember he used to knock around with the Ryan Twins, Paul and Barry, going to the Speakeasy and the other clubs like the Cromwellian but I wouldn't call them friends. Steve was always very much on his own looking out at the world through a child's eyes. His favourite film, he always averred, was LORD OF THE FLIES. I find that pretty revealing.

He was very, very close with himself. I remember when he was going out with Patti d'Arbanville and her asking me how the hell she could get closer to the guy? So I should know? I wasn't the one in bed with him. All you have to do to be in the bed too is listen to the words of LADY d'ARBANVILLE. Did Steve really think that his lady was so cold or was he just telling the world to conceal the fact from himself that he was being distant, removed ... Only able to see how cold she looked ... Unable to even get close to touch how cold she was that night? I never knew and nor, most likely, did Patti. Steve never volunteered close information like that. All we really know about him is gleaned.

When he had relationships, not only sexual ones, he became very jealous of them even though in many cases he did nothing to promote or sustain them. You often wouldn't realise how close you were to him until one day you suddenly got cut dead or, in my case, sworn at. I remember the occasion of my wedding which no one knew about. I had to have it like that as marriage was a huge step in my life and I had to do it by myself and for myself and Jenny if we were going to make it work. No one was invited. Later, when Steve heard the news, he was not only upset, he was angry, as though he'd been specifically excluded. My other friends understood or at least accepted my motives immediately. Steve didn't. Did he think of me as his property, that I had to inform him or was it that he saw me taking the first step in achieving something he wanted for himself, a stable family unit?

I have an idea that there was something very black following Steve, all references to moonshadows apart. If that isn't the right picture then perhaps it was that Steve felt a darkness inside himself. He had a dark side. It was to do with energy, misplaced or mishandled energy which ran counter to the great control and discipline he rigorously applied to himself. His self-will was a lot of stuff had disappeared. The car was found a few hours later but never was found Steve's new friend or the loot!

He took up the challenge of the new times and his new career with typical ferocity. He was a true pioneer in many ways, especially in the innovations he made in touring. Big tours. Steve's tours were always productions. There was always something more than the meat and potatoes, PA only and sod the set tours which had characterised touring for so long. But then, until the late sixties, the idea of an artist or a band touring on its own with just a single support wwould have been strange. Tours went out laden with pop stars; there'd often be six, eight, even ten acts on the same tour doing a couple of songs each.

Gradually it became to be like theatre, a new kind of theatre. By the seventies, it was theatre. Steve helped to introduce the use of computerised monitors, mega-lighting rigs and visual effects and moveable sets and, in America certainly, helped move rock out of the standard clubs and auditoria and into the stadia and arenas. As I've already said, by 1976 and the MAJICAT tour, he had animals - tigers, rabbits, pigeons. That was difficult to get together but it worked. I thought it was really sad he only ever did one more gig after that, the UNICEF concert.

He was really so much better known in the States. I know prophets are traditionally unheard in their own countries and Steve's career proved this to be the rule. His appearances in 1971 at Doug Weston's TROUBADOUR in LA and then at New York's GAS-LIGHT were milestones. In a very short time, he was huge; his concerts became legendary. The TV special he did for Peter Asher with DOCTOR JOHN and LINDA RONSTADT was wonderful and the special he did with LEON RUSSELL too - magnificent. I wish there was more available of him on film but he never did promotional videos. When they became commonplace after QUEEN's 1975 BO-HEMIAN RHAPSODY, Steve was already well into his 'reluctant star' period. BANAPPLE GAS is on film and of course there is the wonderful cartoon film of TEASER AND THE FIRECAT he initiated and drew for. He was a very talented artist. His line drawings of members of the band were accurate and actually displayed more insight into character than I would have imagined.

I must add that Steve was also very helpful to other musicians, performers and artists. Linda Lewis, AMERICA and Linda Ronstadt all benefited from being his support acts. He really liked their music and if he respected someone, he would go to great lengths to be of help. As much as Barry Krost was always there to support and guide and plan, Steve was greatly helped in his American career by Peter Asher and Nat Weiss, Asher being James Taylor and Linda Ronstadt's manager and Nat Weiss, a shrewd but extremely kind New York lawyer who had been long associated with Brian Epstein and the NEMPEROR company.

Steve was always very professional as a performer. Sure, he milked silences and pauses to create just the right mood of reverent expectation in which he knew his songs would go down well, but he never let his audiences down. We mustn't think of Steve as too holy. He was always in for a bit of excess. He jumped into a swimming pool in Barcelona and broke his leg the night of a very big concert. Plastered up to the hip, he managed to go out on stage and of course the audience went wild. Same once in Youma, where he cut his hand very badly and still went out and played. They loved that.

I think he was searching. All the time. For better work, yes. For some way of being able to fit in, certainly. The religious aspect of his life was always important. He went though enough phases and aspects of religion before he found what he felt he truly believed in. Many things influenced him. New places. Foreign things. Japan encouraged his interest in Buddhism, even accelerating his interest in it way past radical into pure Shinto-ism, that Buddhist discipline which is so male-oriented, including the warrior-like, almost violent male aspect of man versus men into the more conventional, less extreme areas of that philosophy. At a different time, THE BOOK OF THE I CHING, one of the Confucian adjuncts to Buddhist basic philosophy, was consulted so frequently that there were days he'd never leave the Fulham house if he felt the auguries he had deduced were inauspicious or inappropriate. He didn't apply the interpretation necessary to allow the poetic Confucian images to free, rather than enslave his life.

However, Islam was another matter altogether. I realised very early on in the process of Steve's acquaintance with the Muslim faith that his involvement was more than transitory and explained this to Barry Krost. We were all used to Steve's passing involvements which I felt he often wasn't fully able to explain. I often thought he talked rubbish he was so impossible to follow. The involvement with Islam was obviously serious. Steve began to realise that here was a faith he could follow and which could be everything to him not just another burden to carry around.

I never understood why. I remember the last time I spoke to him. I'd stopped working for him full time by 1977 as there was no touring to do and his recording work was easily serviced by a new generation of road crew. I'd moved to CBS. I asked him: "Why have you packed it in? You gave so much pleasure, man. What's wrong in giving people pleasure? I can't understand. Why?"

He replied, in Islamic terms which surely meant a great deal to him that he felt Allah would not approve, that it would be wrong for him to continue. I wish I understood. I still do.

But it wouldn't have been Steve's style. He was one thing or the other. No grey, no in between, no compromise. His friends Kelvin and Cheryl who had been Muslim for several years, Richard Thomson too ... They'd converted and seemed to be enabled to continue with their professional lives. Steve obviously felt he couldn't. He had to immerse completely at the deep end, swallow the sword to the hilt. Steve was not a person for merely swimming along with the flow, skimming the surface.

But he's still a star. In his community. I understand he still makes music and that he even had a hit in Turkey some years ago with a version of an Islamic chant. There you go ... I wish he could have carried on. It's ironic to me that the song he's still most identified with especially in his own country is his rendition of MORNING HAS BROKEN which was written long ago by Eleanor Farjeon as a hymn".

CHAPTER TEN

ROYALTIES
AND LOYALTIES

There were windows overlooking Curzon Street both in Barry's office and in the general office where I worked on the very top floor. I vividly remember the day that Steve, Barry and I were standing at the windows looking down into the street at the people coming and going at the National Westminster Bank opposite and Steve turned to Barry and asked: 'Are we rich yet?' At that moment, Telly Savalas came out of the bank and I remember because he was noticeably bald in days when men with little hair never thought of not disguising the fact. It was before Telly was KOJAK. He must have ended up almost as rich as Steve, never ever to have to go the bank by himself again!

Much has been made of Steve's dilemma based on the 'my art versus my soul versus my money' dialectic and I have to admit I have as hard a time with this theory now as I would have had a hard time with it then, mainly because, personally, I was having a pretty hard time financially throughout the time I worked for Barry Krost. My fault, I know. I should have left and got a better job, even a proper job but it nevertheless pains me to remember that other than a lovely Tom Gilbey sweater Barry gave me one year for Christmas and numerous second-hand cast-offs, other than small cash bonuses which came our way at Christmas (and then only after a great deal of carrot and stick, shall I or shan't I from the Boss) there were very few crumbs from the rich men's table.

I can only remember Steve's generosity once. What he bought for the women, I've forgotten but he bought all the male members of the office staff a shirt one Christmas. Mine was a blue, denimy kind of shirt with a rounded fat collar. I remember it so well because it never fitted and I kept it for many years.

True, Steve was never personally conspicuously extravagant. He didn't drive a particularly fancy car. It was a black Citroen DS19, I believe, the sort whose rear end rose or fell with hydraulic pressure which was being constantly thraped round London by Steve who was, incidentally, an appallingly dangerous and terrifying driver in those days. Although he didn't spend conspicuously on himself, I believe nevertheless that Steve liked money as much as you and I and the next person. I also believe he needed money, not for what you or I might need money for and probably for no reason that was particularly clear even to him at the time. However, Steve knew what money could do and he knew that it was better for him in his circumstances to have total control over the most money he could get. If the expression 'control freak' had been coined in those days, it could have most certainly been applied to Steven Giorgiou.

If he had a hard time at all about money, I think it was with what other people thought about his having so much money. But that was the only hard time he had. The Cat Stevens image which had been sold in many ways so glibly by the record companies, lapped up so eagerly by the press and music pundits and finally bought so blithely by the record-buying public was of a simple, saintly sort of guy who had few needs and who was as spiritual as the light by which we thought we saw him so clearly. It has to be said that, again in many respects, this was a true rendition of the essential Cat Stevens.

Steve Giorgiou, however, was a different kettle of fish. If Cat Stevens was very much the victim ... I wonder who the bully was? Steve Giorgiou? Or was the villain, mere circumstance? Was the oppressor only, in fact, a spectre, a sense of the past, memories perhaps of other unknown abuse ... more willis than moonshadows?

Listening to Steve's work now, it was the 'hard done by' strain in the lyric content and the tortured, fractured rhythms, tossing and writhing as though undergoing nightmares of their own, which struck deep chords certainly in me. Oddly, the songs worked the same for me as they did for the confused soul in middle-America who, perceiving herself to be in a godless and mortified state fashioned a diadem from the branches of a Crucifixion plant and sent the crown of thorns through the post one day. We did indeed shiver with revulsion. But again, you see, I have to confess that although I was horrified, I so understood why this American fan had done what she had done. It's what makes penitents believe they see tears on plaster statues, real blood flecking the temples of wooden models of the crucified Christ. Christ was sold as the ultimate victim and it is this perception, readily dressed up, decorated and paraded which has made the symbolism so potent over so many years. Humility, abstinence, persecution, even self-deprivation have accompanied the general perception of many of humanity's proclaimed prophets. It goes down very well. It also pays not to have TOO good a time. At least, not to be SEEN having too much of a good time.

I'm not saying that such qualities or impressions were con-sciously created or striven for by Steve as he wrote but I am saying that if I felt that I could wipe away my tears feeling that I wasn't so alone after all and go back to work once again the following day after having lain sleepless in my bed listening to Steve's albums, his songs must have had the same potent effect elsewhere.

Many of the girls and the women who worked both for Barry and Steve were all footloose and fancy free in the love stakes to a greater or lesser extent and we were all exploring in the same rigging, finding out who and what each of us was in the individuality stakes. It was a great time of companionship, hard to sustain and impossible to repeat as we all fledged, flew the coop and settled with our particular partners. I think that without exception, how-ever much ninety nine percent of each of us wants coupledom or is still looking for it, there is that one percent which resents the enslavement as we remember those rootless days of our youth.

Emancipation was having a remarkable effect not only on both women and gays. A lot of people on most continents, having been through the initial rebellion and catharsis of the sixties, were beginning to see through life's plot and more than a large minority now saw that life as they'd been told it should be lived was nothing more than a conspiracy in which they wanted no part.

However, it was sexual emancipation which was integral in this new-found confidence. If there's no need to hide being gay then there's no need to worry about staying in a job you hate with people you don't get on with. If a woman doesn't feel she has to be married by twenty one and pregnant the next year, there are many opportunities life will afford her. If people decided they didn't want to be part of the mainstream, they didn't have to be and Steve's music egged us on.

Those of us who worked in the music business then were only too happy to be inseparably associated with the work we did and we were proud to be considered as part of a new breed of professional young people, men and women alike, who had acquired respectable and respected business and office skills in that specialised area not via an apprenticeship or training scheme but in the much-vaunted university of life. I cannot emphasise how much we all lived life one day at a time. Even by the seventies, anything could happen to you in London and much of what could happen usually did, to us.

The very real phenomenon of co-incidence, of people just turning up in your life are both major features of every rock 'n' roll and showbiz story. Hard to believe, perhaps but things really did 'just happen, mum'; opportunities did simply present themselves as witnessed by all these stories of Steve's life and career. Once you'd taken the idea of opportunism on board, even though our lives seemed precarious to many of our parents, fretting about our health and moral welfare, the reality was that we lived a life which assumed a strangely structured arena.

I think it's rather comforting to have had a bit of a past. Of course, even at twenty, everyone of us had had a past although most of it was so immediate that it tended to be of little value or consequence. Our past then certainly did not make us particularly interesting people.

When you're a little more advanced in life with three children and a husband, you tend not to get too many chances to add to your past. Instead, having accumulated your history, it is one of life's luxuries to lie back and appreciate that history. The exercise makes you feel rich indeed. And, when you think that your past has both incorporated and facilitated many other people's futures, the worth of the treasure of your history doesn't merely double, it becomes actuarially incalculable.

Chrissie Neal, as she then was, worked at Barry Krost's office for several years before leaving to become Ray Cooney's assistant as he was preparing to found THE THEATRE OF COMEDY. Chrissie finally left show business to have her children. Chrissie Speller, as she now is, lives with her husband Peter in Edinburgh although she loyally still proclaims her London roots and regularly comes south to visit her father in Eltham.

CHRISSIE SPELLER: "In 1971 I was working at Deloittes, the accountants, although the idea of becoming a fully-fledged accountant never appealed. I'd been to school, after all, and the idea of more endless exams wasn't what I had in mind for my life. It was such an exciting time to be living in London and jobs, to me, were for earning money to enjoy those times. However, I also realised that jobs themselves could be a little more exciting than the one I had and so I didn't need to be held back when I saw an advertisement in the EVENING STANDARD for someone to work in the accounts department of a show business company. I wish I could remember the wording because that advertisement was very important to my life. Silly, isn't it, how little notice you take of things at the time? You never think when things are happening, 'Gosh! I ought to remember this because it's crucial!'

My interview was with Neville Shulman, a West End accountant whose company looked after the affairs of Barry Krost's theatrical agency and also those of the agency's biggest client Cat Stevens. Well ... talk about in like Flynn. However, there was a hurdle. Even though I was initially employed by Neville, he thought it best that I see what kind of company I would be ultimately working for and to meet Barry Krost formally.

In the taxi on the way over to Curzon Street, Neville tried as best as he could to forewarn me. Neville obviously thought I was going to be tremendously shocked, put off, even offended by the den of outrage whence he was leading me. *"Some of the language ..."* he started to say ... *"I'm sure they don't mean it ..."* he tried to explain ... *"Not the usual sort of people ..."* The more Neville tried to shelter me from the blast, the more I became determined to take the explosion full-face.

By the time Neville and I had waited the five minutes or so before seeing Barry, I'd already overheard one conversation between two roadies about a gang-bang, had seen more fluttering male hands and watched more theatrical kisses being blown across rooms than most girls from Deloittes would see in a lifetime. Shocked? Oh definitely, very definitely. Put off? No way!!

Although I used to make frequent trips from Wigmore Street to Curzon Street to get the artists' cheques signed, I met few of the celebrities the company looked after. It was not until the office Christmas party in 1971 that I eventually met Cat Stevens. Steve's accounts were always kept entirely and scrupulously separate from those of Barry and the agency. It was Joe Goumal who was in charge of Steve's accounts at Shulman's although Joe got more than just a job out of it. He also found a wife as he later married Sandy, Neville's secretary.

I'd become very friendly with the Di Hughes who'd been brought in to be Steve's secretary/assistant and it was Di who introduced me at the party as I would never have imposed myself on him by making my own awkward introductions. Steve was wearing a bottle green velvet cord suit. He looked very tanned and attractive! He was also absolutely charming and very friendly and natural.

It's amazing how quickly the 'gob-smacked' feeling when you meet people you admire and respect evaporates. Not that it ever disappears entirely because stars always exude that indefinably 'different' quality as human beings but working life takes on an almost ordinary guise. To say that Steve became just an ordinary chap to the people who worked around him would be a gross distortion of the truth of the situation. Even before I went over to work full-time in Curzon Street, I had sensed the politics which seethed around Steve.

The keyword is control. Like you have a control in accounting, control is fundamental to the working of business politics because control means power. The longer he could keep me and my everyday work on his premises, the more control Neville Shulman could retain over the financial workings of both Barry Krost's and Steve's growing empire. And that's just one example of control. It also happened with everyone's jobs. People were very, very jealous of their territory, especially those people closest to and most dependent on Steve. A lot of people behaved as if their own status and future was not only dependent on their jobs but was actually conferred in the first place by those jobs. I'm not saying that there was endless back-biting and jockeying but I often felt quite hurt when someone bristled and spat because they thought their territorial imperatives were being threatened.

I know Steve, especially towards the end of his career, was upset at being in the middle of this power-pulling arena. Could he have felt that the control he had always been able to retain and exercise himself was being ever-so-gently wrested from him? Indeed, I imagine that to fulfil the dual role of being the creative and performing force as well as overseeing the running of the vast finances that his success generated was becoming very difficult for Steve. Of course, when a career burgeons, it's like any business which expands more than anticipated. More and more employees are taken on just to keep the ship afloat and on course. In Steve's case, Alex, his brother-in-law was brought in to be purser and chief officer.

By the time I moved to Curzon Street I had an assistant, Lesley Johnson. I'd found the process of interviewing very difficult. I found it impossible to decide and ultimately settled for one final criteria ... birth sign. The Libras and the Virgos came and went and Lesley got the job not only because I had a feeling she would do the job very well but because she was a water sign and fitted in with the Pisces/Cancer/Scorpio configuration which characterised the environment.

Once again, Neville Shulman was very worried about putting a tender, timid seventeen year old like Lesley into what he obviously still regarded as a dangerous hotbed of perversion and immorality. Lesley took to the life like a duck to water and proved as un-shockable and un-flappable as I.

I must mention too that there was enormous kindness around. The people who worked on the team were very close and looked out for each other, sharing what could often be huge upsets and crises in each other's lives.

The worst excesses and most lewd suggestions of the roadies and the boys in the office we interpreted as the behaviour of little boys who had never grown up. I remember soon after arriving at Curzon Street, I'd dressed up to go out in the evening with Peter and was wearing a velvet something-or-the-other with a velvet choker, all the rage at the time, round my neck. Barry bounded up the stairs and exclaimed: *"You look like some French tart!"* before rushing into the loo.

For a moment I was horribly taken aback until David E hastily assured me that Barry meant his remark as a compliment. If he hadn't, he would have simply ignored me. I also have to say, that none of the boys' grosser teasing was ever directed personally or meant cruelly although it took newcomers some time to get used to. My poor long-suffering Peter, a very good-looking boy indeed, had to put up with some very saucy comments from Barry and David E whenever he came to collect me from the office! The teasing was never badly motivated and served, I think, to integrate us all whatever our sexual orientation for there was nothing that 'the boys' appreciated more than when their own taunts were returned with interest!

There were drugs circulating too. Not as many as might have been thought and certainly never condoned by Barry but they were around and available if you'd wanted to participate. I never did and neither, I fancy, did too many of my colleagues most of whom, like myself, being high enough on the energised atmosphere alone.

Steve never joined in any of the ribaldry or badinage. He was quite happy to smile sometimes but more often than not he ignored a lot of the mayhem that was going on around him. He always had a point when he came up to the office and would sit at the corner of his secretary's desk, looking over papers or talking to someone or the other on the 'phone. Steve was not one for just hanging about. He was always focused. He was also assiduous. He questioned everything, always wanting to get to the bottom of something which didn't immediately make sense. And anything to do with money brought out the most particular in him.

We certainly worked very hard. Everyone stayed late and after some intolerably low rates of pay had been rectified, no one counted the extra hours. Good thing too for there was certainly no overtime structure to cover extra work. Devotion was not only expected, it was presumed upon and, strange but true, it was usually forthcoming. There were perks, I must admit. Once someone had given Steve two first class air fares to Copenhagen and because he couldn't use them himself he told Di to use them and to take a friend. I got to be the friend. Somehow Barry's chauffeur arranged to take us in the Rolls to the airport in great style and we had a fabulous weekend doing the town in Denmark.

However, amongst the apparent hedonistic chaos, we were very professional. I think most of our clients were happy with what we did for them and I know Steve's career was extremely competently handled. He had little reason to be dis-satisfied with any of his own or the team Barry had assembled. He had a temper, sure, but although I often saw it vented via the telephone at some unfortunate person at the other end, he never yelled at me or Lesley or David E ... I like to think he respected us and in some ways, I even think he was a little afraid of us. I know I felt he was generally not comfortable with women; not afraid, as such but there is a certain way in which a man treats a woman which makes her aware that he is slightly held back, slightly in check. Of course, there were also the times when he could ignore you completely.

He was certainly a man of extremes. Either effusive and extra friendly or nothing at all. I certainly think that Steve saw us as part of his security and I feel that he trusted us, although he would never have told us so.

When it came to my leaving, he was not merely demonstrative but genuinely upset. *"They've just told me you're leaving!"* he exclaimed and threw his arms around me and hugged me and wouldn't let me go. *"Why do you have to go? I don't want you to go!"* There was no reason for him to care two hoots but I honestly don't think he did want me to leave.

The last time I saw him was at a Dusty Springfield Concert at Drury Lane in 1979. It was the IT BEGINS AGAIN tour. Steve was sitting in a box and Lesley Johnson and I went up to see him. He was awkward. Not unfriendly at all but very withdrawn. As Yusuf Islam, he had already converted. He mumbled something about having been a bit reclusive of late and that he didn't come to 'these kind of things much' anymore. It was an odd moment. Cat Stevens had all but vanished into memories.

But mine are very precious memories. I once announced that I could sew. Plans were being laid for the LEON RUSSELL TV special that Steve had agreed to do. He needed something to wear and it was at the time when embroidered things were fashionable. There and then, Steve ran out and returned later with a jacket that he wanted me to embroider. He was famous for his spontaneity. He didn't know from Adam whether I could sew but he went with his instincts.

He couldn't have bought a plainer jacket. It was white, cotton and bought from a catering supplier in Wardour Street in Soho. When I asked him for clues as to what he'd like, all he said was that he thought purple would be a good starting theme.

No sooner had I started dying it and braiding all the pockets in lavender than I was taken into hospital. No peace for the wicked, I suppose. I finished the braiding whilst in bed and embroidered a moon and star on the top pocket. I wanted to do more and was very dis-satisfied with the result that Peter later dropped off at Curzon Street. I needn't have worried. Steve loved it and wore it not only for the TV special but for a long time thereafter.

He wrote me a letter which, of course I still have. He never called me Chrissie. Everyone else did and Steve was always different.

'My dear Christine, The jacket is magical. 1st night I wore it the sky put on a show. Get better ... and better, love Steve.'

When David E contacted me about being in this book, he sent

us copies of two or three other contributors' sections. Peter, my husband read them and felt very emotional, saying that he felt sad that it's all gone, that all that magic and those wonderful years are lost. We've had our rotten times, Peter and I and there's so much that really should be forgotten in life. But you can't forget. Facing up to awful things in life gives you a lot in the end although you don't realise at the time. And it's the same with all those good things. They're not gone. They're not lost. They're quite safe where you last put them. All you have to do is remember."

Since Lesley Johnson worked for Barry and then for Steve in Curzon Street, she has worked at Johnny Stirling's Pendulum Music and latterly at Warner Chappell. Lesley is one of the constants of the music business. She was and remains one of the most dependable and caring people in the industry.

LESLEY HATCH (née Johnson): "It was 1973. I was only seventeen and hadn't been working long. I'd only had one job, as a junior with the English Speaking Union in Chesterfield Street in Mayfair. I'd come up from the Isle of Dogs everyday to the West End by bus and tube. I'd left school at the first possible opportunity and I'd done a business course there as one of the last things I learned. Anyway, someone had bought up the English Speaking Union together with its premises and so as I knew redundancy was very much on the cards I joined an agency and almost immediately was sent off for an interview with what was quoted as a management company, looking after the careers of several well-known stars.

The address I went to was in Wigmore Street where Chrissie Speller (nee Neal) ran the accounts department of Barry Krost Management although the headquarters of the company was in Curzon Street. The job being offered was to work with Chrissie helping her with the accounts which were run from the offices of Barry and Steve's accountant, Neville Shulman.

I hadn't the first idea about figures and had indeed been very glad to give up maths at school as soon as I was thirteen. So, thank heavens Chrissie liked my face because she employed me. I didn't waver about taking the job. She quickly explained that the company looked after not only Cat Stevens but also Colin Blunstone, Mike d'Abo as well as several well known film, television and theatre names. Steve's accounts were also done at the office, (Later, I believe, supervised by Derek Bloom on a day-to-day basis) from which we worked but they were and remained an entirely separate entity from the week-by-week accounts and accompanying payments which had to be made to Barry's theatrical clients. Actors, I soon learned, were very quick off the mark if money they were expecting wasn't forthcoming.

Chrissie went over to Curzon Street once a week to have Barry sign cheques but it was ages before I got a whiff of what the business was really about and it was ages before I met Steve. To say he didn't even know of my existence then would be an understatement. Finally, the accounts department moved over to Curzon Street when extra space at number twenty seven was rented and I got to work every day with Barry, David and all the others. All the others of course included Alex Zolas, Steve's brother in law who was married to Anita, Steve's sister and Alex brought his steady, calming influence to bear as much as he could on the turbulent goings on in the office of a busy rock star.

After Sarah Harrison, Steve's secretary, left in 1975 and then David Evans, Barry's assistant, left to go and work for John Reid when Barry had decided to live and work permanently in Los Angeles, I was asked to take over Steve's daily business as his assistant and I did it gladly.

I must say that Steve was not an easy person to know and to many people he was not an easy person to deal with. His temper tantrums were often levelled at those around him and at those he worked with but never did I find myself at the receiving end of his temperament. He once said to someone that I was too calm for him and maybe that was the truth.

He had that quality which so many stars have of making you want to look after him. I know I felt that I mothered him and our relationship probably worked because my sort of mothering didn't involve any censure, expectation or disappointment. He told me several times, right up to the final stages of his conversion to Islam that he trusted me implicitly and of that confidence I am very proud.

Now that I have been asked what I thought about him, I find it difficult to start. I realise everyone's probably said this but he was a very, very private man. I can't stress that aspect of him enough. There were things about him I presumed, assumed, thought, imagined but about which I never really knew. Steve was not a good explainer. This sounds an odd thing to say about a perfection-ist but it's true. He knew very well what he wanted out of life and out of his work. He had very clear ideas in his head but they often remained stubbornly within his head and the 'outing' of those ideas was often a painful and lengthy process often involving fairly random methods. I have a feeling that some of the most important moments of the development of his life and career came by acci-dent. People he met on planes, impromptu trips or expeditions, unexpected birthday presents ... There were many occasions when all the items on that list of possibilities shaped his life. I think Steve was often happier in the company of strangers, people to whom he could explain things about his inner feelings which he was unable to do with those with whom he was more professionally and personally involved.

As with all perfectionists, the meticulousness rarely, if ever, shows. You can't see the joins between the contrasting patches of pleasure and pain which go to make up the final tapestry which you and I go out and buy, whether that end-product be a painting, a novel or a record. You, we, the punters, aren't aware and if we are it's only because we are being made aware for a reason. Steve was no different. The long road to his own ultimate fulfilment was not paved with perfectly hewn stones with neat interlocking edges but was often very bumpy and uneven indeed.

His songs touched very deep chords in those who listened to them and obviously meant a great deal. I think Steve's childhood although outwardly happy, was actually for him, filled with areas of great trepidation. As the youngest, the baby, he was definitely doted on but being very intelligent and very sensitive, he grew up very aware of black and white. Judgements were swift and his sense of right and wrong was sometimes merciless. I suppose I say this in connection with the huge importance which childhood, children, and child-likeness had in his life.

To say that he himself wanted children badly at that time is also an understatement. To also point out that many of his songs deal with the relationships not only between fathers and sons but between adults and children is also necessary for anyone to have any appreciation or understanding of what made him tick. I don't know precisely what made him so passionate about childhood and about the quality of being a child but something in his own childhood had made him vulnerable to the point that associated images well up all through his work. He said to me, after he'd made his irrevocable commitment to convert to Islam and I'd told him that I wouldn't be staying on in his employment, that he supposed it was now finally time for him to grow up.

His work elicited powerful responses in people. Over the years I worked for him, we received a myriad fan letters. One fan totted up a record thirteen letters written and posted on one day. People wrote from prisons and hospitals merely to tell Steve how much he had done to change their lives. Obviously being a fan (short for fanatic) is to be in a state which sometimes borders on the hysterical but some of the letters we received were from people who were definitely psychologically un-hinged in some way but in whom, Steve's songs had assumed an extra level of meaning. Many of these letters remained un-read by him but their persistent arrival made me realise that there exists only a very fine line between what we recognise as sanity and what passes for madness. Steve was always very conscious of his work and its effects. The day when a Crown of Thorns arrived through the post from an American female fan was one when a shiver of what I can only describe as revulsion went through everyone who worked at Curzon Street. We were a very sober bunch for the remainder of that particular day. Steve knew nothing of this gruesome token.

That Steve wanted and sought fame and fortune at the be-ginning, I have no doubt but the very process of becoming rich and famous was essential in Steve's development for he realised through experiencing fame and fortune that the control he wanted and went to such lengths to have acknowledged would ultimately never come from within himself. Steve needed that control to be imposed on him from outside.

By the late seventies, Steve was seriously and painfully at odds with his lifestyle. Although his life displayed all the trappings of anyone as successful as he would have been expected to acquire - flat in Brazil, flat in Cyprus, house in Walham Grove and then a penthouse in Highgate, first-class jet-set travel - they were mere window-dressing for a store that was essentially out of stock and heading for a bankruptcy. The bankruptcy in Steve's case was certainly not financial. If it had been, the situation would have been easier for him to deal with. Steve's store was bankrupt spiritually.

I watched him for several years as he sought the right way to get out from under. His involvement with UNICEF was the start of an awareness of non-music biz life which he used to shift the focus of his life away from himself. I'm sure it was no co-incidence. To be as successful as someone like Steve, you have to be pretty single-minded, determined and also blessed with a fairly massive ego. You also have to shoulder the ultimate responsibility for yourself, your actions and their results and effects far more so than people who are more integrated into a family environment or who have peers who are able to keep wandering feet firmly on the ground. Steve sought many ways to achieve the perspective he so obviously craved.

Strangely, I think Steve was looking for ordinariness; not ordinary in that he wanted to be unrecognised, nor that he wanted to be un-noticeable but ordinary in the way that he didn't want to see himself as anything special. His fame he always seemed to take quite reasonably. In England, we could walk down a street and no on would recognise him. In America, we could walk only the short distance from a car to an entrance and he'd be mobbed. No; celebrity wasn't his problem.

For Steve, the seventies was a very long decade and it must have been tough when faced with the sacrifice that his choice of future had thrown up. It was all or nothing and Steve had a lot of 'all' to give up.

Steve's conversion to Islam was not an overnight sensation. His increasing involvement with Islam was a gradual process of exploring all the ways in which he could convert and be most comfortable - And I don't mean comfortable in the material sense. Many people have converted to Islam and have been able to carry on with the work for which they have been known. It was obviously impossible for Steve to do this. Steve wanted a lifestyle as well as a religion and Islam has obviously enabled him to achieve both.

The implications of this terminal drift away from mainstream music business life and onto the strict path of Islam were never so sharply brought into focus for me as on one specific occasion when Steve had returned from being away for a long time. Usually, he would bound up the stairs of the office and greet me with a huge hug. On this occasion he came up to me and merely held out his hand. I must have looked fairly taken aback but I remember shaking the proffered hand. I also remember that it was never the same between us from that moment on.

I think Steve had a hard time loving and a hard time being loved. He had so many expectations and so many self-imposed parameters, both of which limited his ability to involve himself. I also think that he was often ignorant of those people around him who really did love him. I mean love to include admire, respect, care for, support, defend ... All those things which I'd do for my daughter, which anyone would do for their loved ones and there were a lot of people in all the organisations which Steve was involved with - management, agency people, record companies certainly and also publishers. Steve took a lot for granted and he tended to forget very quickly. As success overtook him, he seemed to withdraw. Perhaps stars use up people faster than the rest of us ... I believe that he had a propensity to seek the love and attention of people he basically knew would let him down or fall short of his expectations and as an inevitable result, despite his angry railing at the situation, he suffered all the more when the ultimate rejection came. He hated being used and yet he permitted himself to be used. There were so many who didn't use him, who worked long hours on his behalf with whom he relaxed but never seemed to fully recognise.

To me, it's a very sad story. I wish the work could have gone on. I wish we could have had as much joy as we've had emotion. I wish I could say that I thought his life had been truly happy. I know I wish he could have met someone earlier on in his life who would have helped him to discover who he was by loving him and being loved by him, patiently and with kindliness, with understanding and tolerance. But then, we could all have done with meeting that person, couldn't we? And, as we know, he did finally meet someone and, as far as Yusuf himself is now concerned, he now has the one thing he always valued most, a family ... His wife, his four daughters and, finally, his son."

As testament has already declared, rock 'n' roll is a notoriously male-dominated arena. Sure, there are female stars but are their management offices and record companies staffed by a majority of women? The whole ethos of touring, of being 'on the road' is essentially masculine - humping roadies and roadies humping, groupies and ra-ra, locker-room, prowess-proving sexual tyranny.

It's changing, slightly. The theatrical world had always held open a few more doors through which the women agents, casting directors, producers and directors struggled at various points over the last few years but, thankfully, in greater and greater numbers. One of the pioneers in London was Sara Randall.

Sara was Barry Krost's colleague in the late sixties and early-seventies. She wasn't tempted to remain although the thought of her as a rock 'n' roll doyenne doesn't spring immediately to mind. She is a highly successful theatrical agent and has run her own company, Saraband Associates for twenty one years. Her clients are legion and celebrated. Her own work extends into an active participation in directing and appearing in the superb programme of plays, musicals and entertainments mounted by The Tower Theatre Company at their historic Islington home.

SARA RANDALL: "I worked with Barry for about seven years at the suite of offices he had at 32 Davies Street. There were several offices. Barry and I shared one whose windows looked out onto the mews at the side of Claridges Hotel. Gordon Black occupied another room and there was a sort of board room - at least, a room used for meetings. In the reception area there was a big old plug-board telephone switchboard. In the accounts office, Sarah Harrison and Sally Moore worked with Tony Payne and Sarah Radclyffe who was William Piggot-Brown's half sister and William was Barry's backer.

I arrived when Bea Narizzano left Barry and she, I believe had followed Lila Burkeman. Bea was a literary agent and it was this function in Barry's Agency which I was employed to continue. I had worked for Peter O'Toole and had lately done some casting, one of the actresses whom I had cast being Fenella Fielding. When Fenella was asked by Barry to become a client of his, she kindly suggested me to fill the post Barry was recruiting for.

Although I was employed as a literary agent, I soon found myself doing everything. Although Barry and I worked in the same room, I wasn't party to any of the negotiations regarding those whom I call HIS clients. There was a distinction. There were clients for whom Barry would allow either Gordon or I to handle affairs of a less significant nature whilst he made the bigger deals and there were clients whom no one else would have even been allowed to talk to had Barry had his way.

Steve was one of these, along with the late Peter Collinson who was then enjoying major success as a director/producer, Silvio Narizzano, another director and ex-husband of the soon-to-be-dead Bea and John Osborne and Jill Bennett. Steve was a welcome and somewhat exotic addition to Barry's client list being neither of the film nor the theatre nor the television worlds. I had obviously heard his previous work when he was in his pop star phase and had enjoyed the songs and so of course I knew who he was when he first came in to the offices but because I knew that he was strictly 'off-limits' work-wise, for a long time I really had little to do with him. Barry was very private in a lot of his dealings and negotiations and meetings about Steve's business were either done in the meeting room in the suite or took place outside the offices altogether. I was aware that he had just recovered from tuberculosis but other than as a frequent visitor to the offices, I knew almost nothing about him. He seemed to be very modest and, as a woman, I reacted to him in an entirely non-physical way. I thought he was good-looking and had a sweet face, I thought.

As far as charisma is concerned, I can't think of someone who became such a huge star who projected the power of their personality, their drive and determination in a less overt way. I was used to the presence of the very famous and so many of these fairly radiated that magnetic aura which engulfs you, envelops you as soon as you are in their presence. O'Toole had it, Jill Bennett had it, Peter Finch too. Curiously enough, Chris Blackwell the owner of Island Records whom I met a few times when Steve started recording for them had massive charisma in that dashing, cavalier way. But not Steve. Not for me, anyway. Perhaps if I'd been a teenager ...

I do remember that he was always most natural with children. My daughter Natasha must have been about seven when MONA BONE JAKON came out. She was with me one day when I asked Steve to autograph a copy of the record for me.

'No,' he replied, 'but I'll do it for Natasha.' He signed the record by means of a feline paw print and the device: 'To Natasha - Love from The Cat'. She was, needless to say, thrilled.

There was very little that could rattle Barry's chain but there were three people at this time in his life who could - Tony Beckley, John Osborne and of course Steve. Steve could make Barry very nervous indeed. But whatever he was to Barry and to others, he was always extremely nice to me. He was always courteous and polite and we did talk. He seemed to value what I had to say about his lyrics and I must say that I did find the change in the nature of the lyrics on TEA FOR THE TILLERMAN compared to MONA BONE JAKON rather bore out my reactions. I found the MBJ lyrics although lucid and undeniably poetic often deeply gloomy and not in the least upbeat or optimistic. I'm glad he realised that a poet can still be soulful without being depressing. That said, I was not at all surprised that his work became so popular. Its literary quality shone through then and it survives today. I find the lyrics still very relevant. FATHER AND SON I find most evocative and MOONSHADOW is another favourite. I think it's the ultimate test of any good piece of work - song, poem, play, novel - Is it relevant a quarter of a century later? Not many artists can claim that distinction.

I worked most closely with Steve on the TEA FOR THE TILLERMAN book which Bernard Jacobson published. Barry had sought my opinion, obviously, when the idea of Steve's publishing a book had come up and I was very glad to look over the text which Steve brought in along with the illustrations as the work progressed. The book could have been published by anyone but as money wasn't the main motive, working with Bernard Jacobson at least allowed Steve the necessary control over quality and workmanship.

It was a beautiful book. Someone, somewhere, quite unsolicited sent in an illuminated copy that had been most lovingly and painstakingly achieved. Steve certainly inspired great devotion.

Although not a great rock or pop fan, I have to confess that Steve's records are ones I still enjoy and will often play them late at night either on my own or when people are visiting. He comes over so clearly on records whereas in live performance I never thought he quite achieved a comparable success."

There is so much more to know about Rose Tobias Shaw than can even be guessed at on first meeting her. She came to this country as an American from America and, thanks to her late husband Maxwell Shaw, stayed on to become in many ways, more British than the British.

Rose's film credits are so numerous that even the biggest Hollywood and British film stars should be envious. But Rose isn't an actress.

Rose is extremely well-read and has an insight into literary property which many film-makers have found invaluable. But Rose is not a producer.

Rose knows more about actors and actresses than their own representatives and her interest in many of them has lasted longer than the interest of a dozen different theatrical agencies. But Rose is not an agent.

In her world Rose has been a star for over thirty years. She has the directness and bluntness associated with Hollywood and yet she has the sophistication and perspective which many see as British. When she says yes she means it and grown men breathe easier. When she says no she means it and the same men have been known to weep. She plays excruciatingly fairly and her word in the film business is a done deal. She is kind and encouraging and funny and we wonder if she'll ever let us have the benefit of a biography.

Rose is a casting director; in the opinion of many, she is the casting director's casting director.

ROSE TOBIAS SHAW: "I'll start off with a story. Into a room full of people comes a short, fat, Jewish faggot, smiling brilliantly like he knows he's just made an entrance. Maybe people look, maybe they don't but he's made an entrance. For those who've looked, they know what they see and they're wary. For those who haven't looked, he wants them not only to look at him but to remember him, even to love him for what they might otherwise shun.

'What! Isn't anyone going to say hello to a short, fat Jewish faggot?' exclaims Barry Krost, like he's Max Miller or Jack Benny or any comedian starting his act in front of a cold house. With a line like that, not only does he get everyone's attention, he also gets a laugh. His audience is disarmed. He has eliminated any threat he may previously have posed; he's drawn them intimately into his world which he has made to look open and defenceless and totally non-threatening.

What most of them won't have realised is that, encouraged into a tacit tolerance of the newcomer, they have also let slip their own guard.

I had a short association with Barry Krost for a few months in 1973. I'd been aware of him for several years, of course but by the time we worked together, his meteoric rise on the strength of Cat Stevens' phenomenal success had made him so much more prominent in my industry which, at that time, was solely films.

I had been asked by Ross Hunter to cast his musical version of LOST HORIZON, James Hilton's classic novel in which Ronald Coleman made such a hit over thirty years before. Casting Directors are sort of like conductors, like conduits. Their job is to bring to the attention of the director and producer the best talent that is available to do the jobs on offer. And by available, I mean not only living and breathing but free to work at the time the film has to be shot. Sometimes we get it right and sometimes not.

LOST HORIZON was a not. It was a botch from start to finish. Olivia Hussey was no longer the sweet ingenue she'd been opposite Leonard Whiting in ROMEO AND JULIET but Ross Hunter specifically asked for her. I wondered about Olivia when she came for the meeting. I thought she was a little, well, bigger than I'd remembered. We found out later that she was five months pregnant. Liv Ullman proved once again that, although a fine actress in her own language, she isn't in English ... In the same way that Yves Montand didn't translate, as far as I'm concerned.

Of the men, Michael York I thought was a little wet and of course there was that unforgettable moment when Sir John Gielgud appears like God out of a whirling snowstorm and in impeccable tones utters the immortal line: *"Hello, my name is Chang."*

Amongst all that mix 'n' match, Peter Finch stood out like the bright light that he was. And Peter Finch was Barry's client and he afforded me my first real professional contact with Barry. Peter was riding the crest of a wave then and was at the peak of his career. Consequently, there was very little negotiation. I'm sure Barry got whatever fee for Finch that he was asking and I found him, under those circumstances, very easy to deal with. Looking back, I also think Barry was softened slightly as he was thrilled to be dealing with Ross Hunter, the producer of all those Doris Day and Rock Hudson movies of yore.

Anyway, my work on LOST HORIZON, which was made for Columbia, came to an end and being a freelancer, circumstances had not supplied me with another movie to work on immediately. As a freelancer, like an actor, you immediately think you're never going to work again. So, when Barry suggested that I change course and move over into management and come and work for him in Curzon Street ... well.

I knew Sara Randall and respected her and had encouraged her when she decided to leave Barry and set up on her own. Barry had been left with a very interesting client list - John Osborne, Cat Stevens, Angela Lansbury, Ian McShane, Mike Hodges the director, Tony Beckley ... There were some incredibly good and interesting names on which one could work up a really promising management business which would have access to every side of the industry. And so I thought, what the hell, I'll give it a go.

I never was introduced to Cat Stevens. I introduced myself to Steve on the stairs one day. Angela Lansbury I was never allowed to meet. If John Osborne came to the offices, he and Barry met behind closed doors and I was never allowed to have anything substantial to do with Peter Finch. Ian McShane was more outgoing and was for some reason made more available to me, perhaps because I was responsible for him being in Herb Ross's THE LAST OF SHEILA. From the very first day I arrived, Barry and I never once sat down and discussed strategy or the development of the business in any structured way at all ... Like HOW were we going to build this management business he had talked about?

Barry was always too busy, always rushing off. His attention span seemed to have been terminally blighted. When I look back, he was hardly ever in the country. On the way to Heathrow, he would arrange that I accompany him in the limousine only to find that there was invariably someone else there or that we would stop off on the way at his home in Walham Grove which negated discussions of any meaningful length.

I realised after a very short time that Barry didn't run a business, he winged it. He was a very lucky man that his moment came at a time in the development of show business when anything went. The whole process of adding on pop music to the body of the business already gorged and giddy with the explosion of television and movies around the world had put everyone on a high. When you're on a high, anything goes ...

Having accepted that my future was not going to be in management, I decided that I had better get back to casting at the earliest opportunity. It became clear that Barry's idea had been to associate with me so that I could fend for him during his absences from London which Steve's burgeoning international career necessitated. As far as I was concerned, the idea didn't come off. I remember going to the Festival at Cannes to hold Jerzy Skolimowski's hand whilst his film was being shown because Barry had promised to be there and ultimately didn't make it. The nicest part of those few months was being right next door to the White Elephant Club. I didn't have far to go for my lunch.

It's an odd business. There are really very few companies which have succeeded in total management of the careers of so many clients involved in so many aspects of the business. Sure, there are people like Kris Kristofferson who can make that cross over from one area of work to another and of course Streisand is the exception which proves the rule. Barry was trying to do too much. He had Cat Stevens, after all.

As far as Steve himself is concerned, I thought he was very

sweet. I also thought he was physically a very beautiful young man. I am a classical music person and was not at all familiar with his music but I thought he was a poet. Without doubt. Very simple, yes but nonetheless a poet. And I thought he was a wonderful performer. Simple, straightforward. I loved that memorable concert at the Albert Hall and was so impressed by the way he enthralled his audience. There were no screams or yells during his concerts. You could hear every word he sang and the audiences were so reverent."

CHAPTER ELEVEN

HELPING HANDS...

The Bernard Jacobsen gallery is a great space for seeing pictures. You feel immediately re-assured as to the status and quality of the work you're viewing. Bernard's gallery and the one he had for several years in Los Angeles are merely the outward reflection of a sensitised and sensitive art lover, whose own persona and life have equipped him to be both appreciative and encouraging of artistic talent. No wonder Cat Stevens found that he was able to work so well with Bernard when together they produced the TEASER AND THE FIRECAT book.

Bernard began his career as a print publisher, dealing more in etchings and lithographs, many by David Hockney. Nowadays the gallery invariably displays the work of painters such as the current exhibition of Ivon Hitchens' landscapes, quintessentially British, nay English, canvases in the sense of location, substance and colour but yet composed with that erudite, almost careless expertise obviously hard-won from a lifetime of work and years of studying French painters like Cezanne. Whatever Bernard hangs on his walls, it simply breathes, 'The Best'.

BERNARD JACOBSON: "It's all so long ago now but I always remember it as a wonderful, golden time. Meeting Barry Krost and then being introduced to Steve and working with him on the TEASER AND THE FIRECAT book was amongst the more fortunate experiences of my life. I thought Barry was just wonderful. Charming and adorable. He could also drive you crazy!

I'd spent 1968 in the United States, working in a gallery in New York. I came back to England in 1969 and opened a tiny gallery of my own in Mount Street. When I say tiny, I mean cupboard. I could almost touch the opposite walls by standing in the middle of the space and holding my arms up. But it was Mount Street and it was £10 a week, including a secretary and the rates and the bills. There was a little daylight at one end and I called it my L-Shaped Room.

After a year or so, I decided that moving on was the only alternative and found premises at 10 Clifford Street, opposite where I am now although the rent on that space doubled. I swallowed hard and took it. In those days, the rent was £20 a week! I was very much into etchings and lithographs then - David Hockney and Ivor Abrahams, Peter Blake and William Tillyer as well as Andy Warhol and many others.

One day, after lunch I think, in walked Barry Krost. It was as simple as that. I remember it was after lunch because he was in buoyant mood and he bought something, I think a Hockney print. I feel he'd agree when I say we became instant friends. There was an immediate rapport which then grew into a sort of fraternal thing, real affection. Sometimes it was as though I was the older brother and he, the madcap, devil-may-care younger, wilder one. Then, the tables would be turned and it would be me who'd feel all little-brotherish. He'd always fool around, sit on my knee, that kind of thing and it was all so outrageous that I never thought anything about his behaviour until one day I confronted him with my assistant whom I deemed vitally short of a boyfriend. She adored Barry too but when I steered the situation around to trying to make a date between them, Barry came out. And very wittily did he do it and left me in no uncertainty as to his preference. I like that. I like sexual people, people who burn on a sexual fuse. I miss it today. People, and surprisingly a lot of people in the art world, don't seem very sexual. Rather above it. Makes for cold work, I think and a cold world.

Anyway, Barry led me into his world and it was a very warm world. I'm not sure how he felt about mine. He certainly bought from me but he never got really involved in the art business. His world was so glamourous, so exciting. Initially, I felt absolutely innocent and didn't quite understand all the ins and outs of the operation Barry ran at his offices in Curzon Street. I know it was intriguing and as the years passed, progressively more exciting. You'd walk up those stairs at Curzon Street and as well as Cat Stevens, you'd bump into Peter Finch or Mike Hodges or Angela

Lansbury, Ian McShane ... A host of names. There was a great family sort of atmosphere there too, as though everyone really cared.

Barry was very generous with his contacts and his friends. We really started to hang out together a lot and he brought many of his clients and friends into my gallery to the extent that he'd always tease me by telling me how much commission I owed him! People like Peter Finch and Michael York are two that spring to mind.

And of course, there was Steve.

I can't talk of these years and Steve without talking about Barry almost in the same breath. To me, they were pretty much inseparable as light in my life. And, in each others' lives too, although their talents and potential led them in very different directions. They really were like brothers, very much at and as one in many things. They certainly enjoyed each other's company enormously.

Apart from them being possibly taken for brothers physically, they had something of the same intelligence. A native intelligence which didn't depend on academic knowledge at all, the sort of knowledge that I and all my colleagues in the art world had built up and worked from. Barry's and Steve's cerebral ability was almost street-wise, almost non-intellectual but yet pulsating with intelligence if that makes sense. Barry's took the form of a quick, almost butterfly mind, a humming bird's instinct for darting about from one honey flower to the next. He was a superb deal-maker, a fantastic wheeler-dealer. Steve needed that talent to convey his creativity to the world.

I also think Barry legitimised Steve too. Barry was into movies and theatre and knew a lot of people from across the showbiz spectrum. In those days, pop stars, rock stars, call them what you want, hadn't yet crossed the divide which separated the heights of art from the depths of the popular. Steve was very eager to be considered an artist and Barry, physically taking him into the company of writers and directors and actors, also physically helped push back the boundaries of what was acceptable to the cultural establishment, not only because of the money which came with pop music but because a lot of it was bloody good. Steve bought from me, some of his purchases being presents for Barry. It was odd that way he had of buying for others. He certainly used his money but it was never for himself. I didn't feel he was acquisitive for himself.

In a way they were making up the rules for themselves as they went along. They had to. After all, they had both strayed, almost unbidden except by great good fortune, into unfamiliar territory. There was no protocol or even the sketchiest of manuals about how a rock star should be a rock star. Now I look back on it, Steve especially was very much on his own but then so was Barry... There was no training course you could go on to teach you how to be a manager. Like swimming, if you're pushed into the ocean without a life-belt, what can you do but swim for it?

Steve had many facets to his talents. I vaguely even remember something about his having written a musical too. Anyway, he had apparently told Barry that he wanted to do a book and Barry simply put the idea to me. It started, of course with the TEASER AND THE FIRECAT album cover. And so we talked.

Steve and I went out lots of times together, walking around Mayfair, the area round the gallery, just talking. He handled being out in public, being a star in public very well. In England he wasn't mobbed, not like he was in America, but people definitely recognised him. One couldn't help being aware of muttered: "Look, there's Cat Stevens!" as we walked along.

One of the things which drew me to the idea of being involved with Steve and a book which as yet didn't even exist was that I too had my ambitions, one of which was to attempt to lessen both the common perception and the red-blooded reality that the art world was somewhat elitist. It was 1972 and I'd been in the art world for four years. It was time for me to move on, not geographically this time but with what I wanted to do with my life. I too wanted to push back boundaries and widen horizons but the way I had decided I'd like to make my mark was by softening the forbidding face which I felt the art world showed the rest of humanity by making entry to that world more accessible and available. By working with a rock star, what better way of doing it?

I don't know how much of the storyline of TEASER Steve had already worked out when we first talked but the book was developed in the sequence of story first, then illustrations. It was a new experience working with a star as opposed to working with artists. Certain artists, painters I'm talking about, are a mass of self-doubt, always needing encouragement and pats on the back although at the same time displaying an often ferocious suspicion of any criticism whether real or implied. Steve was totally different.

After we'd made the decision to work together, that I would

publish his TEASER book, I saw no work in progress whatsoever. The whole thing, text and twenty illustrations, arrived as a package. There it was. Complete. Finished, delivered, just like, I presume, an album is delivered to the record company in the form of master tapes. No self-doubts, no "Is it good?" or "God! I just hate it now" angst that can accompany new work from even very established artists. Steve knew exactly what he wanted and what he was prepared to give.

I was still reeling from the way that the project had come together and couldn't quite believe it was all happening. After all, it wasn't the sort of book that Barry would have had any problem selling to any of the major publishing houses. No one except the highest of the high-minded would have turned down a Cat Stevens book. Steve was by this time an international superstar and the overseas sales potential of a book by him would have been at least as big by 1972 as John Lennon's IN HIS OWN WRITE had been almost a decade earlier. I kept on thinking: "*Why me?*" But as it was me and there was no one else hovering behind me, waiting to snatch the book away from me, I got on with it.

Steve very much wanted to communicate. By quite simply and sincerely addressing the book to the children of the world he was floating his creation to the adult world too for the grown-ups would be the ones who bought the book to give to their children.

We sat down and worked out together the selection of the eleven languages into which the text would ultimately be translated. I wanted Japanese and French, for example, whilst Steve insisted on Chinese and, obviously, Greek. I don't know how Welsh got to be on the list, perhaps because of Alun Davies, Steve's guitarist but Welsh was certainly one of Steve's insistence. I arranged for the text to be translated and when that had been done via translation agencies, we were ready to finalise the design of the book. This was the preserve of Gordon House who did all the catalogues for the gallery. Brian Aris who now works so selectively that only Sting and few favoured others get the benefit of his talent, took the fabulous photograph for the reverse cover of Steve squatting on a floor cushion. The paper we selected was of excellent quality, the highest available and the printing was done by the Hillingdon Press at Uxbridge. The book was bound in soft cover.

TEASER AND THE FIRECAT was published later in 1972. It became a cult book in Great Britain but in the United States where, having sold the rights to Scholastic Magazines in 1973, the book was published at a lower price and, with no objection from Steve at all, printed on lesser quality paper. It was a runaway best-seller, moving hundreds and thousands of copies. It became adopted as school learning text and I should imagine many thousands of American children used it as one of the books which fostered their literacy.

I'm very proud of it and regard it very much as an important part of my own retrospective. My sons, Scott and Jesse now twelve and fifteen respectively, have introduced it to their schoolfriends amongst whom they are kind of mini-stars as their dad is the one who published the little book. I have to say that however far I drifted from further involvement in rock and roll after Steve and I and, to an extent, Barry and I saw less of each other after 1975, having children at least keeps you up to date with Cat Stevens music which, along with a lot of seventies oldies, is enjoying a renaissance with the re-issue of TILLERMAN and TEASER on compact disc.

Publishing the TEASER book quantitatively proved just how right I was in seeing the art world as somewhat removed from reality. Up to that point, I had always thought that my friend David Hockney was famous. No, I thought he was VERY famous. David will forgive me, I'm sure, when I say that his fame was as nought when compared to someone like Cat Stevens. We were literally deluged with mail ... It came by the sackful and what I had published wasn't new record, which would have been pounced upon or a film, which would have been more immediate ... It was a book. A little book.

For many devoted fans, this book was yet another way they could feel themselves a bit closer to their favourite and by writing to the address inside the book, it was another avenue open to them for direct, one-to-one contact. To say I was taken aback by the response would be a gross understatement.

I realise now, in hindsight, that however close I thought I'd become to Steve, I never really knew him at all. On those walks we went on, we'd talk about many things but never anything personal. I wouldn't have known who, if anyone, he was going out with for example. I suppose it didn't cross my mind then that it was odd that I didn't know. I think that this privacy he maintained even with people he worked closely with had something to do with the uncertainty that his religious quest engendered. I know Barry was very confused by it. The seriousness of Steve's involvement with

Islam was one which I honestly don't think Barry really understood and, therefore, which he found very hard to accept and run with.

But, as we now know, Steve was only too serious and there was a drifting apart. With all of us. I saw Steve very much as an innocent, almost a character in the Tenessee Williams mould. There was something I can only describe as slightly dark there, something un-revealed, probably because it was un-revealable except in the poetry of the music. It certainly came over even in the TEASER book. The text is not at all soppy. It has a hard edge. It was very well-conceived, well-thought out. It was aimed at children but there was undoubtedly an adult inference. Some might say his songs were sentimental but they all had a hard substance, sometimes a very tough core idea.

Although I declare this with great affection both for Steve and for all our times together, I can't honestly say that had he not been who he was I would have encouraged him to take up a living as a professional artist.

He had an undeniable illustrative talent although the individual illustrations for the TEASER text display a power and authority which make them more like poems than work which could be readily utilised by a graphics editor in publishing. As illustrations of his own work however, they are highly individual, unmistakeable in style and very expressive of the creative individuality. Steve had an obvious facility and a great eye for what he considered as acceptably perfect for publication or release. He was, as would be expected of a perfectionist, fastidious in our discussions concerning the production and therefore the ultimate quality of the TEASER book.

He also had a canny eye for detail. I always smile when I remark on the way he chose to paint the hole left by a missing knot in one of the wooden slats of the fence depicted in the cover drawing of TEASER AND THE FIRECAT. Through this hole we see the continuing rail to which the fence slats are nailed. It's just a little detail but as with all those known for their meticulous eye, it could so easily have been omitted or not even thought of.

I like that little detail. For me, it sort of crosses the T in Cat and Stevens. After all, he could have been just plain old Cal Slevens."

What Cat Stevens achieved in the few years of his reborn career in the 70's was phenomenal. He was continually pushing back boundaries, driving forward the development of his work and showing the way how to always give audiences something new, the way ahead for others to follow. Sadly, few have done so. Very rarely have any of the big careers which have now spanned three decades creatively encompassed as many areas that Steve essayed in his seven short years.

Of the cartoon film of MOONSHADOW Steve had special reason to be proud. However, trying to trace anyone who had any recollections of the making of the cartoon film of MOONSHADOW which Steve used in concerts proved difficult. I wasn't sure if the film was ever used anywhere other than in the concert context. If would be sad if it hasn't, because like the book of TEASER AND THE FIRECAT, it is a little jewel. Finally, Bev Roberts emerged via enquiries made of Roger and Val Woodburn and Brian Harding.

BEV ROBERTS: "Yes ... MOONSHADOW was made by us at TRICKFILM in about 1972, I should think. I have a feeling that the whole project came about because of David Putnam and Sandy Lieberson at VPS. I think they knew Barry Krost. Anyway, we got chosen to make the MOONSHADOW cartoon.

We were a pretty significant animation studio. Charlie Jenkins and Pete Russell ran it. Charlie had consolidated his reputation by creating the ELEANOR RIGBY and ALTOGETHER NOW sequences in the Beatles' film YELLOW SUBMARINE.

The studios were in Charlotte Mews, all a part of Soho and the film area. I suppose I've been involved in Soho all my working life from those days of the early sixties when we'd go to THE MACABRE in Meard Street and THE HELLFIRE, two of the better coffee bars. The Hellfire had Gerry Mulligan and Lester Young on the juke box. You went to coffee bars for the music as much as anything else. I was living in Regents Park in 1962. There were five of us, including Jimmy Jacques who wrote THE HAND JIVE. I remember our kitchen was papered with old copies of DOWNBEAT, the Jazz magazine. Previously I'd had a room in Kinky Hall in Westbourne Grove. It was a rooming place with a bar that was open all night. Johnny Hawkesworth lived there and I remember Jess Conrad was always around at the Regents Park flat. But we didn't socialise much where we lived. The West End and Soho were always where we went.

It was the days when wacky baccy was beginning to be everywhere. Two pounds fifty an ounce then. We'd go to RONNIE

SCOTT'S where it first started up in Gerrard Street before it moved to Frith Street and Jimmy's at the bottom end of Frith Street was always the best restaurant. Big plate of stew and a huge plate of bread cut into doorsteps. White-tiled tube of a place. It's still there but not the same. I remember Jack Spot was a very prominent figure on the scene in those days, fabled as head of London's underworld. He had a club in Kings Road Chelsea and we used to go there with Ray Merrill who sang with the Stapleton band. When the club closed early in the morning, they'd just used to leave us in there. Never even bother to throw us out. The whole of the West End and Soho has changed now. It was the eighties that finally did it. It became very false and over-commercialised.

Steve was very much a West End boy. He knew all this, same as we all did. When I first met him, I remember sitting in Lacey's in Whitfield Street with Charlie Jenkins and being pleasantly surprised that Steve was a really ordinary sort of bloke. Obviously you were aware of who he was but there was no fuss about him. He came over as pretty sane and the early seventies were a pretty mad era. You could tell he came from just down the road. He came across as very personable and quiet and he could laugh a lot as well as having a serious side to him. I remember talking about vegetarianism that first time we met and Steve saying did anyone know that tomatoes screamed when you cut into them? It sounds as though that was when he was into his buddhist thing. But everyone talked about things like that than. It was an era of finding out.

I was aware of his work too. We'd used two tracks, LONGER BOATS being one of them, for a film we'd made in 1970 for Vogue in New York. It was a ten minute film of that season's autumn collections featuring designers from all over the world and photographers like Bailey, Penn and Avedon. Steve's music worked really well but then I wasn't surprised. I'd always liked it. Good, clean tracks.

I must say we were a bit vague about why he wanted to do the cartoon but the whys didn't matter really. It was a job and we just got on with it. Although, independently, I was first aware of the character on the album cover, I think it was the TEASER AND THE FIRECAT drawings Steve brought in first. Looking at them again, I'm struck by how much their style and execution reflected what I thought of him as a person. They're very individual. Couldn't possibly have been done by anyone else.

The process of making a film like Steve's usually took about three months at TRICKFILM. It starts by listening to the track and making a scene by scene and link by link breakdown according to the lines. Talking about it again, the scene I vividly remember is where the sea goes up into the clouds! From this, a storyboard is produced with each scene sketched out.

When the producer, in this case Steve, has approved the storyboard and made any changes, then the animation process begins and there are several people involved in this process. Errol Lecain, who sadly died in his early fifties, was the animator on MOONSHADOW and he worked with Sue Day. Errol as the chief animator on this one did the key drawings and Sue did what is known as the 'in-betweens', which are basically the movement drawings, the sequence which when seen at 'x' number of frames per second gives the impression that TEASER has turned round to look at the moon.

Both the animator and the 'in-betweener' work with a back-ground artist who, believe it or not, provides the backgrounds! On MOONSHADOW, the backgrounds would be, for example, the fence, the ground and the sky on that famous TEASER cover illustration. Over these backgrounds which are reproduced however many times a sequence required them, the animators, working on paper, overlay their drawings, each set-up slightly differently drawn than that which pre or proceeds it. There can be two or eight or even, though this would be a record, thirty two overlays. The built-up layered work is then given to a 'paint and trace' artist who transfers the assemblage to a piece of celluloid, a 'cell'.

This is the work which is photographed and usually, I was the rostrum cameraman, the person who takes the still photographs of the finished artwork before the editor strings them all together but on MOONSHADOW I was in charge of the dub. Here, the voice-over, the sound effects and the music track get 'dubbed' on to the film. We were using the original album track. No re-recording took place. Arthur Mullard and Spike Milligan were the voices, a brainwave piece of casting by Pete Russell. Sound effects come from a library. You just pay a licence fee and you can get any sound you choose.

Steve was so easy to work with. As far as I can remember, after the story board, he never came in much and certainly never to check or to oversee as a producer, and in this case, the star could have done. After all, he was paying for it. It was as though he'd made his choice and just trusted us to get on with it. Having said that, it wasn't as though he didn't care. He was always interested in the process and it was obvious by the way he picked things up and cottoned on that he was very bright and very eager to learn about new things.

I only ever saw the film screened at TRICKFILM. I never saw it in concert although I know someone who saw it when Steve played Drury Lane and loved it. I wish we could see it again."

No sooner had Bev materialised than a few weeks later, blanket advertisements appeared on British television announcing the latest re-launch of an album entitled THE VERY BEST OF CAT STE-VENS. Part of the MOONSHADOW film accompanied the advertise-ment. I'm glad to see that commerce still has its fingers on the buttons. I wonder why the public can't be allowed the same treats?

Continuing this theme of Steve's continual itch to learn, to try out new areas of possibility for his work, I have to of course include the film of HAROLD AND MAUDE. Sadly, the account of it has to be mine for both the creative parents are now dead. Hal Ashby, its director died first followed by Colin Higgins, its writer and creator in 1988.

HAROLD AND MAUDE surfaced in Steve's life in 1972.

At Curzon Street, Barry had been getting calls for some time from a production office at Paramount in Hollywood and the calls were about Cat Stevens doing some music for a film. There were obviously dozens of calls enquiring about Steve. Would Steve do this? Would Steve do that? By 1972, everyone in the office was pretty much aware what Steve would be likely to do and what he wouldn't. He obviously wasn't a supermarket opener nor a prospective reader-out of nominations at BAFTA and he also, as far as we were aware, wasn't currently in the market of writing any music other than for his own albums. He had only once allowed his music to be used on a sound track, Jerzy Skolimowski's film of DEEP END.

Barry must have taken one of these Hollywood calls because a script duly arrived. The arrival of a script in the office was not an unusual event. Scripts arrived daily in both posts and that they were sent at all usually indicated that they would never reach the person for whom they were intended. For people like Peter Finch and the other major stars Barry handled, a financial offer or at least a ballpark conversation about money came before any script. Because Barry wasn't at all fond of reading, it was my job to be the script reader.

I'd probably get through about ten scripts a week, in addition to my other work; I'd write little reports and clip them to the script cover and perhaps, just perhaps, Barry would skim through the ten line report.

HAROLD AND MAUDE was already being made. The movie was all but in the can. Barry's picking up the telephone was not a live or die situation for HAROLD AND MAUDE, but, the producers were obviously pretty insistent that the script get to Cat Stevens.

I laughed myself off my chair as I read HAROLD AND MAUDE. Like the movie itself when I eventually came to see it, I didn't want the last page to come. I not only laughed, I cried and cried and laughed and cried some more. HAROLD AND MAUDE was as moving and as funny with just the pictures in my mind as it was when it ended up on the screen.

I suppose it's the purity of it, the utterly sacred nature of the energy that Colin was writing about. I've seen it, and indeed experienced it, between two men, two women, a man and a woman, between a younger and a very much older person. It has nothing to do with sex or wayward, disturbed emotions. It has to do with something so deep-seated and so absurdly powerful that when you weep over it, you feel that at that moment, if you died, you wouldn't be scared and you wouldn't regret and you'd be glad to be who and where you were because you'd experienced that incredibly deep, penetrating and all-pervasive feeling of total knowledge. It's unendurable pleasure, it's holy and yet painfully mortal. It's about incredible strength and helpless vulnerability. It's about riding every emotional continuum a man or woman, girl or boy could experience. I think it's what being human is all about. It's life and death. It's indescribable because it is pure love.

I begged Barry to read HAROLD AND MAUDE and begged him to talk to Steve about it. It transpired that the production wasn't after new music, they wanted to use the songs from TILLERMAN and MONA BONE JAKON as they existed. As it turned out, they were to get much more ... I stand to be corrected but I think it was the first time a film was to attempt to employ contemporary pop music as a sound track.

Well, the long and the short was that Barry must have arranged for Steve to see the film and then Steve talked to Paul

Samwell-Smith and they thought it was a great idea and off they went to LA and HAROLD AND MAUDE's soundtrack got married to the Cat Stevens dub. Paul and Rosie Samwell-Smith had two wonderful Siamese cats for years called Harold and Maude.

HAROLD AND MAUDE was not a box office success when it first came out. It is now, of course and it is legendary and seminal, the stuff of every teenager's emotional bankroll. It was a huge success on the continent, especially in France where Cat Stevens was such a huge star. HAROLD AND MAUDE played continuously at one Paris Cinema for, literally, years.

Colin Higgins died in 1988. I couldn't believe that the world had been robbed of the promise of more wonderful work from the creator of SILVER STREAK, FOUL PLAY, NINE TO FIVE and THE BEST LITTLE WHOREHOUSE IN TEXAS. By the time he died, Steve had been in retirement for a decade having last released product in 1978. Surely Steve had had as much if not more to say than Colin Higgins?

Steve wrote two extra songs for HAROLD AND MAUDE, neither of which have ever been released in the UK or the USA except on the soundtrack of the film. It's not true about death having no sting and graves having no victory. Death and graves have it every time.

Chapter Twelve

SHAKING HANDS
WITH MIDAS

A lot of people were inevitably attracted by and to Cat Stevens and, concomitantly, to Barry Krost. The Midas Syndrome is well-documented. Why it is so widely thought that by rubbing shoulders with gilded people, some of that gilt will rub off is a mystery but yet it's one of the motivating rationales of the business world, no matter what the product. Success is supposed to be contagious even though it has been proved decidedly to be merely infectious.

Lots of hopefuls beat a path to Barry's door. I remember Lynsey de Paul taking a couple of meetings. I remember David Essex coming up those stairs. I remember Mike d'Abo, eager for another career after MANFRED MANN. When Mike signed a management contract with Barry Krost, I remember thinking, *'When is this empire-building going to stop?'* I honestly couldn't see that we could do justice to all of them. But still they kept coming as Steve's career went from strength to strength. Barry later explained his philosophy to me in no uncertain terms. If they move, sign 'em. If they stop moving, dump 'em.

Colin Blunstone became a client of Barry's in 1972. He is both blessed and cursed, for his voice is one of those in the annals of music history that is so distinctive that it is unmistakeably his. He is a sensitive writer as well as one of rock's truly gifted interpreters. Perhaps, for Colin, the best is yet to come for there is an audience out there which not only remembers him from the time of THE

ZOMBIES and later from his seventies hits but which, now grown up alongside him, is waiting to hear more.

COLIN BLUNSTONE: "I wasn't sure that I was going to have a lot to contribute but now I've been prodded into thinking and recounting, there were some important aspects of my own life and career which were very much influenced by Cat Stevens.

THE ZOMBIES, which consisted of Rod Argent, Chris White, Paul Atkinson, Hugh Grundy and myself, got together whilst we were at school. I was at St. Albans Grammar school whilst the others were at St. Albans' School, all except Chris White who although at my grammar school was two years older than I and as such I didn't really know him at school, age gaps being what they are at such tender years. I was never supposed to be the lead singer. It was Rod who was the real driving force behind getting a band together and to start with he had me earmarked as the rhythm guitarist. Our first meeting was very inauspicious. It was on a street corner in St. Albans and I arrived with two black eyes and a bandage across my face holding in a broken nose, a trophy from a recent rugby match. Things just happened for us, really but by 1967, after completing our last album ODESSEY AND ORACLE, it was reluctantly agreed that the time had come for the band to break up. The ODESSEY album, sadly, had not attracted any significant record company attention.

As THE ZOMBIES, we had been touring almost continuously for the past three years. We worked under the formidable management of Tito Burns who was also our agent. People like Tito, Dick Katz, Harold Davison were all-important to young bands in those days. If an agent like Tito heard and liked your record, his contacts throughout the business were so strong and so powerful that he could ensure you exposure on the three major television shows which then made hit records. There was no radio promotion then as commercial radio only just about existed in the form of the pirate stations like Radio Caroline on ships outside the three mile offshore limit. ITV's THANK YOUR LUCKY STARS, Rediffusion's READY STEADY GO! and the BBC's JUKE BOX JURY and later TOP OF THE POPS ... These were the shows that made hits. Tito's links had been forged for many years and held up in variety shows too so that many artists looked after by Tito and the other major agents were able to cross over into more mainstream entertainment.

However, I decided that I needed to take a break from the

music business altogether and so much to everyone's amazement, including my own, I took an office job in central London, working for the Sun Alliance insurance company in St. James.

Working in an office was a revelation! It was frantic but stable and secure. There were many new people to meet and skills to learn. I ended up working in the burglary department. I was enjoying myself and slowly beginning to forget about ODESSEY AND ORACLE, a strange title bestowed upon the work by Rod and Chris.

It came completely out of the blue when TIME OF THE SEASON, a track from that forgotten album became a huge hit in America. A lot of its success came because Al Kooper from BLOOD SWEAT AND TEARS had heard some of the album and had liked it so much that he pushed it very hard with CBS. In the USA, the ODESSEY AND ORACLE title was ditched and it was re-titled TIME OF THE SEASON.

In my new found office world it was not really easy or encouraged to take private telephone calls but as news of THE ZOMBIES' success in America became known, I was bombarded with offers to record again.

One of these callers was Mike Hurst. Mike had been a member of THE SPRINGFIELDS together with Tom and Dusty Springfield and had since become a record producer. One of the main reasons I decided to record again, with Mike, was that he had produced those great early Cat Stevens tracks I LOVE MY DOG, MATTHEW AND SON and I'M GONNA GET ME A GUN. That orchestral style of production was very fashionable at the time and I liked the 'Mike Hurst sound' a lot for which he used excellent arrangers, people like Phil Dennys and Alan Tew.

And so, faced with Mike's persuasive and infectious enthusiasm and remembering his successes with Steve, I found myself back in a recording studio but I was thinking of it more as a fun project rather than a full-time career. As Mike Hurst's affairs were managed by Mel Collins and, being assured by Mike that Mel had also looked after Cat Stevens' affairs, I also went to see Mel at his Townsend House offices in Dean Street.

When Mike suggested I should re-record the old ZOMBIES hit SHE'S NOT THERE, I thought ... Why not? At least I already knew the words! He also wanted me to change my name to James MacArthur until it was pointed out that there was a James MacArthur in HAWAII-FIVE-O. And so I eventually became Neil MacArthur, spending a whole year in that guise. This may all sound a little haphazard and in truth it was. I can only say in my defence that I still had no intention of becoming a full-time musician again and that I just got 'carried along by the flow'. And, in due order, as Neil MacArthur, I became a client of Mel Collins for the purposes of the six sides that Mike recorded at Olympic Studios in Barnes.

SHE'S NOT THERE, put out on the Deram label for Decca, became a minor hit, charting somewhere in the thirties but two other singles that followed didn't fare so well. As far as I can remember my relationship with Mike Hurst seemed to just slowly fade away and with it, my incarnation as Neil MacArthur. Sadly, a band in the USA called THE ROAD also had a hit with SHE'S NOT THERE at the same time I was having my second hit with it in Britain and so I was never able to use Neil MacArthur as any kind of springboard in America.

However, by now, the music business bug had bitten again and it was a pleasant surprise when my old friends Rod Argent and Chris White offered to produce and write for me. I decided finally to retire from the hectic world of commerce to pursue more ethereal goals once again.

I started working with Rod and Chris in 1970 and the album ONE YEAR became the first of a deal we got with CBS, co-incidentally using Active records, Mel Collins' record company, as the conduit. Eventually the Denny Laine song SAY YOU DON'T MIND was released as a single and, thankfully, had chart success in 1972 when it reached number fifteen.

I had been able to write four tracks on my ONE YEAR album and was becoming increasingly aware how important it was to write in order to develop a career and maintain some form of credibility as an artist. My new-found interest in writing led me in the direction of publishers in general and Rondor Music in particular where I had long discussions with Derek Green and Bob Grace. It seems that some of my more cynical mates had noticed that my song-writing productivity increased at the slightest hint of a break-up in any of my relationships with girlfriends ... Did they? Would they? No, I'm sure that tottering relationships would never have been given a helping hand by those eager to see a couple of new songs ... Would they?

Seriously though, my reborn career seemed to be taking shape apace and CBS were pushing very hard for me to find a manager with some kind of international reputation. For my part it seemed that everything was going pretty well as it was. I was working with old friends and together we were making hits.

However, when Bob Grace suggested a meeting with Barry Krost, CBS were very, very keen.

Here my path crossed with Cat Stevens' again. Managed by Barry Krost, Steve was having incredible worldwide success. Barry was a very powerful negotiator and was one of the world's great characters. I signed a three year management deal with him and we immediately completed a very good publishing agreement for me with Rondor. Jackie Krost was brought in to look after my day-to-day career and I got on with my second album for CBS.

I only met Steve a few times but I greatly admired him as a writer and as a performer as I followed him from producer to manager. As well as being hugely talented, he seemed to me to be quietly determined and surprisingly organised, seemingly always managing to write, record and tour inside any deadline which I was rarely able to do!

In 1975 I left Barry's office and so lost any contact I had had with Steve. My journeys have taken me all over America and Europe since then, though I know Steve has taken a different path. I often think of him and wish him every happiness in his new life.

I'm left with a nagging memory at the end of all this reminiscing. I believe that Barry had spoken to Steve about the possibility of his producing some tracks for me. I don't remember being told how far this suggestion had been taken and so it was with great surprise and completely off-guard that I took a telephone call one night. It was one of those infuriating moments when with a group of friends I was on the way out to somewhere pre-arranged and uncancellable; I had almost left the flat where I was living in West Hampstead when I heard the 'phone. I ran back in to answer it. It was Steve.

He asked me if I felt like coming over and playing through some songs with him. I mumbled, 'how wonderful' or something like that but then immediately made my excuses as I was being called from the hallway to hurry up. We obviously made an arrangement to call each other again but, well ... We never did."

There are so many 'ifs' in every life but never more so it seems than in the life of our subject and his peers. So many imponderables. In tracing back the specific line of cause and effect in Steve's career, areas are reached where being able to be specific is as impossible as alchemy even though the parameters in time and space can be identified when specific events took place. If one wasn't a sensible, logical and reasonably rational person, one could be very tempted into veering off at some silly and very unscientific tangent about fate and destiny and ....

That Steve was a pop star once is a quantum-enough leap of circumstance. That he should achieve not only equal but greater significance later on a second-go-around, is, in betting terms, a virtual impossibility. It has happened to only a very few. Neil Sedaka is one. There are probably a couple of others. Barry's company seemed to specialise in old rockers desperate for a renaissance. Having settled in California, Barry even had a go with Dusty Springfield. Steve was always friendly to Barry's other clients when they met in the office, always polite, even occasionally deferential. After all, he had known most of them on the first go around and there was he having his second.

I know so many who would have liked to have had that second go-around, who were in many ways just as talented as Steve, perhaps even more articulate, more wide-spread in their capabilities and potential but who just didn't ultimately cut the cosmic mustard.

For several years in the early seventies I tried my damndest, and against overwhelming odds in the office, to revivify the career of my friend TWINKLE RIPLEY. Lynn Annette Ripley found fame as TWINKLE in the mid-sixties, the same time that Steve first got lucky. Twinkle was interesting for her songs. She had two memorable hits, the first being TERRY and the other GOLDEN LIGHTS. Both these self-compositions from a poor-little-rich-girl were story-songs, movies-in-miniature. TWINKLE's writing was immediate and very black-and-white; some wanting to be clever and cruel would call it simplistic. But she wasn't merely bubblegum, she wasn't only pop disposable. I knew she wrote well, I knew she had something but I couldn't make it work.

I couldn't make it work because I didn't have the knowledge and, together, we didn't have the luck that Steve and Barry had; all I possessed was ignorance born from being English and not know- ing about American country music. Neither did I have the power, that sheer force resident in my name which would have ensured that any and every record company executive in the world would have taken my call. Barry had that power. Barry could call anyone and speak to them because whoever he spoke to each fancied that one day they might get hold of some bit of Cat Stevens.

But Barry wasn't on my and TWINKLE's side.

It's too late now some fifteen years after the event for me to do anything about my failure but, strangely, it's still not too late for the Twinkles of the world. TWINKLE wrote aching, deceptively simple songs from the heart about loves lost and loves gone wrong and revenge and jealousy and home-making and love-after-death ... Wonderful songs that needed a producer who knew about country performers and an initial record company that was based in Nashville and then a bloody good publicist because Twink's story would have had them bawling on line to buy her music ... She was a country writer without a country. She was a country singer in a land where country is something green, pleasant and rolling and where there ain't no tortured hearts nor no blood on the corn, no hoboes, no dirt roads, no guitars, no guns ... None, at least, to speak of.

What we as audience and it as the industry needs at the moment is a little less ageism. I, for one, want to know about how people feel now, in their mid-forties, long after puppy love has become a shaggy dog story. And what about this luck thing? What IS luck? There are artists who don't appear to start out or make way with any disadvantages and who are bankrolled to the tune of thousands and funded with the expertise of those who are paid to know what it is that makes something work at a particular moment. Making something work is perceived to be a buyable talent, an over-the-counter facility. It's not. It's luck. It's something so indefinable that dilettantes like me have had to resort to calling it the 'X' factor.

We know about the material having to be sound, the artist-producer relationship being fecund, we know about the need to have the record company solidly behind you, we realise the importance of strong management reflecting the essential interest of the artist, we understand the cumulative acceleration of interest that successful reviews of live performance and enthusiastic initial airplay can generate ...

We know about good publicity, angled just right and spread evenly not to cause any competitive backlash, we know about good photographs ... we know all that. We know a lot of it's about fashion but we know a great deal of it's ultimately about luck. We also know success can in the first place be contrived; we know about THE MONKEES, the VILLAGE PEOPLE all those shooting stars that shot their way out of orbit. So why don't we know what the 'X' factor is?

Just what is it that makes hundreds of thousands of people go out and part with hard-earned money just to be able to listen to something?

Why, when we know so much about what doesn't make a hit, can we not do something for the legion of 'Disappointeds - Kent', 'Still hopings - Surrey', 'Always waitings - Essex'. Why can't we make stars?

The answer is that we can. We do. We are the people who make stars.

But we do it as individuals, as uncontrollable individuals not as a mass, a conformist market phantom at the beck of some industrial Svengali. What we, you and I, do when we hear a new song or a new artist is to react emotionally. Something chemical happens. If it happens right and for long enough it's like falling in love. It's chance and yet it's meant. It's unpredictable and yet in hindsight it's entirely logical.

And at the other end, when it's all over, it's like falling out of love. It happens equally quickly. There was a falling out between Cat Stevens and his public. All very predictable except that it was Steve who fell out of love with us.

CHAPTER THIRTEEN

ONE TWO, ONE TWO...

In the abscence of any replies to enquiries directed at the concert and tour promoters I had contacted hoping for their contribution to this account and being also constrained by lack of finance to pursue the American and Japanese promoters, I persuaded Carl Miller to help with both more background and detail to the Cat Stevens gigging years.

It is interesting to remark on the ultra-sensitive reactions which are often forthcoming from sources when approached to be part of historical books like this. Paranoia is too glib a word to describe the resounding silence which often follows an enquiry. Without people's memories, accurate assessments cannot be made and assessments will be made despite the silences. All that the silences ensure is that initial starting points, could very well be wrong and the resulting assessments therefore rendered inaccurate and invalid. Rock music is too important just to be ignored. There is already a Professorship of Contemporary Music established at a German University where the incumbent's background is in classical music. There will be more such Chairs established as time passes and the category of literature as an academic study is expanded to include the best and the worst and the most esoteric of the popular. This category has to expand as more and more people buy recorded music as opposed to literary fiction as published in paper books. The book is a dying piece of information technology.

As to the tarnished side of the coin, I would be the first to acknowledge that there is also a market for slime and sleaze, stories of sex and wrecked hotel rooms and impossibly wicked uses of a whole range of confectionery but these stories last a day and they're used the next to wrap up fish. Proper books with personal accounts and un-sensational conclusions will never go away despite their never being read by a large number of those who should figure in them.

Can these people even read, I wonder? They can certainly write as I often receive Christmas cards from them. So, to save them sending any more Christmas cards, 'Peace on earth, goodwill to all men (and women).'

Thanks, Carl. Take it away. One two. One two ... One two, one two.

CARL MILLER: "It's been the fate of many roadies and tour managers to go deaf and I thought my time had come way too early in my life. I'd only been working for Steve for a few months in 1971 and I'd been doing the sound for him on a lot of the small University gigs we'd been doing as well as in the studio or at rehearsals. I couldn't believe it but it was true. I was going a bit deaf. You have to remember that this was in the days before specialisation, before separate sound engineers who would delicately balance sound equipment for hours to achieve perfect acoustics.

'I think I'm going deaf, Steve.'

'Oh,' said Steve rather snidely, *'then that explains everything!'*

'Perhaps I should hand on to someone else?' I suggested.

'What? And leave?' Steve queried in disbelief.

'No. Hand on to a specialist. Someone who just does the sound and nothing else. Then I'd be free to get on with all the other stuff. You're getting bigger not smaller, y'know.'

'Of course!' Steve exclaimed. *'Let's get him in, then!'*

His reaction was immediate. His sense of what was right for a situation regarding his shows was not only unerring but exploratory and experimental and he would listen to everything, to every suggestion. He had no fear of forging ahead and was unstinting in expense to achieve the best. He was incredibly professional, was never late but always early and if you asked him to be somewhere at a certain time, you could rely on him one hundred percent. That was the up-side of working for Steve. His was a great academy to start off in and many road crew and technical staff have been pleased to have his credit on their CV. The old Cat Stevens crews are still rolling on very nicely with outfits like GENESIS in all its forms - Phil Collins, Peter Gabriel - George Michael, for whom Albert 'Spot' Laurence works - and Barry Manilow.

Cat Stevens shows became well-known for their hallmarks of originality and their impression of being just avant-garde enough to captivate the audience and lead them further down the path of their own imaginations rather than frighten them off unknown territory by creating an atmosphere they weren't comfortable with. Steve began touring in the early seventies when rock acts were not known for their theatricality. Even people like THE WHO, already authors of a rock opera, would go on stage and just play ... just the PA and the basics. Not much different in principle from when THE BEATLES played Shea stadium with a simple PA. No wonder no one could hear them above the screams.

To give credit where it's due, Barry Krost was the source of the Nile on this front. Steve must have sensed more than just business-wise that Barry was the right manager for the direction he wanted to follow for his second go around. Because of Barry's vast theatrical experience, it was he who galvanised Steve's thinking about presenting and formulating and building shows, about lighting and design. Barry turned a Cat Stevens gig into a performance and then into a show and then into a concert in the classical and theatrical sense. Steve knew very well what he wanted but he needed others to help him achieve it.

The Drury Lane concert in 1972 saw all these strands brought together in full flower for the first time. From Steve's name being displayed in neon on the marquee to the way the stage show was lit, presented and dressed, Steve's audience was spellbound and a standard had been set which every artist and band since has been affected by.

Eric Barrett who was James Taylor's lighting man had been flown in from America; he went on to work with Bowie and Madonna. Del Newman had been engaged as the conductor for an ad hoc orchestra specially recruited for the performance; John Thompson who has since created sound for both STATUS QUO and IRON MAIDEN sat behind the desk. Putting all that together and introducing the various components of the evening hidden behind drapes and curtains, building the show without the traditional support act from small beginnings to huge climaxes was innovative in the extreme. Everything down to the bazouki players!

We'd started doing gigs to promote MONA BONE JAKON and TEA FOR THE TILLERMAN in 1971. In those days it was Steve, Alun Davies, Larry Steele, me and a Ford Transit. There were a few calls from the mainly student audiences for some of the old Cat Stevens stuff as it was on the strength of those hits that he was being booked. Steve never gave in but once, when he played I LOVE MY DOG. I can't remember the place but I do remember that he sang it very tongue in cheek. Oh ... And once later on, under very great pressure from the audience, he did POP STAR in Boston but again, very tongue in cheek.

The early gigs were just that ... gigs. There was no thread or strand running through them. There were no such things as tours as we know them today. There were the circuits, the Odeons and stuff which had always been the venues for the fifties and sixties merry-go-rounds where up to ten or twelve acts would be on the same bill, like variety. Steve was one of the people to change all that forever. He was the first I believe to actually name a tour - BAMBOOZLE was the name of his 1974 World Tour and others like Bowie with THE MOONLIGHTING TOUR and Elton with the LOUDER THAN CONCORDE TOUR were soon to follow suit.

Those early gigs in England came out of a variety of agents and promoters. Richard Cowley at Chrysalis (which became in turn Cowbell and then World services), Andrew Miller, Adrian Hopkins, Barry Dickens and also Harvey Goldsmith. It certainly was far from star time in those early days. We got the booking and off we went. No fuss, no razzmatazz.

The first American tour in 1971 didn't seem all that big-time either. For a artist who was getting great airplay and whose second album was selling very well, it was all rather small-town. We played Doug Weston's TROUBADOUR as a return gig was part of the original deal whereby Steve got to play there with Carly Simon in 1970. Jock Maclean was on that tour with me. Jock, who is now a vice-President of Showtime and Paperview Inc., worked at the time for the New York lawyer/manager Nat Weiss on James Taylor and Carole King Tours.

In New Orleans we played THE WAREHOUSE, where Don Fox was the promoter. THE WAREHOUSE was an old railhead building with the tracks still functional out back. We did our usual sound check in the late afternoon. By the time we'd finished it was quite dark, one of those thick, humid Louisiana nights. Larry, me, Steve and Jock decided to go out and sit at the edge of the railway track and do a little looking at the moon. As we sat peacefully appreciating the luminous state of the mother goddess, the tranquillity of the scene was suddenly shattered as a bank of lights and beams were turned on us and someone started ordering us through a bullhorn to stay where we were ... It was both the local and the Louisiana State Police. We were grabbed and pinioned and spreadeagled over the fronts of the police cars and were decidedly mute in our response. It would hardly have paid us to announce that we were Cat Stevens and his entourage ... like who the fuck's Cat Stevens?

Anyway, the commotion brought Don Fox out from the venue who was told by his brother-in-law the Sheriff that: *'We just got some hippies here, Don!'*

'Hippies!' Don replied in alarm, *'they're my fuckin' artistes!'*

We got off any charges, thank heavens and the gig went well. I remember Jose Feliciano joining Steve on stage in part of the set. However, my lesson in the deep-down-South facts of life wasn't quite over. Way back then, before sophisticated payment and banking arrangements, it was part of the tour manager's job description to collect the gig money after the show in whatever way the contract had specified. On THE WAREHOUSE occasion the fee was to be paid in cash which amount was somewhere, I recall, between three and five thousand dollars. In Don's office, he handed me the bag containing the cash but the bag felt very much heavier than even five thousand dollars ought to have felt. I looked inside and there was the dull metal barrel of a .38 revolver. Before I could say anything, Don said: *'You're so goddam dumb, you better take it or you won't even get back to the hotel. Leave it with the desk clerk and I'll collect it in the morning!'*

The next tour of America was very different. We were on planes with both crew and gear and where we weren't on planes, there was a five vehicle tractor-trailer truck convoy with the tour tucked in it. Also, by the time of the next tour, we were under the aegis of Nat Weiss's syndicate. That sounds ominous but it was far from it. It was comforting and it made life much easier to have the big guns of rock 'n' roll with all their experience, expertise and business machinery covering you rather than gunning for you.

Nat Weiss was Peter Asher's associate and this relationship became the basis for the loose but entirely functional association which developed encompassing Nat and Peter, Barry Krost, Robert Stigwood and others including, I believe, John Reid. One could be forgiven for thinking that one really had stumbled on the Gay Mafia. In 1971, it was the strongest management syndicate in the music business and has never really been emulated since even by the corporate version established by Lieber Krebbs.

The artists represented by this cabale collectively dominated the rock scene at the time. With the photograph taken by David Bailey, Cat Stevens along with his peers was adorning the front covers of TIME Magazine. Rock music was bigger than mere big news.

The pool of intelligence gathered in the syndicate by the participating managements and their representatives about venue capacities, grosses, overheards, legal matters and inter-state legal differences, tax affairs, banking and financial arrangements even down to the strengths and weaknesses of local promoters and their competitors stood everyone in good stead. No longer did the gig money come in a brown paper bag with a gun to protect it and you!

The syndicate maximised the artists' income in safety and under the law and controlled secondary exploitation such as television and other media rights. Nat Weiss too had incredibly strong connections with the record company magnates, people like Ahmet and Nesui Ertegun and his connections were of general benefit to all involved.

A major saving which the syndicate achieved immediately was the elimination of any agency commission in making a booking with a promoter. Vincent Romeo at CMA, which ICM was called then, was Steve's agent for the first couple of years. After Vincent was head-hunted and left to move to London to manage the affairs of Paul and Linda Macartney, Barry really began to save although he was always, always looking round for the best deal for Steve, despite his ties, for in so doing Barry was also maximising his own income and potential and maintaining his viability as an independent operator. Typical of the promoters we worked with were Ron Delsener in the New York area, Barry Fey in and around Denver, Peter Asher in southern California, Bill Graham in the Bay area, Martin Onrott in Canada. Via Barry, Steve got some very, very good deals.

All this, you might say ... Ah, yes, but there was more to come for we were STILL giving away T-Shirts! Merchandising, as it became established, was virtually unknown and there was a feeling current that it was in some way infrading to make money out of posters and material which we considered merely advertising and promotional aids. That state of affairs didn't last long as you will well have appreciated over expensive years of concert-going! What happened was that the pirates turned 'legit'. Although merchandising was born in the States, it was soon developed in England by people like Mick Worwood and Adrian Hopkins. By the time of his last tour, Steve was well aware of the profits to be made from merchandising but he remained fastidious to a degree about the quality of what was sold. I remember the motif on the MAJICAT T-shirts was somehow finished in gold already.

The touring thing was faster growing than the proverbial rolling snowball. Very soon, every act had its own stage show. Though some parts of the music industry must in some respects now damn those who started it, the mushrooming size and therefore costs of touring a major rock act would have been started by someone. Better, in my opinion, for it to have been begun by people with a great deal of sensitivity and taste and style like Nat, Barry and the other guys. Though the punters obviously paid for it in the end in the way of increased ticket prices, they certainly gained better value for their money.

Standards of technical and engineering specifications were also becoming more sophisticated and exacting. Steve, for example, employed the use of the first customised and computerised monitor speaker system for his stage and studio work which was designed and built by Chuck Conrad, the ex-SHOW CO engineer who we met via CROSSROADS AUDIO in Dallas, Texas. Chuck's wife Diane chalked up another first for the Cat Stevens Show by becoming the first female roadie I'd ever come across. Our sound engineers in the States were legion and legendary. The Clare Brothers, Gene and Roy, Barton Ciatti and Mike Johnson. Thanks guys!

The tours did seem so small in those days compared to the monsters encountered today. I'm referring to the numbers of dates rather than the personnel although even the people were fewer. Now it seems normal for wives and girlfriends and children, even babies, to come along quite naturally. In those days, wives and girlfriends usually stayed home. Patti d'Arbanville occasionally came on tour when she was around but none of Steve's other girlfriends did. Speaking as tour manager, it would have been a nightmare for me to have had anyone personally close to me being on tour too. My day began when I opened my eyes and finished when I closed them to grab what sleep I could. Even thinking about the welfare of someone close to me would have detracted from my ability to cope. Easier perhaps for the musicians with specific hours of sound-check and performance to actually function but even there, few of our guys brought family. People were also younger then, too; not so many had married or produced a permanent family by the early seventies, least ways, not ones they'd readily admit to and want to exhibit!

Our first proper tour in the UK was basically one which followed the old Odeon circuit in 1972 when we were promoting TEASER when the MOONSHADOW cartoon was shown, the first pop promo film to be made specifically for a three minute single track other than what the Beatles had culled from their full length feature and cartoon work.

However, it was in 1974 and the BAMBOOZLE World Tour that our operation came into its own. Again, I'm surprised at the size - only forty five dates across the world and not always the big venues like today's tours. Nowadays, acts do many more than this. In England alone you can more than outnumber forty five. In London, Steve played venues like Drury Lane and the Albert Hall whereas now, under the same circumstances, it would be at Wembley or Earls Court, like Elton and the others, for several nights.

Having said that, it warms me to think we played all the classic venues in rock 'n' roll history. America saw us on the BAMBOOZLE tour at places like the Shell Auditorium in Hawaii, the Santa Monica Auditorium and the Greek Theatre in Los Angeles, in San Francisco we'd played the Filmore West and were at the Oakland Coliseum, in Chicago at the Stadium, in Philadelphia at The Spectrum, the Coliseum in Nassau, New York and ultimately on July 17th 1974, Madison Square Garden.

It seemed also to be the time when stars from other firmament began to want to be associated with the rock 'n' roll people. It was the start of the era of the guest list, the back stage pass and the photo opportunity. Not that the late Steve McQueen was in anyway a publicity seeker but he, just as an immediate example, and Ali McGraw were big fans of Steve's and would come along to the shows. Rock started to shake off the sleaze and was fast acquiring a glamour all its own recognised by the media. Hype became possible, publicity horizons expanded for all sides in the publicity bargain.

The social and political establishment throughout the world

too began to see possibilities in association with this new cultural phenomenon of rock music stardom and was not slow to fashion relevant, mutually beneficial entente. For his own account, Steve became very much involved with UNICEF, the United Nations International Childrens Organisation. On the Japanese leg of the 1974 BAMBOOZLE tour, on the twenty second of June to be precise, Steve played a concert to a capacity crowd at the Nakano Sun Plaza in Tokyo. The concert was recorded and the resulting album, SATURDAY NIGHT, issued via A and M Records on the King record label for the benefit of UNICEF. The operation was geared through Steve's charity fund which he had created and which he christened the Hermes Foundation. Steve was developing a far greater affinity for children and animals than he was with human beings. As far as SATURDAY NIGHT was concerned, Steve had been loathe always to do cover versions but in the way that artists are sometimes blinded by their preconceptions, Steve didn't realise that he had reached that status where he could have song Hickory Dickory Dock and people would have gone ape. Sam Cooke's ANOTHER SATURDAY NIGHT included on what was really a compilation live album was a chart success for him when he needed one a lot. However, its success highlighted a gnawing, nagging doubt for the success of that cover version came at the start of the time when I believe Steve thought he had dried up creatively.

Although he didn't like touring as such, Steve found that travelling from place to place and seeing new and different environments gave him inspiration. He began to buy homes in foreign countries, the itinerary for later visits being another stimulus for his creative juices. Beirut through which we passed was a place he loved seeing and when he started visiting UNICEF centres in the third world, another avenue for inspirational travel opened up.

For Steve, the idea of touring was fine; the reality of it for such a reluctant performer was not fine. For a while, the songs kept coming. After FOREIGNER which he had used to explore a totally different direction, he was forced back onto the track. The songs on the subsequent BUDDHA AND THE CHOCOLATE BOX album, itself purportedly a title born from an experience at an airport, had certainly been written over and above the basic fund of songs he'd started out with. EIGHTEENTH AVENUE was, for example, also about being at airports and always finding yourself in the slowest line in front of the slowest check-in clerk. But it wasn't a happy creator who started to wonder how long he could go on for, worrying where the next song was going to come from and, worst of all, after inevitable public scrutiny and comparison, would such a song stand up?

Steve's lyrics had been taken so literally that their meaning had multiplied, probably outstripping whatever meaning he had initially, consciously intended. Steve was in a bit of a trap. The songs that had appeared in his albums hadn't been written in sequence as the albums had been issued but they appeared to have been. Current and future writing therefore had to be seen to match up in quality, content as part of a development of the artist as human being. I sensed that Steve was having trouble identifying with himself. I think he always had had that problem but the situation was becoming unmanageable especially in the light of the tension in his relationship with Barry. It wasn't that Steve had ever expected Barry to be on tour all the time. Barry would only ever show up usually at metropolitan gigs - Paris, London, New York, Los Angeles. Most of the time, Steve was on his own. This time, the more he was left, the further away he drifted into new realms of thinking and attitude towards himself and his future. He became more and more inadequate in dealing with people.

Touring, shows and live performance for a time masked Steve's fears. The MAJICAT world tour of 1975-76 was a huge feat of show-business engineering rather than an exposition of wonderful new work but even the production values couldn't disguise the unhappiness which spread down from the top, floated down over all of us like acid snowflakes. There was no one who was exempt from the possibility of a bollocking and none more than the crew, especially the department heads who came to expect a daily dressing-down from Steve when even the slightest thing was not as he had ordered or envisaged.

Recruiting road-crew had been a growing problem for the last two years we toured. Bad reputations, like bad news, travel fast especially in the narrow confines of the rock world. By the time of the MAJICAT tour, I was having to offer crew way over the going rate to join up. If the meanest roadie's daily rate was £50, I'd have to offer £75. The difference came to be known as the Grief Factor. The crew enjoyed their pay packets, sure. They didn't much enjoy the working atmosphere. I too had had my moments, one in particular concerning a promised bonus which my wife and I were intending to use as a deposit for our first house. It was £3000, a lot of money in those days.

I was at first fobbed off and then my repeated requests bounced like a ping pong ball from Steve to Barry and back again ... 'Talk to Barry,' said Steve ... 'Talk to Steve,' said Barry. I got to such a pitch of rage that one day on the telephone from Arizona, I told Barry that if my wife wasn't in possession of a cheque by that afternoon, I'd be gone and he could come out himself and sort out the mess.

I got my cheque. But it left a crummy after taste.

I could never fathom why Steve could be so unstinting in his commitments to the facilities to make his show the best he could and then fall down so badly in the way he treated those who made the facilities work. There was a part of Steve which begrudged the money, which made you sweat or dare for it, pushing your requests to the point where you'd threaten resignation before he'd accede, just to see ...

On the MAJICAT tour, at the Munich Olympic Hall, I remember the start of one such an incident. By that time, with most of the European promoters we worked with, Barry negotiated deals for Steve's appearance based on a 90-95% basis of the capacity fees at the venue. This total can vary according to two variables, the ticket price and the number of seats. As the ticket price was agreed and printed, Barry asked me to check the seat total as often as I could. I happened to do a seat check at the Munich venue and I discovered an extra number of seats which would have generated, for Steve, an extra income of $5000. I approached the promoter and confronted him with the situation and asked breezily what he was going to do about it, the implication being that if I had discovered the 'oversight' on one occasion, how many other venues had been similarly doctored?

We were due to leave for Paris the following day after the gig. Before we left, the promoter came to me and begged me obviously not to tell Steve or Barry and dumped a suitcase into my hands in which was the 'missing' $5000. I assured him I would do what I could to smooth over the matter of the undeclared seats ...

I said nothing to Steve on our way but when we'd booked into the Paris hotel I went to his room. I showed him the suitcase and merely said that I'd received the 'sweetener', our kickback from the German promoter. Steve thought I was talking rubbish but realised as soon as he opened the case what my implication was. He was delighted, running his hands through the money, quite like a child with five thousand M and M's. Then he tipped all the money out onto the sofa, sat down and pushed all the money behind his back, dividing the amount into two, one in each hand.

"Which hand do you want?" he asked me, grinning. *"You can have whatever there is in the hand you pick. Go on."* So I said whichever hand I said and he handed over about $1000 and kept the contents of his other hand for himself. Typical! He had to do that macho thing, challenge me instead of merely splitting whatever had come by good fortune his way.

I never told him the truth about the source of the money.

As it turned out, the confrontations increased as that MAJICAT tour went on. I don't know if it was on that tour we played in Belgrade but there was a showdown there between Steve and I when the political police with their AK 47 rifles pointing at me told me that the show was not to proceed with the houselights down. Steve said he wouldn't perform and that I was to go out and tell the police that they would be responsible for the consequences. I replied that I wasn't going but that he could go and tell them. I then let slip about the rifles and the dark glasses and reminded him we were in a Communist State. The show went on with the house lights up.

It's all a bit like JURASSIC PARK really. We create the monsters out of our own test tubes. We allow them to get as monstrous as they get and then, like Frankenstein, we cavil when they won't behave as we want them to. Confrontation one minute; big hugs in the dressing room the next. Such a load of contradictions that I was getting confused and far too tired. I felt he was relating to fewer and fewer people and was hovering in a limbo in almost every area of his life, thought and work. I remember suggesting to Barry at one point that he put Steve on artistic ice as it were for a couple of years to allow him a breathing space but by that time, that sort of advice wouldn't have been constructively followed.

As it was, Steve put himself on ice. The last concert he did, the UNICEF show at Wembley with Gary Numan, he did because the show wasn't selling and he was persuaded to join the line-up. The show sold out within two hours of the announcement of Steve's participation.

Will there ever be just one more?"

CHAPTER FOURTEEN

THE LOST AND FOUND, BOUGHT AND PAID FOR.

Lesley Johnson as well as others has testified to the significance which Cat Stevens' songs have had in the lives of thousands and thousands of people. The following merely illustrates the point. I wish that I could advertise for the many, many other stories and include them. This recollection concerns SAD LISA.

Garo Necessian is an Armenian Lebanese. What that actually means, I am still unsure although his family I know is Christian and they lived once in Beirut, a beautiful city in a beautiful country that was one of the jewels of the Levant.

Garo's father died in 1971 just two years before the unrest began between Lebanese army and the PLO which initiated a sea of troubles which any amount of opposing could not and did not end. Garo remembers that his father was once loyally warned by one of his Palestinian employees to leave Ashrafiyeh, a peaceful neighbourhood and the strongest Christian enclave in East Beirut where the family lived before open war finally broke out in 1975 ...

Whilst fighting raged and opposers opposed those who were opposing yet other opposers, a once-beautiful country was being torn apart, limb from limb and head from heart. Many families either left Beirut, fleeing for their lives and found it physically impossible to return. There was no safety. Anywhere. Garo's family did not leave and remained locked into East Beirut.

For eight months, Garo lived in a boarding school in the mountains overlooking West Beirut at Souk-El-Kharbe. The school was both international and ecumenical, multi-cultural, multi-racial and multi-religious. And mixed sex. There were Lebanese, Palestinians, Saudi Arabians, Egyptians, Jordanians and Kuwaitis, in which number the Al Saba family, the royal family of Kuwait, were listed. There were Christians, Christian Falange, Shi'ite Muslim and Suni Muslim ...

The school was in a predominantly Druze area, the Druze sect originating, Garo believes, in Jabal Druze in Syria. They were predominantly Muslim with a predilection for militia activity. Their fanaticism was well-documented as was their intense secrecy concerning their faith itself. In those days, the opposers in the civil strife were, mainly, the extremely right wing Christian Falange (who supported either Jemayel who became president in 1982 or ex-President Shamoun and neither faction were at all sweet about the other) versus the Druze and the Palestinians and the Muslim factions.

Gradually the Palestinians had been able to involve other fundamentalist political Islamic groups when it was realised that the Christians were being aided and supported by the Israelis. At the very end of the various allyings, of course, the radically extreme Hezebollah, (The Party of God) backed by Iran, emerged to further complicate the situation. When Shamoun's cause sank after the his 'Tiger' militia and the Christian Falange fell to the combined Muslim and Palestinian forces in the ex-President's home town of Damour, the Christian cause united.

And still the boarding school remained multi-cultural and multi-religious although after the fall of the Shamoun-focused Falange in May 1975, attendance started to wind down.

GARO NECESSIAN: "... food was in reasonable supply until late 1975 when everything became very scarce, including electricity. By this time there were only four students left in the school. There was a five year old girl from Tripoli in Northern Lebanon. There was an Egyptian boy who was about seven, an Iraqi about my age and me. I was around fourteen.

It was Joe, a very much older guy, a Christian Falangist, who introduced me to Cat Stevens, handing me a cassette as he was packing up and moving out. Other than a Shirley Bassey tape, it was about the only cassette that was left. In all probability it was a pirated tape as I have a feeling that there were more songs on it than comprised TEA FOR THE TILLERMAN.

I used to play SAD LISA again and again and again. I would

play it, wind it back, play it, rewind it, play, rewind ... That is, as long as there was electricity and even when there was a current, as long as the transformers in the cassette player didn't burn out; the power was of such variable voltage that the song often ran slow.

... SAD LISA, it was such a sad song. I felt so stuck, so low, so trapped, unable to go anywhere, unable to escape. I remember just the way the words seemed to ramble, sort of floating over the music. But still sad ... So sad.

I didn't consciously hear the song again for quite a while until I bought a copy of TEA FOR THE TILLERMAN in Camden Lock one Sunday. I played the song and it brought back exactly the feelings I had had at the time. Nothing had changed.

Of course I got out in the end. I was lucky and now I'm here and to an extent those years are behind me now but I can't help thinking of the song every time I see my niece. She, co-incidentally, is also called Lisa and she was not even born during that terrible time. She arrived about 1982 as she's now eleven.

But she's autistic. Not badly, in fact rather mild as far as autism can ever be mild. But it takes so much to get through to her. She seems to live in a world of her own, sealed off from the rest of us.

SAD LISA. Once it was my song and now it's hers. I sort of understand what it might be like for her."

And, indeed, what it must have been like ultimately for Steve, growing increasingly isolated amidst the brouhaha which surrounded him?

If London had a lot to do with the start of these ramblings, America had a lot to with the end of them. And, come to think of it, the middle. America was and is of key importance in the music business and therefore in the thinking of the artists themselves whose work falls under that microscope created by the scrutiny of the music machine. Steve never even got to lick the Big Apple the first time around. I think on the second, he was determined to eat it core and all.

Steve must have learned a great deal from that first trip he made to America as a performer and current recording artist with Alun Davies in 1970. Although TEA FOR THE TILLERMAN had already been recorded but the tracks for TEASER had yet to be selected. Steve's future was still very much up for grabs.

When an artist first hits America's spot, the effect produced by the cumulative acceleration of radio airplay as station after station, and then chain after chain of stations across the country pick up on the material is more like a Richter shock than a mere wave frequency. The effects can be devastating.

America empowers. It gives you control.

It makes you feel that you can do anything, be anything, go anywhere however and whenever you like. America makes the possible likely, makes opportunities out of dreams; it can make monsters from mere mutations, delusions from pretences, compulsions out of idle ambitions and addictions out of harmless weekend tokes.

America gives you control of everything except yourself. The self-control has to come from you. Sometimes, they forget to put that bit on the packaging.

Transatlantic jet flight as a common phenomenon was only just over a decade old when I first went to New York and then to LA in 1974. I'd gone at Barry's behest of course and at the company's expense. I therefore first glimpsed America from a very privileged perspective and was immediately seduced. It seemed that the speakers on every radio were playing Cat Stevens.

However, strange to confess, in Lotus Land with the hedonists I was always able to somehow remind myself that: 'You get nothing for nothing and very little for sixpence.' I'm afraid the price of paradise was always too steep for me. Barry and Steve, on the other hand, were now well able to afford it. Steve, after all, had conquered the whole of it and Barry ... well, he wasn't much interested in Omaha or Nebraska but there were a few square miles of the state of California with which he became infatuated. Hollywood. Los Angeles. Beverly Hills. Malibu. Burbank. He had, to be fair, tasted the lotus fruit once before. For reasons about which I'm not altogether clear but probably to do with London, his family and his internal struggles with his moonshadows, Steve never gave in to America. Nor did I.

But Barry, however, did.

There is something sacred about friendships between men, the David and Jonathan sort of friendships, the kingmaker friendships. At the same time as they can render the weak strong, at the same time can they expose the strong to debilitating weakness. To be empowered takes support. Remove that support too quickly and the barbells drop.

Male friendship is, truly, a double-edged sword. When

friendships go wrong, they truly go wrong. When friendships are also business relationships - yes, even playing employee to someone else's employer is a business relationship - something as solid as a rock, as immovable as a mountain can turn out to be deceptively frail. Riven through and through as rock can be with complicated and often invisible fault lines, the ultimate damage is often irreparable. Imperceptibly, perhaps for years, water has seeped into these fault lines. Tears have flowed, bad words have been spoken and never exorcised ... Frosts have frozen, thaws have melted and the tears, as water, have flowed deeper into the fault, expanding and contracting and making the rock eventually crumble and the mountain to finally tumble.

The more time Barry spent in California, the more he liked it and the less he wanted to return. In a way I could understand it. Life in London, in Britain, was poky compared to LA. It was parochial, slow, backward. Barry wanted to conquer LA not only for business and professional reasons but because he was at that age and at that point in his life where a man needs a lift. You only had to be a gay man and ride down any street in the designated areas to realise that lifts there were to be had a-plenty in LA in the mid-seventies. Barry went through a fair few fallings-in love before he met Doug Chapin and before the idea of moving permanently to LA first took root, then shape and finally place.

Barry left London. It was as simple and as quick as that. As final and irrevocable as the moment when you fall out of love, the moment you turn from boy to man, from woman to mother, from unborn to quick. Of course he left material things behind - shoes, winter coats, furniture, a couple of Hockney prints - but the main item he deliberately left behind was his old life and everything and everyone associated with it for we all knew he had left us. Tony Beckley, me, the office, Steve ...

You can't have relationships on the 'phone. You have to live with the person, touch them, wait for them, be quiet with them, know they're not unhappy ... and be able to ask why, eyeball-to-eyeball.

The others I can't answer for, but as for me ... ? I'd lied for Barry, cheated for him, deceived for him, protected him, comforted him, encouraged him, censured him, sulked, made up and shared with him. I loved Barry. That was the problem.

Yes, I was pissed-off when he left. I was hurt, let down, betrayed ... I thought he'd robbed me. I hurt then and I can still feel the pain now and if I felt like that, what did the others feel? And, in all compassion after all these years, how the fuck did Barry feel?

Someone once opined, I was told it was David Hockney but it's probably apocryphal, on being asked what LA was like: *"It's like the Holloway Road but with perpetual sunshine."* Its not. I live near the Holloway Road and I know that even at it's furthest end and even on foot, it would take me no longer than an hour to get home. I think that if only in this respect, Steve and I were a little alike.

In 1975, we were all back in LA for yet another series of meetings. Barry was now resident, Steve and I and Sarah Harrison (then Steve's secretary and assistant) and Jackie Krost, Barry's brother, were visiting. Sarah and I had just flown in, in fact. It was her first visit and the occasion was, I believe, a joint celebration of Steve's and Barry's birthdays. Anyway, Steve was, obviously, the joint guest of honour at his own party and the party had been organised by Barry at a restaurant. There was an uncomfortable atmosphere from the word go. Jackie Krost gave Steve a straight-jacket for his birthday. Jackie doesn't have a bad bone in his body and the beautifully painted device was supposed to be a joke. Oh, dear. Then, the cake came on and the candles were the sort that don't go out when you blow them. Another joke. Harmless? Oh, no.

Steve was not thrilled with the jacket and actually hurt himself when he burned himself trying to put out the candles on the cake. The tension and the embarrassment in the atmosphere worsened and Steve's now-obvious distress communicated itself to me, to Sarah and to Jackie. He left and so did we.

Outside the restaurant we sat in back of his limousine while Steve got very cross and then very upset as he ranted that the party wasn't for him at all, but for Barry. It didn't take a degree in psychology to realise that he was feeling very, very alone and cut off and helpless and rudderless and I knew from that moment on that there was no future for any of us in terms of our past. Barry and Steve had lost it, Barry and I had lost it, Steve had lost it. We all had. It was time for us all to move on. I realised that what I needed was a new job. I realised what Steve needed was a new life. As it turned out, as well as changing jobs, you can also change lives.

Prince Rupert Loewenstein is a man of many talents. He is also a man who exudes authority, not of the didactic variety but the quiet, confident and reasonable authority of an oracle. He is, in fact, exactly what he has made his career. He is a consultable authority, a conduit of auguries and his pronouncements organise his clients' financial futures into a decipherable and practicable code.

Prince Rupert first came into Barry's and Steve's lives sometime in 1973. At that time, Prince Rupert was a managing director of the city merchant bankers Leopold Joseph. His reputation, and that of the bank, as the wise financial adviser to THE ROLLING STONES must have been one of the main reasons why he and Barry Krost first met. It is no understatement to record that Barry and the Prince got on extremely well. That Steve and the Prince should also have got on very well might be a surprise to some but given Rupert's deep and instinctive appreciation of the arts and of the essence of creativity itself, I'm sure Steve initially felt immediate empathy with this accessible, worldly and essentially avuncular man.

PRINCE RUPERT: "I believe that Barry and Steve were, for the seminal part of their association, ideally suited. Barry was so straight forward and so honest that one felt there was nothing he would not do for his client, no corner he wouldn't fight in any part of the world. They had a tremendously strong relationship. One could feel the closeness and also see the very real joy that each derived from the other's company. Barry legitimised Steve. Pop singers, rock singers ... In those days, they had no credible place in the show-business firmament. Barry was excellently equipped to steer Steve with all his many talents into the areas that other managers would not have been able to essay. To my way of thinking, Steve's career was handled with enormous taste and style and made it very mush easier for subsequent artists to be more widely and deeply appreciated.

So ... With so much right, what went wrong?

I fear, fundamentally, that for many reasons, Steve began to mistrust Barry's judgement. May I say categorically that so far as I am concerned and that so far as I was privy to their business relationship, I do not believe that Steve had any foundation for such thoughts.

When Barry introduced me to Steve and showed me his own set-up at Curzon Street, I could not have been more delighted. To advise on and establish the financial arrangements that Steve wanted in order to protect and secure his future while working with a creative manager is one of the areas I believe I am best at and one in which I am most confident. To be able to so with Barry taking care of the everyday aspects of the organisation, maintenance and furtherance of the Cat Stevens career was an ideal arrangement. I had confidence in Alex Zolas, Steve's brother-in-law who had been brought in to oversee the running of the day-to-day business arrangements of Steve's life and with all these building blocks in place, we put together an arrangement which Steve found satisfactory.

It must be remembered that these were the days of punitively high taxation. Top rates on earned income were eighty three percent and this rate kicked in at £15,000. The rate on unearned income was an incredible ninety eight percent. Of course, Steve had sold a very large number of records, millions, but bearing in mind that he was a British resident and therefore subject to paying tax at these rates, there was not, un-surprisingly, an enormous surplus. However, whilst perhaps not exactly laughing all the way to the bank, the journey would have been one which Steve could have made with more than a wry smile.

Being experienced in dealing with record contracts and their implications, I assisted Barry in the renegotiation of Steve's recording arrangements especially in America where Nesui Ertegun of Atlantic Records had come in with a far higher offer for Steve's recording than Jerry Moss of A and M was at that time prepared to commit. In short, the negotiations veered in the direction of Atlantic and many drafts of the proposed contract were submitted to both sides. Finally, the day of signature arrived and, in front of the Atlantic lawyers, in front of Barry and myself, Steve decided not to sign. It was, to say the least, momentous and the shockwaves continued to ripple outwards from the epicentre of that moment for several years.

Of course, in the months preceding this 'decision', I had sensed the relationship between Barry and Steve becoming different. A sense of strain, perhaps? Certainly an appreciable change in the closeness that had marked their association. I'm sure there are many people who have their own versions of the rationale but whatever the individual reasons bearing on Steve's decision to cut himself loose from any contractual recording commitment, the effect showed a lack of trust in what Barry had prepared as a blueprint for his recording future. Without such trust, the artist-manager relationship has no alternative but to founder.

It was a strange day. It was not as though Steve had not been consulted in the preceding months and it was certainly not the case that Steve had been given no chance to effect the form and shape of the contracts himself ... Steve was not only forthright but experienced in contractual arrangements and had been dealing with lawyers for many years.

From there on it was only a matter of time before Steve's commitment to the edifice that he and Barry had built to house his career ceased. Barry and Steve inevitably went their separate ways.

My personal opinion remains that Steve could have been suffering from a massive case of artistic cold feet. I think every truly creative artist suffers thus and Steve was undoubtedly a great talent, both musically and lyrically. He is in that 'jongleur' tradition from which the great minstrels and troubadours of history have sprung. What these wanderers speak and sing is entrancing and captures the hearts and minds of anyone with romantic tendencies. Could it have been that, as many actors believe at the close of a long run of a great success that they will never work again, Steve felt himself written out, that he could not foresee being creative again?

With no contract between them, Barry must have felt little inclined to remain in London committed to a client who would not, in business terms at least, commit to him and who might never work again. Barry was a very intelligent man and as an artists' representative had assembled a client list which was more at home in the cut and thrust of the Hollywood arena than in the respectable but comparatively sluggish world of British television, films and music.

From 1974 onwards both Barry and Steve began processes which would effectively shut the connecting door between them. Barry moved permanently to America and Steve began to explore further and further the religious path which would eventually lead him to Islam.

Although Steve was not formally intelligent and certainly not well-educated - I doubt for example, that he could easily and quickly precis a ten page document and render it into twenty lines of concise summary - he was certainly very bright street-wise, with an unerring sense of opportunism, he peddled an image which he knew was immensely saleable. I also happen to think he wrote well. Who knows ... Perhaps he didn't even realise himself just how good he was.

He effectively undertook his own career arrangements after 1976 and assumed Barry's company's tenancy of the Curzon Street premises. His family became more involved with his business life although I feel that he regarded this as a mixed blessing. He seemed to alternate between embracing those near to him only then to distance himself in the company of total strangers.

Sadly, litigation marked the end of my business relationship with Steve but I seem to recall that I last saw him in either 1978 or 1979. I went to Curzon Street and was asked to remove my shoes. By this time, I think Steve was very close to converting to Islam. It is a religion with no monastic tradition. One is Muslim and one remains in the world and one cannot, it would seem, be alone. I felt strongly, as Steve told me of his wishes regarding the dis-establishment of the financial arrangements to which he had committed, that he needed some time alone and I suggested that, in the tradition of Greek orthodoxy which was after all the faith of his father and in which I imagined he had once been involved, that he seek to spend some time in one of the Greek mountain monasteries such as Athos and think things out.

I also remember wondering aloud to him at that meeting, what reason stood in the way of his working now and writing some more music and making another record. He replied that he felt that his new religion prevented him and so I asked why it was that the music which had brought so much pleasure and calm satisfaction to so many people throughout the world could possibly be deemed unacceptable to God.

He heard me out but, suffice it to say, went his own way and never really worked again."

CHAPTER FIFTEEN

FULL CIRCLE, FULL MOON

I don't think I can even call myself an agnostic although if the word has come to mean someone who is suspicious of religion, then my hand goes up. I'd like to be religious very much. But I can't be because I don't know.

I'd like there to be God, the unseen hand, guiding us, even killing us with deft certainty, giving us through faith and belief the assurance that there is a purpose, that there is a plan, that we're all going somewhere, that it really does mean something despite the murdered babies, the raped geriatrics, the maimed and mutilated soldiers, the dead refugees, the lost loved ones...

I can't think of a single established religion or philosophy that doesn't promise something better at the end of the mortal path; that being with god, a part of god, at one with the whole and indivisible un-sliced wholemeal loaf is the temptation which is supposed to be able to help each of us make it through our current, uncertain lives.

I think it's always easier to cope with life, and therefore with death, if you're not the centre of your universe. If you are, there's nowhere to escape to without the whole kit and caboodle of you veering wildly off-centre and off-course and hurtling away out of control into chaos and darkness. And madness ... For turning irretrievably in on yourself as the only means of escape from the world is what some madness is. It is, surely, pure thought? Pure being, untrammelled by the intrusion of any worldly consideration? But then, none of us wants to be mad, do we?

Other than drugs and palliative addiction, god emerges as the very natural and understandable alternative, one which you don't have to make yourself which has already been made for you, off-screen. Like they tell you when they're recruiting: god takes away so much of the pressure, so much of the strain. There's that comforting parental quality about a relationship with god. Conversion is a re-birth indeed. It makes legitimised children again out of grown people, it allows adults to gratefully grasp the helping hand and follow where the greater, less ignorant, more experienced, capable, un-shirking, immortal being leads.

The thing with god and the famous is, of course, not only pertinent to the Cat Stevens story. The feeling for the need for god in both famous and un-famous circles is more than common and doesn't always manifest or culminate in an actual religious embodiment. In the late 1930's when he had become phenomenally successful almost in a way never before seen, Paul Robeson wrote acknowledging *"... a conception I'm getting about God. My career has been so strange and so seemingly guided by some outside influence."* Later, expounding on the "higher plan" to which he alludes, he talked of: *"... truth necessary to create TRUE beauty"*, adding, *"So God watches over me and guides me. He's with me but lets me fight my own battles and hopes I'll win ..."* (Courtesy Martin Bauml Duberman PAUL ROBESON. Bodley Head via Alfred Knopf Inc.).

Robeson was an interpretative creative artist working with a creative team and he had to struggle. Steve, solo, bore the total brunt of the creativity which engendered his work and had to struggle more, both with the world and with others as well as with himself. The struggle isn't only inside; once out, the artist still has to struggle first to be recognised and then to survive. For where do you go once you've reached the top? That dilemma comes NOT when THEY tell you you've made it to the summit of the highest peak there is, but when YOU KNOW YOURSELF that there's nowhere else to go.

It must be so weird to find yourself the one who gets the career that 'takes off'. If it was me, I think I would need to ascribe the mystery of the miracle to some greater purpose. Writing as I am from the other side of famous, it would all seem so pre-ordained, so decreed. It is, after all and after all the struggle, the incredible made believable. And that is just what god and religion are all about to converts ... the incredible made believable.

One has to be very careful about words these days. Writing now with the secular, psychotherapeutic meaning of the following danger words in mind, I do believe something holy happened to Steve. Those first four, seminal albums (for I personally include

CATCH BULL) of his renaissance were his apotheosis. Their creative content and the commercial success they achieved enabled him to leave earthly, everyday concerns aside and to consciously and conscientiously look for God in areas of purer existence. As a monk or a nun or any religious or truth-seeking being has found, our corporeal world is a difficult place to find God for longer than an ephemeral, temporal moment. In order to feel with certainty you have the best chance of enjoying a spiritual eternity, god is best sought *"... when the hurly burly's done, when the battle's lost and won ..."*

Rupert Everett, actor and writer and, by way of this particular utterance, sage, has written:
"You get what you want in the form you deserve".

Ever since I read this sentence I've been applying it to lots of people and situations and although the maxim sounds cute, it also furnishes a convenient jumping-off point when considering the global nature and significance of, for example, a relationship, a career, even a life.

I think everyone who strives and heaves and pushes and forges ahead because they nurse a sore ambition will ultimately get somewhere along the road they wish to travel but there are always and inevitably hidden costs and how far they will travel always depends ...

Let us therefore assume you achieve the success and the fame you've sought but when it arrives, like something you've ordered from its photograph in a catalogue, its not quite in the form you wanted. You see a rose in a crowded florist's window and although you buy it, without the ugly, prickly stem, the beautiful petalled bloom which is what you wanted to buy initially is useless - but unless you think to wear gloves, you have to bear the thorns pricking you in order to hold and smell the flower.

What you want is never quite what you're ultimately allowed. What you end up doing is not quite the work that you had originally aimed for. I, just as an example, always wanted to be a proper writer, one of those who is well-considered and who would be invited to celebrated literary occasions and be consulted and respected and looked up to as I once sat reverently at the feet of W.H. Auden in the Junior Common Room at my university college. But that sort of career will never happen for me. I'm not cerebral enough, not sufficiently well-read; I am - in music terminology -

too much country and not enough classical. And I am not complaining. I am perfectly content to write novels that tell stories about characters, books which I hope have some craft and a little humour and which people enjoy even though the work doesn't set the world alight nor earn fabulous financial rewards.

I think what Steve got was just what he deserved both in terms of his talent and his ambition but it, obviously, was not at all what he wanted.

True, the pivotal emphasis in the music business shifted, just as Steve's renaissance was taking place, from the song to the artist. Albums were not merely random collections of individually pretty, catchy or commercial songs; they were declarations of the state of the artist's mind and soul, designed to be shared with the buying public. The artist became the product via the music. The artist became a kind of prey and many were unwittingly devoured.

To avoid that fate, the artist found him or herself obliged to remain open to the scrutiny of the buying public, accountable to their un-elected interrogators, those members of the press who themselves came to form an entirely new section of the journalistic media. For some artists, the pressure of the intrusion was too great. Some, like Steve, most in fact, invented another persona to cope with the intrusions. But, the alter ego, the Cat Stevens ego, wasn't quite sufficient. There was still Steven Giorgiou's ego, state of mind and welfare to be accounted for. There came a point when the mutual compromise between the two became supportable by neither one. Steve was too much like a chameleon, changing who he was for the benefit of different people. There is no core being who was at the centre of Steve's existence who was the same to all people. Different people knew a different Steve. Unlike a chameleon, however, it is impossible for the human being to continually change and then change again to suit what he or she thinks of are the expectations of others.

Together with the industrial shift of emphasis from the song to the artist came the emergence of the artist as controlling power behind their own throne. With requisite professional advice bought and paid for and therefore available to be taken or ignored, artists at last and at least had the chance to steer their own careers. The lessons had been learned from the rip-offs of the fifties and sixties and the control over the generated wealth began to be re-assumed by those who created it. But few succeeded. Too many other people had too much to lose. The financial gains and losses were too great.

It takes time and energy and attention to control and to manage wealth. It's a job in itself bringing with it huge responsibilities, often requiring the making of burdensome decisions and even the taking of nail-biting risks. It's the job Steve Giorgiou had to do as well as being Cat Stevens.

As a people-pusher, Steve was a useless diplomatist and made a bad manager. The qualities of selfishness and insensitivity, pig-headed determination and iron-willed self-discipline which had enabled him to establish his artistic success were irrelevant, unless greatly mollified, in dealing with others and it is the ability to deal with others that is the pre-requisite in any business. Without a manager, trusting hardly anyone, Steve was stymied. As a businessman, Steve would have rarely have thought or considered the needs and wishes of others. He had never needed to learn about politics and when he needed the knowledge most, he was let down by his own ignorance and inability.

The prospect of continuing to be Cat Stevens must have been very unappealing as he continued along the road he had been allowed by luck and talent and chance to travel. He'd come much further along that road than most but now he had only the perspective of no perspective to focus and guide him. The once so golden trail was rapidly turning into a dangerous and flimsy path over a footing which was becoming progressively thinner and more brittle as time past and his experience made him acutely and un-settlingly aware of the many dangers.

When we're young we tend to be blithe and careless and unaware that we are in fact treading on a surface beneath which lies not only a sea of troubles but a miasma of tears. As we get older and we realise that life is not only about the good times but also about the bad, trouble, as Steve himself wrote about, shows its face more and more often and threatens more frequently to break through and drag down those who fall prey into its sadness. We often arrive at a point where we feel that the slightest jolt to our increasingly precarious confidence and commitment could trip us and, as we fall, cause the surface supporting the edifice of our lives to crack and give way. And, that way lies a sort of madness.

I've been there on those days when you feel like weeping from the moment you wake up, when you never want to leave the house, when all you want to do is be alone and, maybe, remain alone forever. Maybe even to die appears considerable as the alternative of being drowned in that sea of tears is just too much to cope with.

In those circumstances, neither you, nor I nor Steve like ourselves at all and any escape route is better than staying both where and who we are. Steve finally escaped.

DISCOGRAPHY

GREAT BRITAIN ONLY

(Courtesy Island Records)

FIRST RELEASES
(Albums and Compact Discs)

ILPS ICT 9118	MONA BONE JAKON	*14:70*
ILPS 1CT 9135	TEA FOR THE TILLERMAN	*10:70*
ILPS 2C1 1CT 9154	TEASER AND THE FIRECAT	*9:71*
ILPS 2C1 1CT 9206	CATCH BULL AT FOUR	*9:72*
ILPS 9240	FOREIGNER	*25:73*
ILPS 2C1 9274	BUDDHA AND THE CHOCOLATE BOX	*3:74*
ILPS 2C1 9274	GREATEST HITS	*7:75*
ILPS 2C1 9370	NUMBERS	*11:75*
ILPS 2C1 9451	IZITSO	*9:77*
ILPS 2C1 9565	BACK TO EARTH	*10:78*

RE-RELEASES
(*Albums and Compact Discs*)

ILPS 9706 (Europe Only)	MORNING HAS BROKEN	:82(842472-1)
ILPS 9823 (USA/Europe)	FOOTSTEPS IN THE DARK	:84(846137-1)
CID 9154	TEASER AND THE FIRECAT	1:87
CID 9135	TEA FOR THE TILLERMAN	3:87
CID 9206	CATCH BULL AT FOUR	3:87
CID 9118	MONA BONE JAKON	3:87
CID 9310 (842309-2)	GREATEST HITS	3:87
ILPM ICM 9135	TEA FOR THE TILLERMAN	
ILPM ICM 9154	TEASER AND THE FIRECAT	
IMCD 34 (842778-2)	CATCH BULL AT FOUR	5:89
IMCD 35 (842351-2)	MONA BONE JAKON	5:89
IMCD 36 (842352-2)	TEA FOR THE TILLERMAN	5:89
IMCD 70 (842685-2)	BUDDHA AND THE CHOCOLATE BOX	10:89
IMCD 72 (842332-2)	FOREIGNER	10:89
IMCD 104 (842350-2)	TEASER AND THE FIRECAT	4:90
ITSOD 12 (514283-2)	TEASER AND THE FIRECAT TEA FOR THE TILLERMAN	11:92
IMCD 168 (842309-2)	GREATEST HITS	3:93

SINGLE RELEASES

WIP 6086	A. Lady d'Arbanville	*6:70*
	B. Time Fill My Eyes	
WIP 6092	A. Father and Son	*10:70*
	B. Moonshadow	
WIP 6102	A. Tuesday's Dead	*:71*
	B. Miles From Nowhere	
WIP 6121	A. Morning Has Broken	*12:71*
	B. I Want To Live In A Wigwam	
WIP 6152	A. Can't Keep It In	*11:72*
	B. Crab Dance	
WIP 6163	A. The Hurt -	*NO LABEL COPY AVAILABLE*
	B. Silent Sunlight	
WIP 6190	A. Oh Very Young	*3:74*
	B. 100 I Dream	
WIP 6206	A. Another Sat'day Night	*8:74*
	B. Home In The Sky	
WIP 6238	A. Two Fine People	*6:75*
	B. A Bad Penny	
WIP 6276	A. Banapple Gas	*2:76*
	B. Ghost Town	
WIP 6387	A. Remember The Days	*5:77*
	of The Old Schoolyard	
	B: The Doves	
WIP 6407	A. Sweet Jamaica	
	B. Is Dog A Doughnut	*WAS NEVER ISSUED*
WIP 6465	A. Last Love Song	*2:79*
	B. Nascimento	
WIP 6594	A. Morning Has Broken	*4:80*
	B. Moonshadow	
IS 123	A. Morning Has Broken	*5:83*
	B. Moonshadow	